The Story of

CHRISTIANITY

from Birth to Global Presence

The Story of
CHRISTIANITY
from Birth to Global Presence

JAKOB BALLING

WILLIAM B. EERDMANS PUBLISHING COMPANY

GRAND RAPIDS, MICHIGAN / CAMBRIDGE, U.K.

Originally published in Danish under the title *Kristendommen*
© 1986, 1996 Politikens Forlag A/S

This English edition (translation by the author)
© 2003 Wm. B. Eerdmans Publishing Co.

Wm. B. Eerdmans Publishing Co.
255 Jefferson Ave. S.E., Grand Rapids, Michigan 49503 /
P.O. Box 163, Cambridge CB3 9PU U.K.

Printed in the United States of America

08 07 06 05 04 03   7 6 5 4 3 2 1

Library of Congress Cataloging-in-Publication Data

Balling, Jakob.
[Kristendommen. English]
The story of Christianity: from birth to global presence / Jacob Balling.
p.   cm.
Includes bibliographical references and index.
ISBN 0-8028-3944-4 (pbk.: alk. paper)
1. Church history. I. Title.
BR145.3.B3513   2003

270 — dc21

2003049063

www.eerdmans.com

contents

CONTENTS

Contents

preface

A short interpretative account of the history of Christianity must by necessity leave much out if it is to say anything worthwhile about what it does not leave out. The reader of what follows has a claim to a word of preliminary information about the guidelines chosen by the author, his principles of including and of leaving out.

Christianity is, in the widest sense of the word, a historical religion. Therefore, this book is a book of history, and dwells at some length on things that have been done and said in the past but that — often in less than directly obvious ways — are living elements in contemporary Christian life and thought.

It is in view of that contemporary relevance that I have aimed at working out and clarifying the long lines of continuity and development in the historical process, while leaving out many of the events that in a bigger book could have been included to illuminate the nuances and multifariousness of the process, as well as making clear to what extent any construction of coherence is put to question by the individual, unmistakable person, event, and action of the past.

The tracking of coherence is in this book tantamount to an attempt at describing the great Christian complexes of ideas and actions — earliest, Mediterranean, old European, modern European and American, and global Christianity — as well as an attempt at determining what binds them together mutually and with Jesus of Nazareth. That means that the account as a whole is mainly orientated toward Europe and toward what has come from Europe — it is, in that sense, Eurocentric.

It is in some respect necessarily so, considering that the mainstream of Christian history — as far as it is known — has as a matter of fact run through the European daughter civilization of antiquity and through its offshoots in other parts of the world. But the price that a short book has to pay for giving a passably differentiated account of that mainstream is that non-European, and indeed east European, forms get a more sketchy treatment than could otherwise be achieved. As the reader will be sure to see, that price has been paid here, although I have strived to communicate at least an impression of those forms.

Further, the following account is socially orientated. In other words, the main emphasis is laid on those elements of Christian faith and conduct that are common to most Christians of the past — those that are "normal," "orthodox," and "churchly" — in preference to those that are specially linked with ideas and experiences of outstanding individuals. Certainly, to leave them out would mean a failure of the entire enterprise, but they are included only when I have judged them to have had broad historical effects and common relevance. Here, too, a price has to be paid; i.e., that of leaving out such dimensions of Christian thinking as are represented by men like Eckhart and Kierkegaard, and of neglecting some individual aspects of more centrally placed figures such as Augustine, Aquinas, Luther, and Grundtvig.

Finally, in several places the book tries to sketch out some information and reflections about the general historical context of Christianity. But such sections cannot compensate for the knowledge of the general course of history, which can be found in books made for that purpose. In what follows I have certainly tried to place the Christian religion where it belongs, namely, in common human life, as a religion that undergoes a multitude of influences from its social and cultural contexts, and influences them itself. But of that life and that context it has only been possible to account for the most decisive features.

The publication of this book in English has been made possible by grants from the following Danish foundations and institutions: Queen Margrethe and Prince Henrik's foundation; The Unidanmark Foundation; The C.A.C. Foundation; the Rector and the theological faculty of the University of Aarhus. For this support I am deeply grateful.

J.B.

part one

The Birth of a Religion

1. The Beginnings

At a point of time in the late twenties or early thirties of the first century of our era a youngish Jewish artisan called Jesus became known as a prophet, teacher, and healer in the region of his birth: the northern part of Roman-occupied Palestine. He and his followers regarded this activity as a sign of the definitive breakthrough of God's kingdom, apparent in his mercy toward poor people and outcasts, in his renewal of human life, in his judgment on its destruction at human hands. Somewhat later Jesus went up to Jerusalem where — after having been acclaimed and then deserted by both the people and his disciples — he was accused of blasphemy and sacrilege by the Jewish authorities, and subsequently tortured and put to death by the Romans. Shortly afterward his friends and followers began proclaiming that he had risen from the grave, shown himself to them, and made clear to them that from now on his life — stronger than death — would be theirs too, and that it would be open to everybody willing to put faith in him as their Lord and Savior. As a consequence of this preaching, a number of men and women joined the disciples and began being known as a people apart. This "people" is known as the *church,* after the Greek word *kyriake,* derived from *kyrios,* "lord and master." The message preached by the church is known by the name of *Christianity,* after the title given to Jesus: *Christ,* that is, the King, the Messiah.

This, in the briefest possible terms, is how Christianity came into being. We begin our closer consideration of these beginnings by looking at their background and framework.

2. Palestine and the Jews

The people of Israel — the Jews — were one of the Roman Empire's subjugated peoples. They had had similar experiences before, at the hands of Assyrians, Babylonians, Persians. And just as they had managed to retain their identity as a people under those earlier conditions, so now, under the "Roman peace," they were anything but "assimilated." They were granted wide powers of internal self-government under the "Council of Elders" — an assembly drawn from the priestly and secular elites — in Jerusalem, as well as under Jewish satellite princelings. Above all, they were free to worship Yahweh, their God, in his temple on Mount Zion and in the synagogues all over the country. However, as the history of Jesus was to show, the political and religious freedoms were absolutely dependent on the Jew-

1. This view of Jerusalem from the Mount of Olives is dominated by the Temple Mount. There, Herod the Great (34-4 B.C.) built the magnificent "Third Temple," the scene of a number of Gospel stories, which was razed to the ground by the Romans in A.D. 70. To the right is the great Mosque of Omar with its golden dome.

ish authorities' ability to guarantee the peace and order that the strategic and financial interests of the empire required. The power of Rome made itself unmistakably felt by the presence of legionaries and tax collectors as well as Pontius Pilate, the governor of Judea. It was a power that could be brought into play rapidly and with deadly efficiency if the freedoms were "abused."

The Jewish people had internal problems too. A chasm divided rich from poor, and there was enmity between Jews that were open to Greco-Roman cultural influences and those that rejected any dealings with outsiders. Both sets of tensions were, moreover, involved in the bewildering diversity of religious practices and ideas. Side by side with "official" Judaism — the religion of the temple and the Law — a number of more or less deviating tendencies were rampant: groups like the fanatical purists of the Dead Sea sect at Qumran, armed messianic movements, and many others. Last but not least, a deep groundswell of apocalyptic fervor made itself powerfully felt through extravagant speculations on the beyond and on the impending end of the world.

3. Jesus

Jesus was a Galilean from a fringe area on whose inhabitants the Jerusalem establishment were inclined to look askance. But above all, he was an Israelite. That means that Israel's certainties and hopes were his certainties and hopes also. He shared the conviction that the one true God had chosen *this* people among the whole of fallen and wayward humanity, and that he had established his covenant with this people without ever abandoning them in spite of their repeated violations of the pact. And he shared the hope of an imminent liberation from the powers that held the people captive: sin, injustice, oppression, and foreign dominion. Nothing Jesus said or did during his short spell of activity is understandable without constant recollection of these common assertions, all derived from Israel's Scriptures, the collection of holy books that yielded illumination on past, present, and future alike. It was precisely as an interpreter of the Bible that Jesus stepped forward. But the things he had to say were widely different from what people heard from the experts. As the Evangelist puts it, "They were astonished at his doctrine; for he taught them as one that had authority, and not as the scribes."

What they heard from him was the proclamation of a "kingdom of God" that was coming now, and not just something that was to come sometime in the future. God's "kingdom," his reign among men, and the life of freedom, justice, and community that only he could make possible was already there, in the midst of the people, hidden like the seed in the field or apparent to everybody's eyes like the candle on a stick. It was breaking through, it could not be stopped, and it made all things new wherever it appeared. It implied judgment and liberation simultaneously: judgment because by its coming it tore the veils of righteousness from people's selfish desertion of the commandment of love toward God and neighbor, and liberation because now God was assuming full kingly powers, revealing himself as the Lord of mercy and sending men out into a life of selfless service.

This did not, however, mean that Jesus proclaimed the kingdom of God as something he had "discovered" and was able to point out to his hearers. The decisive difference of his message from that of the "scribes" is to be found in his speaking of the kingdom's breakthrough as something that was tied to *his* person, *his* words and actions. When John "the Baptist," the great preacher of repentance, sent his disciples to ask Jesus who he was, the answer, according to the Evangelist, went like this: "Go and tell John what you hear and see: the blind are seeing, the lame walk, lepers are cleansed and deaf people hear; the dead are raised and the gospel is

5

2. View, ca. 1900, of Tiberias by the Sea of Galilee, a city founded by the vassal ruler Herod Antipas. Built on top of a cemetery in flagrant defiance of Jewish rules of purity, and named in honor of Herod's master, the emperor Tiberius (A.D. 14-37), it was one of the main points of entry for Hellenistic influence in the land of the Jews. (Courtesy of The Royal Library, Copenhagen, Department of Maps, Prints and Photographs.)

preached to the poor. And blessed is he that shall not be offended in me." Thus we are given to understand that Jesus himself is the sign of the kingdom, the new life. The kingdom is received or rejected by receiving or rejecting *him*. It is revealed by what he does when he casts out demons so that limbs are loosened and eyes opened. It lives in the stories he tells about the lost that is sought and brought back, and about the love that removes all obstacles, even the Law of Moses if need be. It lives in the form in which the stories are told: the parable, which in itself is a pointer toward the great things done by God in the shape of something small, weak, and common-place. But above all, it lives in what Jesus does by forgiving sins — not only as one who, in obedience to the Law, absolves the neighbor who has wronged or harmed him, but as one who has the authority to forgive sins committed against a third person or indeed against God.

This is precisely what allows for only two responses toward such a claimant: rejection or acceptance — rejection meaning punishing the blas-phemer, and acceptance, acknowledging that in this man God himself is uniquely at work and calls men and women to discipleship.

Such was the central assertion of Jesus. In this way he let people un-derstand that he did not see himself as merely a prophet like Israel's proph-ets of old, but as the man who at one and the same time transmitted the de-finitive promise from God and was himself that promise incarnate. There is nevertheless reason to suppose that the title of prophet is the appropri-ate one to use when describing him. His claim to be someone unprece-dented, endowed with a unique authority, does not necessarily mean that he saw himself as something different from the ordinary prophet in his ca-pacity as a frail and mortal creature. He was uniquely chosen by God; he had been entrusted with a superhuman task; but a human among humans he was and remained.

The claim that a unique authority was entrusted to someone who at the same time was a Jew among Jews went alongside an equally distinctive pat-tern of behavior — one characterized by a sovereign independence, which nevertheless simultaneously expressed itself in unconditional fellow-feeling for those oppressed by authority. Not surprisingly, whenever Jesus showed a lordly disregard for the rules of the Law as interpreted by the experts, he did it as a sign of solidarity with the men and women whom the current norm system excluded or who were barely tolerated on the fringes of society. In the words of the Evangelist, Jesus was "friend of sinners and publicans." Their sins were as far from excluding them from the kingdom as they were from qualifying them for entry. In his person the kingdom, the new life, had come to those that had no qualifications to display, and the new life revealed its presence by being handed on as unreservedly as it had been given by him. In sharp contrast to the teaching of the "Baptist," repentance and conversion were shown not to be the precondition of God's merciful coming but its con-sequence. The catchphrase of moralists through the ages: "He who is good becomes happy," was turned around to that in which the gospel can be sum-marized: "He who has been given joy becomes good." In other words, when the joy that human beings are unable to create for themselves comes to them undeservedly, then their joy wells over into goodness.

But precisely by being an *euangelion,* a message of joy to the poor, Jesus' teaching caused division in the people and became a sign of contention. Persecution was the natural response to a doctrine that was as politically dangerous as it was religiously and morally scandalous. Behind the words about the foxes with lairs and the birds with nests while the "Son of Man" has nowhere to lay down his head, we can discern an almost tangible experience of enmity. In the words of a modern scholar, the life led by Jesus and his closest adherents, a life of constant insecurity, renunciation of normal family and social ties, and sudden removals from place to place, can be likened to that led by guerrillas — even if it must be emphasized that the word is in other respects inappropriate.

The popular movement awakened by this teaching in words and actions was no political party, no revolutionary conspiracy, no military formation, and no sectarian group. All the same, it appears to have been meant to become an *organized* movement: the beginnings of the new people of God. This seems to be indicated by the tradition that Jesus appointed twelve disciples to be the people's judges and regents once God had carried through his intent. It is also indicated by the seemingly calculated effort to transmit the message to the entire people as quickly as possible by means of men later known as apostles. No time must be wasted, for God would hasten the breakthrough of his kingdom and put an end to the old world, the one in which Satan and his demons were loose and wreaked their work of destruction. "I saw Satan fall from heaven like lightning" is one of the sayings of Jesus that most clearly express this conviction.

According to Jewish belief, the night of the *passah* was when the coming of the age of grace was to be awaited and men were to look out for its signs and portents. Jesus may have shared this belief and summoned his followers to Jerusalem for the feast. If so, he must have seen the definitive breakthrough as something that in God's plan was tied to his person.

Exactly how he may have understood this cannot now be stated with any degree of certainty, for not only are the texts in which the story is told written in a language other than the Aramaic of Jesus himself, but, more importantly, they presuppose faith in the *resurrected* Jesus, the risen Savior who fulfilled God's promises by going through death to life. The authors of those texts are convinced that Jesus was the person meant by the prophet Isaiah's words about the "suffering servant of the Lord," about him who "was wounded for our transgressions, bruised for our iniquities." The Gospel narratives consequently understand the teacher personifying the coming of the kingdom as someone who makes it happen by giving his life for the people, as a victim in the people's stead.

8

The same idea is differently expressed in the accounts of Jesus' last meal in Jerusalem the night before his death. The breaking of bread and the pouring of wine are evidently meant as a pointer to something that shall come: the meal of rejoicing when the fruit of the vine shall be drunk new in the kingdom of God, and the sacrifice that shall make it possible. Like the symbolic acts carried out by Israel's prophets, it is meant both to pull back the future into the present and also to contribute to the accomplishment of that future, when the body is broken as the bread is broken now, and the blood poured out as the wine is poured out now.

Whether Jesus thought along those lines himself is a hotly contested question. But the Gospel words about the bread as "my body, which is broken for you" and about the wine cup as "the new testament [covenant] in my blood" are evidently old enough to have been received as "formulae" by the apostle Paul, who records them twenty years or so after the death of Jesus. To that must be added, perhaps more importantly, that the understanding of the Last Supper as the sign of a self-sacrifice accords well with the way Jesus in his parabolic teaching described God's coming to the people who were rejected by their fellows and by themselves. If this is what real love is like, then it must regard sacrificial death, total abandonment of self, as something possibly necessary. And if this kind of love is seen as that of God himself, then its possibilities are seen as unbounded.

Shortly after the last meal Jesus was arrested on the orders of the Jewish Council of Elders, from whose viewpoint he was a blasphemer and false prophet, and who naturally regarded the popular turmoil caused by his entry into the city as an imminent threat to the peace and order on which a satisfactory relationship with the Roman authorities depended. The council's prestige among the people and its chances of maintaining elbow room in its dealings with the occupying power were at stake, and as a similar consideration was valid on the side of Pontius Pilate, who appears to have had his own, not wholly reputable, reasons to keep himself in the good books of the central government, Jewish and Roman authorities had no difficulty in coming to an understanding. As the Evangelist acidly comments: "And the same day Pilate and Herod were made friends together." The Jews examined the case and delivered the prisoner; Pilate put him to torture and determined his punishment — who exactly gave judgment is somewhat unclear; Jesus' friends and followers took flight; and the sentence of death was carried out in the ignominious and overwhelmingly painful form of crucifixion outside the city gates. Like the book of Isaiah's "suffering servant," Jesus was "numbered with the transgressors" and died "despised and rejected of men, a man of sorrows."

4. Christianity after Easter

Christianity and the Christian church began with Jesus proclaiming the kingdom of God, and with the company of his followers.

But in that form it perished utterly on the death of its founder and the flight of his disciples. "We had hoped that he was the one that would redeem Israel" — such was the low-voiced expression later given by the Evangelist to the feeling of utter emptiness that must have taken hold of everyone. The idea that came up much later about the church having survived in *one* person's faith and hope between Good Friday and Easter Sunday, Mary, the mother of Jesus, tells us more about a distant posterity than about those days and nights themselves. The defeat being a total one, the event that Christians then and now call the resurrection of Jesus was, then, in a radical sense a beginning — a new departure from which a flood of light was thrown on "Christianity before Easter." The experiences described by the disciples as their meetings with the "Risen One" — events that, according to the apostle Paul some twenty years later, had been reported and handed down to him — made clear to them that the suffering and death of Jesus, and their own desertion and shame, far from being the end of everything, were everything's beginning: the entry into Life. By awakening Jesus from the dead, God had acknowledged his claims. Jesus' words and actions, and his promises, were thus confirmed as God's own, and by making the promises his own, God had initiated the work of fulfilling them — a fulfillment to be carried to its conclusion by the Lord's return and the awakening of *all* the dead.

Precisely this assertion was the point of departure for "Christianity after Easter." From that claim everything else followed, everything said by the Christians about the new people invoking the Risen One; about baptism and the meal of rejoicing — the signs of the new covenant established by Jesus between God and humankind; and about the new life in expectation and mutual love, the love that holds everything in common.

With that faith as the center of their existence, some remained in Jerusalem: "And they, continuing daily with one accord in the temple, and breaking bread from house to house, did eat their meat with gladness and singleness of heart." Others carried the message out into the world, with far-reaching consequences for themselves, for their hearers, and for the message.

Most of the individual phases in the spread of the new faith are insufficiently documented in the surviving sources. Enough is, however, known for us to be sure of the two most important things. One is that the spread was a rapid one; the other, that the ties to the Israelite-Jewish milieu to which Jesus had confined himself were cut or loosened with astonishing speed — astonishing in view of the role played in the life of the first Christians by the temple, the Law of Moses, and the Jewish traditions with their detailed and unconditional commandments enjoining one and only one way of living.

One generation after the death of Jesus, a considerable number of Christian congregations were to be found in the eastern parts of the empire and as far west as Rome itself. And after another generation or two, Christianity could with reason be called a universal religion, in the sense that it had rid itself of the bonds limiting it to its local and national origins and reached such a degree of organizational and intellectual independence that it could no longer be perceived as a subspecies of Judaism.

Among the most important causes of these developments were, first, the support initially given by the Jewish communities outside Palestine;

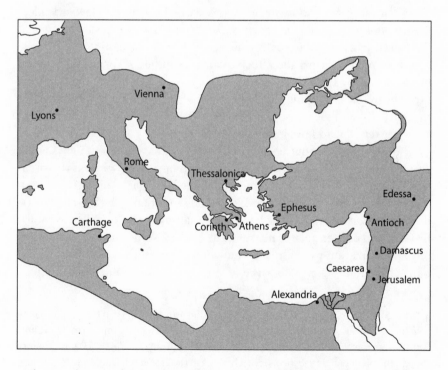

3. The map shows a selection of cities where Christian activity is documented before A.D. 200. Seventy are known with certainty, but the existence of many more can be more or less indirectly inferred.

second, the possibilities offered by the political, social, and cultural unity of the Roman Empire and by its net of internal communications; and third, an individual, the only early Christian known in anything more than the barest outlines: Paul, the "apostle of the Gentiles," a religious and intellectual genius of passion, zeal, and originality.

The most important characteristic of Judaism outside Palestine — in "the dispersal" — is not to be found in the features by which it differed from the Palestinian version. It was undiluted Judaism, governed by the Law of Moses, while conversely the Palestinian form had received some influences from abroad. Most important, from a Christian missionary viewpoint, was the existence throughout the empire of Jewish faith, cult, organization, and way of thinking. That ensured that the Christian message about the resurrection and the kingdom could be understood on its own terms and presuppositions: Israel's knowledge of its history under the guidance of the true God, the God who had made his will and purpose known in his Holy Book. When that is kept in mind, it is of considerably less importance that the missionary message very soon met with massive resistance from Jewish leaders everywhere, who would have no more to do with the risen Jesus than would the Palestinian authorities before his death. The decisive thing was that the message could be heard and understood in its authentic form, and believed by some, during this critical transitional phase. Later on the message was often heard as something different from what it originally was. The fact that such a loss of identity did not become the rule from the beginning is to a large extent due to Jews in the dispersal.

But the story about Jesus would hardly have reached the Jews at all, and it could not have been carried further to non-Jews, without the situation created by the Roman conquest of all the lands surrounding the Mediterranean. Even if the influence exerted on Christianity by the Hellenistic urban civilization, protected by the "Roman peace," was to prove much broader and deeper in later phases of its history, some characteristic traits of that civilization were already vitally important for the very first Christian generations. Their fate was to a large extent determined because pro-

4. "Synagogue and Church." This juxtaposition of Judaism and Christianity, the old and the new "people of God," represented by two female figures, became a common motif in Christian art from the ninth century onward. In this painting (from ca. 1200) in a Danish country church, the blindfolded *Synagoga*, from whose head the crown is falling, thrusts her lance into the Christ-Lamb (not shown) while the crowned *Ecclesia* catches the blood in her raised chalice, as a sign of the salvation mediated by the church's chief sacrament. (Courtesy of the National Museum of Denmark.)

fessional missionaries were able to cover long distances quickly and to make themselves understood everywhere, in the universal Greek language. Above all, it was determined because people in the Mediterranean cities — living in close intimacy, confined within small spaces — could become efficient bearers of the message by the method of one neighbor "preaching" to another. Without this "amateur" mission — deplorably little is known about how it was done — the rapid dissemination of the new faith would be utterly incomprehensible. It can, by the way, be added that without the hopes and longings and fears of this humble citizenry, without their conception of the good life and of what threatens it, important elements of Christian outlook on life during the early centuries cannot be fully understood.

But, as already hinted at, the big leaps were taken by men whose main occupation was the preaching of the gospel and the founding of churches. Only one of them is known by more than a name and a meager amount of personal data. That is Saul, known as Paulos or Paul, a Jew of the tribe of Benjamin, probably born in Tarsus, a city in southeastern Asia Minor, a younger contemporary of Jesus, educated as a theologian and trained as a craftsman in Jerusalem. He acquired his first contacts with the Jesus movement by taking part in the persecution of its members shortly after the death of its founder. This activity was, however, sharply interrupted by an experience the details of which he does not reveal but which convinced him that the Crucified One was a living personal presence claiming allegiance from him as his Lord and Savior. That experience led to his baptism by the Christians of Damascus and then to a missionary activity that in time was carried to eastern parts, to Jerusalem, to Asia Minor, Greece, and Rome. There he died by decapitation, most probably during the persecution unleashed by the emperor Nero in the year 64.

In the course of his journeys Paul visited Christian communities founded by others, and founded some himself. He also wrote a series of letters, through which he kept up his contacts with the churches, gave advice and admonition, and presented his interpretation of the gospel and its consequences, as well as his understanding of its relation to the history experienced by Israel under its God.

Paul has been called the "second founder" of Christianity, or even its one and only founder — meaning the perverter and distorter of its message. Neither of these assertions is likely to advance the understanding of the man or of the genesis of Christianity, even if they can be said to throw a useful light on tendencies in nineteenth- or twentieth-century Christian thought.

Stating this is not equivalent to saying that Paul is an easy figure to make out. But it is clear that the one thing he wanted to say above everything else resulted from a working out of central elements in the teaching of Jesus and the paschal message preached by his disciples. The core of Pauline Christianity is to be found in the claim that God, by acknowledging Jesus and raising him from the dead, had put all human wisdom to shame, shattered all human pretension to religious or moral worthiness in the eyes of the Creator, and opened a road to freedom, community, and joy hitherto blocked by the Law of Moses. Mercy, not precept, was what expressed God's innermost will and purpose.

By this statement — behind which may be glimpsed an experience of having received grace against all reason and deserts — Paul means the same thing Jesus did when he told his hearers of the forgiveness that is the precondition of conversion, not its reward. And he meant the same thing meant by the disciples in Jerusalem in the light of their double experience: that of their Master's victory over death and that of their own desertion — even if the conclusions they drew from it did not imply a breach with the Mosaic Law as a rule and a help in the new life.

But having thus stated a "unity in diversity," we have touched on the most difficult problem facing the earliest Christian church during its expansion beyond the frontiers of Palestine. Even though the Christians of Jerusalem differed fundamentally from all other Jews by asserting that the man who had been rejected by the people personified the fulfillment of all God's promises, they were nevertheless convinced that God's demands on them were the same as they had always been. The Law was binding for them, as it was for everybody. As an expression of the divine order of things, it was inextricably bound up with the claim that life on earth was endowed with a meaning and a purpose. Male non-Jews who adopted the faith were to receive the sign of the covenant — circumcision — and the rules of purity that precluded sharing food with non-Jews had to be observed. When Gentiles began joining the church without getting circumcised, and when Paul stepped forward with his claim about Christ as the "end of the Law," that is, as the one who by dying for transgressors had fulfilled the Law and put every human righteousness to shame, then a serious threat was implied against unity and coherence in a church now making its way into the wider world.

The problem — which was part of the general problem of "history" and "newness" in the Christian life, something we consider below — was never really "solved." No clear-cut decision was ever made in the matter, and only the disappearance — in the wake of external circumstances — of the "Law-abiding" branch of the church rendered the problem less pressing in its original form. But because of Paul's uncompromising rejection of the Law as a way of salvation, and above all because of the community of all Christians in claiming that the resurrection of Jesus was the fulfillment of the promises, Peter and the other leaders of the Jerusalem church entered an agreement with Paul to grant the "Gentile" Christians freedom from the Law, and to divide the missionary work accordingly. The fact that this unclear "solution" did not entail serious consequences is not least due to the circumstance that Paul and his congregations were as determined to maintain community with Jerusalem as they were to insist on their freedom from the Law. Why that was so is a question on which only a somewhat closer consideration of early Christian ideas about Christ, about the church, and about the new life can throw a measure of light.

5. Ways of Faith and Ways of Life

We have just touched on something critically important for the understanding of earliest Christianity; namely, it simultaneously held fast to a set of common tenets and also extended itself in various new directions, according to the answers found in various new situations to the questions raised by the common tenets.

As stated above, the core of the Christian message was the "Word" concerning Jesus' resurrection as testimony of God's loving-kindness toward the lost and of his will to create in them a new courage and joy in living. To this fundamental tenet was coupled the conviction that God's address to humankind entailed the church — a people with a history behind it — and that God's act of revelation through Jesus was endorsed and continued through the new covenantal signs: baptism, by which the new people was taken out of the old world, and the Eucharist, the meal of wine and bread by which the people communed with their heavenly Lord.

These words and actions, and the manifold biblical associations released by them, were used wherever men and women confessed Jesus as "the Lord" — in Greek: *ho kyrios*. This word was known to Jews in the dispersal as the name used for Israel's God in their Greek version of the Scriptures, and at the same time was familiar to the pagans as a title for the savior gods of the mystery cults — victors over death and corruption — and for the divine or semidivine Roman emperor, the mediator between heaven and earth, guarantor of "peace with the gods."

But for many reasons — one of which was the use of the same or similar words in other religions — the words and the actions were open to interpretation in various directions. They raised questions. Not questions about the truth of the paschal message — that was unshakable — but about its meaning in relation to what was otherwise believed and thought, hoped, loved, and feared by Christian people.

Those questions about meaning, relevance, and consequences can be summed up in three main questions; namely, Who is — and was — the Risen One? What is the church? What is the Christian life?

a. Who Is Christ?

Who is he whom we confess as the Risen One? And who was he? For these questions the early Christians were able to refer to a series of answers given by Jesus himself. And at the same time they gave expression to their own reflections. Those two things merge in the tradition. Many of the answers allegedly given by Jesus to the question of who he was — answers that were transmitted and collected by the first couple of Christian generations — are derived from what those Christians knew *after* Easter. It was in the light of Jesus' resurrection from the dead that people first fully understood what it meant to say that one's relationship to him crucially determined one's relationship to God and to God's kingdom. This claim — the only one that can with full certainty be ascribed to Jesus himself as far as the question of his "identity" is concerned — was interpreted by the Christians in two mutually coherent ways. They interpreted it by the words they — in some cases perhaps rightly, in other cases certainly or probably not — transmitted as sayings of Jesus, such as the one about the "Son of Man," the celestial figure that was to return from heaven as judge and savior at the end of time; or the one about the Savior King who would gather the people from the corners of the earth; or the one about the Son who had come from the Father and returned to him. And this claim they furthermore interpreted through their reflections upon it, as theological thinkers and writers, as church leaders, and as rank-and-file Christians: reflections such as those upon the "Word that became flesh," the divine child born by a virgin, the "Second Adam," the cosmic ruler conquering the powers of evil, the high priest who goes behind the curtain offering the sacrifice of redemption, the suffering servant that bears the sins of the world and is "made a curse for us" in order to restore what men have broken down, the Lord who is invisibly present in the meal of bread and wine, the bridegroom whose bride is the church, the head whose body is redeemed humankind.

Three lines of thought are common to this multitude of reflections on the Lord of the church. First, he is everywhere seen as the one who fulfills the promises made in the Holy Book of Israel. He reveals the innermost meaning of that book. It is a book about him, no matter whether it speaks in open terms about the Messiah and about the new pact to be established between God and his people, or covertly, in terms of Israel's kings and its sacrificial animals; or in terms of the brazen serpent in the desert; or of Melchizedek the priest-king who came to Abraham, the people's father, bringing bread and wine.

Secondly, Christ is not just an expression of God's will and purpose for humankind; he is its *unique* expression. God has spoken through many prophets and acted through many kings and priests. But only one is *the* prophet, king, and priest, because in reality he is something more, namely — as some Christians put it — "God's only begotten Son," "the brightness of his glory and the express image of his person." Accordingly, some spoke of him as of an eternal person, one who has always been with God — "Before Abraham was, I am" — and as one by whom God created the world as he re-creates it now through his victory over death.

Finally, everything said about Christ is something said at the same time about created and saved humankind and the life it has been called to lead. He is the one who comes to the people having relinquished his divine glory in order to lead the people back with him into a redeemed life. And everything said about that is said out of a churchly situation, in the context of men's and women's common confession, praise, and adoration.

That is precisely why the other two questions are raised.

b. What Is the Church?

What is the church — that people to which we know we belong because Christ would gather a people to himself? That is the second of the three great questions posed by earliest Christendom, a question to which it has given a number of answers.

Here, too, it is a common presupposition that the new which has happened is connected with the old, namely, with Israel and with its history. That is already evident from the Greek word *ekklesia,* by which the church is designated in the early writings and, incidentally, in modern Romance languages as well. The fact is that this word — "the assembly which has been called out" — is the name not only for the popular assemblies of the Greek city-states, but also — in the Greek version of the Hebrew Scriptures — for the people of Israel in its capacity as a congregation of worship. Consonantly with that, the church is sometimes understood as the

5. A third-century wall-painting of a meal with bread and fish in the Catacomb of Priscilla in Rome. The fact that the meal is set in a room intended for the funerary meals celebrated by the Christians as well as by their pagan fellow citizens suggests one of its meanings. But many other allusions must be taken into account, such as Jesus feeding the crowds with loaves and fishes, the apostles' meal of fish with the risen Christ, the heavenly banquet to be celebrated by the saved together with the Conqueror of death, the Eucharistic meal, and, not least, the fish as the mysterious symbol of Christ, "the One to whom we belong, we small fish who are born in water," as Tertullian (ca. A.D. 200) writes, alluding to baptism. Put together, the initial letters of the Greek words for "Jesus Christ, God's Son, Savior," form the Greek word for "fish." (Courtesy of Foto Pontificia Commissione di Archeologia Sacra.)

"remains" of Israel, or the "true Israel." And above all, the biblical prophecies about what is going to happen when the time of salvation dawns are used when describing the early days of the church. Thus the words from the prophet Joel: "And it shall come to pass afterward, that I will pour out my spirit upon all flesh; and your sons and your daughters shall prophesy, your old men shall dream dreams, your young men shall see visions. And also upon the servants and upon the handmaids in those days will I pour out my spirit."

We can discern a characteristic duality in this way of thinking about the church. On the one hand the Christians want to say: This people really is Israel, the people that was led out of slavery in Egypt, through the desert to the Promised Land; the people that received the Law and listened to the prophets; the people to whom God gave kings and priests; the people allowed to build the temple on Mount Zion. Every promise from God to that people is a promise to us, and God's demands on that people are demands upon us. On the other hand, this Israel is a *new* Israel living a new form of life under new demands, precisely because God has redeemed his promise to become present among it in a new way, in this crucial latter day when the meaning of history is being revealed.

This doubleness appears with a special force when talking about the organization of the church and its common worship. On the one hand this people is the heir of a structured people with fixed rules of governance and clear notions of obedience, with priests and laity, with kings, councils, and citizens. This is what the God of ordered creation has intended, and many of the precepts given to the old Israel can be — and ought to be — adopted as rules of conduct for the new people.

On the other hand, in these "last days" God has put all received order to shame; he has poured out his spirit over "all flesh" and made prophets — bearers of the new message — of everybody. The apostle Paul, who dwells more insistently than anybody else on the "foolishness" of God that has put to shame all human wisdom by the self-abasement of Christ, quite consistently also says much about the seeming casualness and the sovereign disdain of rules wherewith "the Spirit" makes now one, then another speak the word of power and illumination in the congregation of the faithful.

But the same Paul sees no problem in the churches also having more permanent leaders, who give form and order to their daily lives. And above all, he is indefatigable in pointing out that Christianity is not just any random thing that might arbitrarily be dreamed up by a Christian. It is a definite message, reliably transmitted and received, about a past event in which other past events have found their fulfillment. Neither side of the doubleness can be ignored or abandoned. Each of them is essential. Behind them lies in the last resort — for Paul but not for him alone — the conviction that Christ is at one and the same time the "Master" from the past and the Lord of the present. He it is who is as close to you as the word itself "in your mouth and in your heart." His action among the people is at no one's disposal, unforeseeable as it is in its capacity as action in a present that is open toward God's future.

In the "people of the last times" everything is, so to speak, definitive, but always as actualization of history. That goes for Bible reading, prophecy, and prayer, seeing that all of them aim at making real something from the past in the open present into which God speaks. And it goes for baptism and Eucharist, not least in the interpretation given by Paul when he calls baptism a dying and rising with Christ and the Eucharist a communion of Christ's flesh and blood. The innermost point of both these acts is thus to be found in their actualizing in the present the definitive revelation of the mind and will of God as it was carried out in the past by the sacrificial death of Christ.

This distinctive coinherence of "history" and "newness" may with good reason be called the most original expression of early Christian thinking about the church. But by no means does it cover everything that was thought or said about the church. Other expressed tendencies can be said to represent a sort of abandonment of the duality, tendencies such as an unhistorical spiritualization of the life of the people or a stronger emphasis on the church as a structured organization, an authoritative order. Yet other statements contain elements of interest for a speculatively minded posterity, the church being seen there as some kind of cosmic entity, an image of the universal order of creation. Several of those features will have to be considered in later contexts; they emerge again and again as sorts of "eternal companions" of Christian history.

c. What Is the Christian Life?

Once again, the burning problem is about "history" and "newness." The Christian life is a new one. It is the outcome of an unprecedented action by the Creator: his renewal of humankind and of the world they live in. In Paul's words: "If any man be in Christ, he is a new creature: old things are passed away; behold, all things are become new."

But the God of the new creation is at the same time the God of the old one. He is the God of history, Israel's God who has given the Law. As we have seen, the inherent tension between the two assertions had come to the fore as early as in the controversy about attitudes to the Mosaic Law. But the problem of old and new was much more far-reaching than the direct question about the Law. As was the case when thinking and talking about what it meant to be a church, the tension was permanent wherever Christians declined to abandon the specific Christian identity. That is amply documented in the writings of Paul — who at the same time reveals that tendencies toward a loss of identity existed in the church.

As stated above, Paul turned sharply against the abandonment of newness which he found implicit in the demand that everybody obey the Law of Moses. Confronted with Christian Jews who upheld the demand when dealing with Gentile Christians, he insisted that in denying their fellow Christians freedom they denied the cross of Christ — which represented the absolute and ultimate judgment upon, and liberation from, all

6. Dura-Europos, once a Roman frontier town in Eastern Syria, is now in ruins. When excavations were begun in the 1920s, three sanctuaries were brought to light: a Jewish one, a Mithraic one, and a Christian one. The last named is the earliest known example of a Christian community building. It was in use from the 240s until ca. 256 and had room for 60-70 worshipers. The photo shows the house's baptismal basin as well as some wall decorations. A fragmentary painting on the rear wall of the baptismal niche represents the Fall of Man, and Christ as the Good Shepherd. Such works testify to the early existence of Christian pictorial art outside the catacombs. The room shown here is now reconstructed in Yale University Art Gallery. (#Z65 Reconstructed Baptistry overall view, Dura-Europos Collection, Yale University Art Gallery.)

human pretensions of making oneself worthy in the eyes of God. The struggle conducted by Paul on this issue is against what could be called "Judaizers," but it is evidently also against *any* legalistic or moralistic denial of newness, whether it invokes Jewish tradition or not.

But equally important for understanding the early Christian situation is that Paul had to struggle on another front too, namely, against those who could be called fanatics for newness, who denounced each and every past history, Israelite or not, as well as the future in which the history of salvation was to come to its consummation. In their view, consummation had already happened. The "world" *had* been defeated, perfect freedom *had* been achieved, the power of the "old Adam" *had* been broken. Face to face with such enthusiasts as well as with those who gave themselves over to ecstatic forms of worship and neglected the clear, rational, and historically based manner of preaching and prophesying, the apostle pointed at some hard facts: A Christian life was a life to be lived under the conditions of "suffering with Christ" — persecution, doubt, temptation, moral defeat. It was a life led in an "interval," a moment in time where the decisive divine action had been carried out but where God's enemy was still alive and active in Christian minds and bodies as well as outside in the "world." The time of the church was a time where consummation was an object of hope, not of possession; in other words, something that was at no one's disposal. The time of waiting would be short, but it was the time in which Christians had to live.

This position over against the "enthusiastic" version of the attempt to abolish the tension is a remarkable confirmation of the fact that Paul regarded the problem of old and new in the Christian life as something that lay far deeper than the question about the Law. Even when the concrete precepts of "Moses" have been abolished as a way of salvation — which does not necessarily mean that they have been made away with as useful practical instructions for daily life — even then the Christian is still an "old" creature, for two reasons. First, because as a human being he belongs in the "first" creation, made out of God's goodness and his will to maintain an ordered life against chaos. And second, because as a *fallen* human being he gets entangled again and again in his evil desires. Being a Christian is an existence in a frontier area between two worlds, or rather two "aeons" or ages: the old one where Adam's fall is constantly being repeated by all his children, and the new where Christ, the "Second Adam," man as God intended man to be, has proclaimed the law of love and made love possible in the world by giving his life for the lost ones.

This "frontier existence" between two "ages" — in which a conflict rages between the church as it ought to be and the world as it is, between freedom and servitude, "spirit" and "flesh" — is implied wherever the apostle speaks more specifically of moral and social matters.

It is a teaching about obedience — the citizen's toward the powers that be, the slave's toward his master, the wife's toward her husband. In later phases of Christian history these precepts were often torn out of the Pauline context and placed in distinctly non-Pauline ones. The idea that the servants of the God of ordered creation ought to support the powers that be, in order to avoid social chaos, may of course not have been far from the apostle's mind. It is also probable that he was influenced by the paternalism current in his culture and by the depoliticized turn of mind prevalent among the citizens of the empire. But the decisive impulse is to be found in the "frontier" situation just mentioned.

It is, then, no wonder that the teaching about obedience is inextricably bound up with a teaching about love — a very down-to-earth one. The kind of love Paul speaks of makes no fuss of itself, and it is gladly content with being called by the names of unsensational, everyday virtues used by the apostle in the admonitory portions of his letters. "Bearing each other's burdens and thereby fulfilling the law of Christ" — that is what this teaching is aimed at, a teaching about love and obedience in one breath, directed at men and women who are "new" and at the same time "old" and who "have nothing that has not been given to them." The final summing up, so to speak, of how Paul conceived the Christian life is found in the words he uses about himself, but with general scope, in his second letter to the church in Corinth, the passage about those who are "as unknown, and yet well known; as dying, and, behold, we live; as chastened, and not killed; as poor, yet making many rich; as having nothing, and yet possessing all things." The words are unmistakably Pauline, and they are no doubt uttered out of a background of deeper reflection than can be taken for granted among "average Christians" of the first century; but the attitude to life that they reveal was, quite definitely, not special to Paul.

The conception of the Christian life as a life on a "frontier" is fundamentally common to almost all writers of the earliest period. It must invariably be understood against the background of what was said about the resurrection of Christ. The Christians are "new," because Christ has conquered death and because they themselves have — as Paul puts it — died and risen with him in baptism. And they are "old," precisely because they have *not* died and risen again. Both statements are, one could paradoxically say, total ones. In no other way were those writers willing to attempt the task of speaking *both* of that which has come from outside human reach — "that which has not risen in any man's heart" — *and* of that which clearly enough has its birthplace in the hearts of fallen humanity. A couple of generations after Paul, the unknown author of the Gospel according to John gives expression to a similar way of thinking when he speaks of resurrection as something that is a present reality as well as a future one. In that Gospel Jesus is represented as saying not only "I shall not lose anything of what the Father has given me, but I shall raise it on the last day," but also "He that hears my word, and believes in him that sent me, has everlasting life, and shall not come into condemnation, but has gone from death to life."

Such lines of thought are, then, representative of very early Christianity. But they are also important in a larger perspective of time, in two respects. First, they bear witness to an endeavor to connect what is said about the Christian and the church with what is said about Christ. In times to come this endeavor became a distinctive mark of all such Christian theologies that achieved any kind of historical impact.

Secondly, by these lines of thought a perennial problem of Christian theology is indicated with painful precision: how to define the relation between "already" and "not yet." In other words, the tension between two equally necessary propositions, that about salvation having already happened and that about it not yet being a consummated reality. In what follows, occasion will often present itself for noticing, directly or indirectly, what could result from neglecting the problem or whittling it down — but also for observing what could happen when it became obtrusively alive in a number of new ways.

d. Unity and Diversity

As hinted at above, the writers whose "Gospels" and letters and other works comprise our sources for forms of life and thought of the first Christian generations staked out the directions for later developments. That was due not only to the fact that they were regarded as principal witnesses and as "apostolic" figures, entrusted from above with a special task of formulation and transmission, but also because several of them, and above all Paul and "John," were original and seminal thinkers who, in contradistinction to many of their successors, were able to resist the temptation to make the things they had heard more tractable than they were.

Their writings differ from each other in a great many respects. That is not only because an account of the life of Jesus, labeled a "Gospel" (*euangelion*) in the narratives that go by the names of the Gospels of Matthew, Mark, Luke, and John, undertakes another task than does a doctrinal letter to a congregation, such as one of Paul's, or a history of the spreading of the message, such as the Acts of the Apostles, or some sort of congregational sermon, such as the Epistle to the Hebrews, or a prophecy about the end of time and the return of Jesus, such as the Apocalypse of John. But even more because the individual writers were interested in different aspects of the common message and emphasized different elements of it. One can vividly demonstrate this by comparing the way of thinking of Paul and "John" about the "churchly" aspects of the message, or through reading "anti-Pauline" polemic conducted by the author of the Epistle of James, or indeed by considering the mutually contradictory ideas put forward about the "origin" of Jesus, who could be regarded as someone "made into" Lord and Christ but also as an eternal person, descended from his seat in heaven with God.

The "diversity in unity" presented by such differences of thought and opinion is one element of tension in early Christianity. Another is the conflict between the thinkers known to us directly and those more or less totally unknown ones against whom the former write — "Judaizers" and "enthusiasts." Yet a third source of tension is that about which regrettably little can be said with certainty: the tensions between, respectively, the elite

7. The earliest known papyrus fragment of the Greek New Testament, one of the treasures of the John Rylands Library in Manchester, England.

known to us through their writings and the common people whose outlook and practices can only be glimpsed through those same writings. Although those tensions cannot be sufficiently documented through what is incidentally recorded in the texts — instances of the modest agonizings of petit bourgeois morality, of speculations about the power of the stars, of opinions concerning the sacrificial meat on sale in the butchers' shops, of frictions between the poor and the better-off, of gossip among neighbors — there is ample reason to believe that the tension in fact existed.

In any case, one thing is essential for understanding the life and thought of the earliest Christians in general and their internal conflicts and tensions in particular, namely, the difference between "confession" and "theology." The confession of faith in him who "went around doing good"; who died on the cross for the sins of humankind; who rose on the third day; and who was to return as judge of living and dead was simple, accessible, and common to all. It held everybody together by being heard in the gathering for worship where the risen Lord himself was present among his people. Above all, it was no homegrown thing; it had come from outside in the strict sense of that word; it was the message that had been "received" as something utterly incontestable.

Theology was something else — a series of human reflections drawing conclusions on the basis of the confession. Those conclusions and reasonings could be, and often were, in mutual conflict, but they need not in any destructive sense divide those that confessed the faith.

The hammering out of the articles of faith in written words is one element of a general process of consolidation that was active throughout the earliest period of Christianity, but which makes itself felt with special clarity toward the end of that period.

6. Consolidation

In a wide sense of the word, the consolidation of the new religion can be said to have taken place as soon as it became clear to all interested parties that this was no mere variant of Judaism. This fundamental decision about something that Christianity was *not* was, of course, made by the Jews as well as by the Christians themselves.

The decision about what, then, Christianity *was,* as a system of belief and community, was taken at a considerably slower rate. It was a gradual process, lasting until well into the second century at least, and in a number of respects longer. It ran along several different lines.

The most important — the one that in a sense gathered everything else up into it — can be characterized with one word: worship. That is so because it was precisely in the gathering for worship that the Christians learned who they were as a people apart, entrusted with a special message. According to general opinion in the early church, Christianity was something that *happened*, and above all happened in the worshiping congregation. Here the Lord himself was invisibly present; here history became present reality through reading of the Scriptures, through prayer, preaching, prophecy, and singing, in baptism and the Eucharist. And here, more than anywhere else, men and women learned what it meant to be brothers and sisters. As Paul expressed it: "There is neither Jew nor Greek, there is neither bond nor free, there is neither male nor female: for you all are one in Christ Jesus."

Whoever belonged there was thereby a Christian; whatever was acknowledged there was thereby Christianity. The event of common worship was the touchstone for everything else.

This, then, was the framework for the working out of the individual features of consolidation. Apart from the two central events — baptism and the Eucharist — those features were: the creed, the Scriptures, and the ministry.

The creed, in the sense of a short, formulaic summary of the contents of the faith, was a natural part of the ritual for baptism, but it also figured in other contexts of worship. One such formula was the ultrashort one recorded by Paul: *Kyrios Iēsous:* "Jesus is Lord"; another is the hymnic piece, transmitted by the same writer, about him who was in the form of God but took upon himself the form of a slave, obedient unto death; him to whom was given a name above every name, the name at which heaven, earth, and hell shall bow.

But the creed was, after all, nothing but a summing up of what was contained in the Scriptures — Israel's Bible, read and interpreted in the context of common worship, and understood in its capacity as prophecy, a story about the coming Christ. In other words, a book "written for our admonition, upon whom the ends of the world are come." That book, and at first that book alone, was the Bible of the church, a basis for the Christian thinking that we have considered above. But with time a number of more specifically Christian texts were added. Some of them were accounts of words and actions of Jesus, collected and written down in the form of "Gospels," probably during the last three or four decades of the first century. Others were letters or other writings that, like the Gospel stories, were read during Sunday worship and exchanged among the congregations. There was no fixed consensus as to which texts were to be read. Only from the last half of the second century onward do we find instances of normative collections of Scriptures — books that yet later became *one* collection, known as the "New Testament," the "books of the new covenant."

Lastly, like creed and Scripture, the function of church leadership was bound up with vital interests of worship. From the beginning, someone had to uphold order and guarantee the conformity of baptism, Eucharist, and preaching with what had been "received." It was only at a somewhat later stage that this function assumed clearer outlines and began resembling a priestly office. That has, of course, to do with the first Christians' general view of the church as a people where the Spirit had been poured out over "all flesh" and to whom it was said: "You are a chosen generation, a royal priesthood, a holy nation, a peculiar people; so that you shall show forth the praises of him who has called you out of darkness into his marvelous light." Wherever such words are taken at full face value, a priestly office wielding authority over "lay" people is not the first thing that comes to mind.

Nevertheless, in time it *came* to be thought of. There is, in fact, a suggestion of it as early as the turn of the first century. That becomes clear from a letter, written by the congregation at Rome to that of Corinth, in which allusions to Israel's priesthood are drawn in to support an admonition to obey the leaders of the church. A similar line of thought is pursued in the so-called Pastoral Epistles, where a strong emphasis is laid on the leadership exercised by "bishops," "deacons," and "elders" in their capacity as guardians of the "sound words," the received doctrine. And in the course of the second century the idea and practice of a "monarchical" episcopacy began gaining ground — a one-man leadership of the entire life of the congregation, entrusted from above with authority over the rest of the "people." What thus began taking shape was later to become one of the most staple elements of Catholic teaching and practice.

Why and how this development came about is a question to which no simple answer can be given. One may think of the "delay" of Jesus' return, or of the general Israelite heritage without which the church was no church, or of the structures of authority in the surrounding society and culture. Situations of crisis must certainly have played a part, as for instance those deriving from "heretical" contestation of the received message, or attacks from outside in the shape of pagan harassment and persecution. Such situations were likely to support the case for a firm leadership whose decisions could be taken quickly and without debate.

Be that as it may, here we find the clearest sign of the institutional consolidation with which the new religion's period of genesis can be said to come to an end.

part two

Christianity as a
Mediterranean Religion

1. Context and Events

The new religion, which until the first decades of the second century had achieved a degree of elementary consolidation, underwent significant further developments in the course of the following three to four centuries. Those developments took place in the framework of a Mediterranean civilization, created by the cooperative forces of — on the one hand — Hellenistic and Near Eastern cultural traditions and — on the other — the imperial power of Rome.

The lands on the shores of the Mediterranean constituted — together with the areas approaching the Rhine and the Danube, and later, Britain — a cultural and political unity. Among the factors making for unity among these lands, the Mediterranean Sea itself was probably the most important. It is a "law" of preindustrial history that the sea unites whereas the land divides. Across "our sea," as the Romans called it, a lively traffic and a brisk trade went on, with goods coming from all the surrounding areas.

This traffic was one between cities. With that word another of the great factors of unity is pointed out. The ancient city societies — *poleis* in Greek, *civitates* in Latin — displayed a great number of similarities of governmental and social structure and ways of living — originating, as they did, from one and the same Greek city-state tradition. City-*states* is precisely what one may be allowed to call them, notwithstanding the fact that they had been incorporated into the Roman Empire. They enjoyed a wide measure of internal self-government under their councils and magistrates as well as jurisdiction and powers of exploitation over the surrounding country areas.

The municipal power elite that was responsible for the government of the cities can rightly be designated as the third factor of unity and coherence. These men's economic status as landowners and rentiers, as well as their political and social dominance in the life of their city, was everywhere the same. Almost equally important was the fact that they constituted a cultural elite, with a common outlook on life, derived from a "classical" literary schooling.

That normative culture, resting on Greek and Latin literature such as it was read and interpreted in schools throughout the empire, was in itself a prime factor of unity, but it became of special importance by being the common culture of the power elite, contributing to the supralocal coherence of that class of people.

Over the city-states rested the "Roman peace," the Pax Romana, as a

33

force of security, coordination, and exploitation. In local affairs the imperial government by no means played a part comparable with that played by modern states. Nevertheless, with its machinery of administration, defense, military control, and tax collection, organized in provinces under governors in the provincial capitals — the *metropoleis* — it was a force whose presence made itself unmistakably felt, as demonstrated, for instance, in the history of Jesus.

It was a political, military, and financial power, and only in slight measure a cultural and religious one. That was partly because it originated in the western Mediterranean, always poorer in that respect than the East. To that must be added that from time immemorial, religion had been a local concern before it was anything else. The city and its gods; the gods and their city — that was, so to speak, the religious watchword. Consequently, the gods of the imperial city never became the gods of the empire in a real sense. The supralocal religions in the empire — flourishing and expansive cults, many of them — had no connection with the state, and they were, at any rate, too numerous to serve as factors of coherence. One exception confirmed the rule. The cult of the emperor had quite a lot to do with the state, but it was less a genuine religion than an expression of political loyalty. As such it pulled some weight, but it never gained real power over people's minds and hearts.

The hearts and minds of the powerless, subjugated peoples are a quantity to which the historian has very limited access. One thing is, however, clear: they contributed little or nothing to the unity of the civilization. It is of course true that the forms of life of humble city folk, peasants, agricultural laborers, and slaves displayed fundamental similarities from place to place. But it is also a fact that there was a gaping gulf between city life and country life, that linguistic and cultural differences between regions were more heavily felt among humble people than in the elites, and that the people had practically no part in imperial business in any direct sense.

The imperial unity covered, in fact, tension and conflict that could explode in situations of crisis. Both the unity and the possibilities of disunity were important for the development of Christianity as a Mediterranean religion. That will become clear, indirectly as well as directly, in the following chapters. In the present context we confine ourselves to a short sketch of the main phases of that development from circa 100 to circa 450.

The spread went on as it had begun, from east to west and with its main support in the larger cities, whose upper classes in time became represented among the leading groups in the congregations. During this dissemination process the Christians were frequently harassed and perse-

8. *Notitia dignitatum,* a Latin manuscript from the fifth century, shows how persistent was the cult of the emperor in the early Christian empire. After an emperor's accession to the throne, his images were distributed in the provinces and honored there with candles and incense. The illustration shows an imperial image on a table with lighted candles. (Reprinted by permission of Bibliothéque nationale de France.)

35

cuted — first locally and later on an imperial scale — on account of their "atheism," i.e., their abstention from the pagan cults. That was, however, no real obstacle to the church working itself out as a fully organized institution, led by its bishops, with considerable material resources, with a strong grip on its members' conduct of life — in short, as some sort of "state within the state." At the start of the fourth century an important proportion of the inhabitants of the eastern regions appears to have been Christian, whereas the percentage was much smaller in the West where, incidentally, a native, Latin-speaking Christianity was slow in being established.

This was the situation, then, in which the emperor Constantine "the Great" concluded an alliance with the church, with the result that, in the course of the fourth century, the imperial power became Christian and Christianity became the official and exclusive religion of the empire. This sequence of events implied a widening of the possibilities available to the church for influencing the population of the empire, as well as a change in its material circumstances and in the social composition of its governing elite. Those events did not, however, imply any deep-reaching change in its organizational structure, and still less in its message — what the state needed from the alliance was indeed precisely its firm structure and its coherent worldview. It is certainly true that the Christian religion underwent very important changes during the Mediterranean centuries, but most of them had taken place before the alliance with the state, and they took place within a permanent pattern of thinking and practice. It will, therefore, be advisable, in what follows, to consider those centuries as a coherent whole.

2. Mediterranean Christianity — Internally

After the turn of the first century, the Christian religion was present and identifiable in the world at large. What happened to it afterward was certainly not uninfluenced by the surrounding world, its impulses and its constraints. But it happened primarily in the form of answers to questions that were raised inside what could be called the church's own house. Therefore, this "own house" will occupy our attention in the first place, and we begin where the Christians themselves saw the beginning of everything: in their common worship.

9. The early Christian basilica is a legacy of the pagan world. This type of building was used by the Romans for many different purposes, such as law courts and markets. Under the empire, it became common to place an image — for example, a statue — of the reigning emperor in the building's semicircular apse. This practice foreshadows the representation of Christ in Majesty in the Christian churches. The basilica shown here is St. Sabina in Rome (ca. 422-32). (Courtesy of the Danish National Art Library, Copenhagen.)

a. Worship

Christian worship began with the preparation for baptism. This was, in its mature form, a lengthy process during which the candidate was required to participate regularly in the first part of Sunday service: Scripture reading, prayer, singing, and preaching. The early stages of the process are illuminatingly described by Augustine (354-430), the North African bishop, in his booklet *On the Teaching of the Unlettered*. Here the teacher's most important task consists of a narrative covering the whole of history, from the creation through the vicissitudes of the chosen people; to the life, death, and resurrection of Jesus; and further on through the history of the church until the present day, with a concluding glance at the future: the return of Christ, the day of judgment, and the church's everlasting "rest" with God. According to Augustine, this narrative is aimed at making the candidate look at himself as belonging in a coherent divine plan, understandable to everyone willing to listen. The claim that history finds its fulfillment in the church is, then, tantamount to saying that it is fulfilled in the candidate. This knowledge is the indispensable base for his initiation in what *cannot* be understood until it is experienced: God's mysterious action in baptism and the eucharistic meal. The candidate is, accordingly, required to demonstrate understanding by "giving back the symbol," i.e., reciting the creedal formula by heart, as a proof that he has made it his own.

Baptism itself, in the form known to us from Hippo Regius, the city of Augustine, took place in the context of the church's greatest feast, the paschal service, beginning on Easter Eve. It went on throughout the night in an ocean of light, reflected in the cathedral's marble columns and playing on its woven tapestries, and it reached its culmination in the celebration of the Eucharist on Easter morning. In this long feast, full of readings, prayer, and song, the candidates for baptism took part as a close group to whom the bishop and his priests addressed explanations and admonitions suitable for their needs. Everything was done to impress on them that this was to be the most important event in their entire lives. Their descent into

10. Baptismal basin in Sufetula, approximately 200 km. south of Carthage in Roman North Africa.

the baptismal pool, their confession of faith in the triune God, their ascent from the water, followed by their being clothed in white; their anointing with consecrated oil on their forehead and breast; and finally, their first Communion — all this, taken together, signified their passage from darkness to light, from chaos to order, from death to life. Or, perhaps more accurately, through death to life, baptism being, according to Paul, a dying and rising with Christ.

Precisely this idea provides the key to the understanding not only of baptism, but of the paschal feast and the church's worship in general. What is taking place in all stages is exactly such a process of past salvific events being turned into present reality. That appears from the texts being read during the night: such as the one about the creation of the world when God made light and order emerge out of chaos and darkness; that of the passage of the Jews across the Red Sea; or that of Jonah, who was freed after three days in the belly of the whale — a mysterious pointer to the death and resurrection of Christ. It appears also from the symbolic acts and gestures being performed. One of them was the anointing of the newly baptized — something that was later to develop into the separate rite of confirmation. Anointing was the sign of the new Christians' incorporation into a people anointed like Israel's kings and priests and in conformity with their King and High Priest himself: Christ, the "Anointed One." It was, in short, a sign of their membership in a "royal priesthood." Another symbolic rite was the present of milk and honey to the baptized as a sign of their entry into a life in which the full meaning of the Promised Land of the Bible was revealed — the land "flowing with milk and honey." Above all, the Eucharist itself constitutes the great transposition of past things into present ones. When bread and wine are consecrated and "turn into" the body and blood of Christ at the recitation of his own words of institution, then the sacrifice made by Jesus is turned into present reality for the people. And the eating and drinking of the bread and the wine is a sign of the new people's incorporation into their Lord and Savior himself, thus coming into renewed existence as a people, or as branches on the true vine, Christ himself.

From all the words and actions of the feast, light is thrown back on what had been said and done during the course of preparation. Only in that light can it be fully understood what is meant by teaching that the entire history of salvation is "gathered together," concentrated or epitomized in the individual man or woman being taught. Precisely this is what Augustine has in mind in a central passage of his book. There he begins by letting the teacher tell his pupil about the Israelites' first Passover in Egypt when the blood of the paschal lamb was smeared on their doorposts so that the angel of death would pass them by. Then he explains how the innermost meaning of that story is revealed by the blood-stained cross of Jesus on Golgotha. And finally — with an allusion to the initiatory "crossing" of the pupil — he says: "With the sign of his suffering and cross, you shall today be marked on your forehead as on a doorpost — and that is what happens to all Christians."

The Easter service as a whole was a celebration of the events to which Christianity owed its existence; it was, therefore, the most important of all the church's acts of worship. No wonder that baptism, the individual Christian's passage from death to life, was placed in this context. No wonder either, that the normal Sunday service was regarded as a reminder or, better, a making present of Easter, and that the weekly fast enjoined to Christians was fixed on Friday, the day Jesus died.

No wonder, then, that the festal calendar that was gradually established began as an extension of Easter. By slow stages the "church year" came into being, with two new principal feasts, Pentecost and Christmas; with a time of fasting before Easter and a time of Advent before Christmas; with Marian feasts and feasts in commemoration of the glorious deaths of the martyrs; and with a more or less stable distribution of Scripture texts on those days as well as on ordinary Sundays.

Evidently this arrangement is an expression of the way of thinking behind the celebration of baptism and Easter. The church year is structured by the high points of the history of salvation, bound together by biblical texts and tied into a constantly repeated sequence of a year's length, with the constant aim of transposing past events into the present.

Everything considered here points at something centrally distinctive of Christianity as compared with all other religions in the ancient world — Judaism partially excepted — namely, the way in which the "mysteries," God's incomprehensible and uncontrollable interventions in the world of men, are consistently being viewed in the framework of a rationally appropriated historical context.

This distinctive mark was, however, also strengthened by the role played in weekly or daily worship by the rational instruction of every Christian. This is, of course, especially valid as far as the Sunday sermon is concerned. This was the bishop's responsibility, and its point of departure was the day's text, interpreted word by word with constant emphasis on the Old Testament's character of prophetic witness to Christ and, conversely, on the New Testament being a fulfillment, revelation, and clarification of what had been darkly hinted at in the Bible of Israel. This interpretation might then conclude in a consideration of some problem of practical conduct: in a warning against heathen practices, such as astrology and magic, for instance; in an instruction concerning sexual discipline in marriage; or in a tale of horror about what the heretics were up to against the one true church.

Much of this is relevant for what will come under consideration later on. What interests us here is the naked fact that a rational instruction about the life made possible by the "mysteries" was deemed indispensable by the ancient church. The church was a place where God's saving intervention was celebrated by a "sacramental" actualizing of past events and where salvation was experienced by the faithful in a way that ultimately was God's own secret. But it was also a school where knowledge was imparted to all and sundry, and where attitudes and conduct were being formed by conscious channels, laid out by human hands. Last, it was also a place where people ought to be able to have fun, a substitute for the theater and the gladiatorial games. The popular reactions to which surviving texts bear witness — applause for the sermon, sighs and loud laments, beating of breasts, etc. — must, incidentally, often have made the experience of divine service a considerably livelier one than that provided by Catholic as well as Protestant worship of later periods.

b. History

"The law of prayer is the law of faith" — that is the way one of the pivotal perceptions of the ancient church has been formulated. What is meant is that everything that is to be thought and believed about God and mankind comes out of what is experienced as a living reality in worship, and that only what is important in worship ought to be considered relevant for belief. The statement is by no means an unconditionally valid one, but it may be said to be more valid than any other comprehensive judgment. The ancient Christians had, of course, more ideas about sacred history, about Christ, humanity, and the church than those directly occasioned by the experience of worship; and the way those themes became problems for theological thinking was often the result of impulses and challenges from outside. But the point of departure for the reflection with which the challenges were met lay above all in precisely what was experienced as a living presence in the gathering for worship: sacred history, the Savior, the individual, and the people. And something similar can, with reservations, be said of the structures of church government that were gradually worked out. This proposition provides us with a guideline for the following sections. We begin with a look at the thinking about history.

The fact that this thinking achieved a rounded and theologically coherent character was due to two challenges from outside. The earliest one
came from the "dualist" tendency of thought which regarded itself as
Christian and which in at least one instance — that of the "arch-heretic"
Marcion — was in fact profoundly imbued with centrally Christian patterns of thought. Among its other representatives were the Christian
Gnostics and — somewhat later — the Christian version of Manicheism.

A short answer to the question of what is the inspiration for a dualist
view of life may be found in an experience of deep and radical alienation.
That of which the innermost essence of a human being consists, its spiritual nature, its, so to speak, "real I," is in dualist thought experienced as
something radically different from everything else in the world. The essence and will of corporeal nature — including that of man himself — is
utterly at odds with the spirit. An enmity, impossible to allay or conciliate,
exists between the two; and if nothing more remained to be said about the
human condition, the only attitude possible would be despair. But, the
dualists say, there *is* more to be said. The misery is not the original condition; the spirit comes, not from this world, but from somewhere else, from
God's totally different world. Only because of some disastrous event
somewhere beyond human reach has it been taken prisoner by the darkness that confronts the light of God. And, the dualists continue, neither is
the misery a definitive one. From outside, from the divine world, a messenger has descended to the captive spirits, a divine teacher who has made
their true origin known to them and instructed them in how to forsake the
world and thus liberate themselves in order to return to their true home,
the purely spiritual existence.

The dualist thinking, whose fundamental motives and tendencies
may be thus summed up, did not normally appear in this simple and radical
shape. Considered as a whole, it constitutes, rather, a jungle of partially
contradictory speculations and stories. Decisive in our context is, however, that it presented itself as a genuinely Christian thinking, in opposition to the allegedly false and twisted kind of Christianity preached by the
church. Traditional Christians, the dualists maintained, had failed to grasp
the true meaning and concern of Jesus and his apostles. The authentic message was not about the Creator's saving intervention among his creatures,
but a message of liberation from the wicked or clumsy creator of this evil
world and of a return to the true God, him of whom nothing whatever had
been known before the advent of the divine illuminator. Jesus had not become a man of flesh and blood — the heinous substances of creation. He
had not died, and he had not risen again. As a foreigner, a messenger from

11. This sixth-century mosaic in the church of St. Apollinare in Classe near Ravenna, Italy, shows the three great Old Testament foreshadowings of Christ's sacrificial death. To the left stands Abel, the first innocent victim; to the right, Abraham with his son Isaac; and between them Melchizedek, whose person was believed to refer to the future Savior in a double sense: he was both king and priest; and he received Abraham, the people's father, with gifts of bread and wine. On the altar table in front of him are two eucharistic loaves, stamped with the cross, and a pitcher of wine. From above, God's hand reaches down toward the center of the picture, where heaven and earth are united in the sacrament. (Courtesy of the Danish National Art Library, Copenhagen.)

the unknown God, he had only made use of a sort of illusory corporeality in order to make it possible for the captive spirits to listen to his teaching. After accomplishing his task he disappeared, but his listeners — those who had received the salvific knowledge from him and had thus become the "knowing ones," the Gnostics — were eventually to follow him out of the world, leaving behind all who could not or would not listen.

This kind of thinking appeared in its most dangerous form — to the church — with Marcion toward the middle of the second century. The seriousness of the threat he presented to traditional Christianity was not only due to the fact that he — like other dualists — appealed to a widespread uneasiness about Old Testament ways of talking about God and man, or spoke in much simpler and more accessible terms than did many other dualists. Above all, it was due to his having made his own — more profoundly and passionately than other Christian dualists and indeed many an orthodox thinker — something altogether central in the original Christian message. Namely, the assertion — common to Jesus and Paul — that God's was a kind of love that made away with all human pretensions in the matter of salvation. That love, Marcion claimed, could not have come from Israel's God, the god of law, of punishment, and of revenge. If that love was a true one, then he could not be God; and if he were God, then that love was impossible. But, as was shown in the life and teaching of Jesus, it *was* possible; therefore it came from the unknown God, the Stranger.

By the dualist assertions — which in Marcion's case were carried on through several centuries by the church founded by him — the Christian view of history was not only questioned but utterly denied. Therefore, Christian thinking about history took the form of a showdown with Marcion and the other dualists.

One way to meet the challenge was for the church to point at its own existence and give a factual account of its own history and of the way its message had been transmitted. This method was used because of one of the ways the dualists argued for the genuineness of their Christianity. In order to make that plausible, it was not enough for them to abolish or reinterpret the Bible of Israel. It was also necessary to get rid of those parts of the Gospels and Epistles that went counter to their claims. That could be done by postulating a secret tradition from Jesus via the apostles down to themselves. It could also be done by "purging" the Gospels and Epistles, which had allegedly been falsified by insertion of nonoriginal material. That was how Marcion reasoned. He set to work composing the first New Testament, consisting of purged versions of the Gospel of Luke and the Pauline letters — thereby, ironically enough, providing the church with the final impulse to collect and define its own New Testament canon as its norm for doctrine and conduct.

Confronted with such attempts, the orthodox writers argued that the Israelite heritage, as well as the church's understanding of Jesus, had been present in an open and controllable manner during the entire history of the church. Nothing was secret there; everything lay open on the table; as it looked now, it had always looked. This claim, they continued, could be substantiated by an enumeration of those bishops and priests the individual congregations knew to have been their leaders in the past, and who as an unbroken chain connected the church with the apostles — with Peter, for instance, as far as the church at Rome was concerned. This idea of an "apostolic succession" by which the church's interpretation of its heritage had been guarded, and which guaranteed the authenticity of that interpretation, became an important part of the antidualist thinkers' efforts to demonstrate the coherence of sacred history from the creation until the present. But the dualist claims could, of course, not be refuted by that argument alone. The most important task was arguing not only for the antiquity but for the truth of church doctrine. In other words, the task was to make plausibly clear that the God of the Old Testament — notwithstanding everything that appeared to make him different from the "Father of Jesus Christ" — was the selfsame God as he; and that, consequently, salvation came from nowhere else than from where life itself had come, body and soul, animals, birds and plants, as well as everything else in the good Creator's wisely ordered universe.

This task was taken in hand by writers such as Irenaeus from Asia Minor (d. ca. 200) and Origen of Alexandria (d. ca. 254). Both aspired, generally speaking, to place the responsibility for evil where it belonged, and to disclose the unity of divine action through the history of both "covenants." Everything began, they argued, with the God of love. His overflowing love was the sole cause of the creation of man, body and soul. Creation took place because love is something that never lies still and always strives to communicate itself. Accordingly, the purpose of creation was for the human creature to find its fulfillment in freely and joyfully returning the Creator's life-giving love by loving him and all fellow creatures. The freedom, which was there because love is freely given — or it is not love — was, however, abused by man when he revolted against God in selfish and life-constricting pride. By that revolt, not by any evilness or imperfection in God, evil came into the world. But the Creator did not give up on his creatures; his love did not lie still. Against all deserts he kept fallen humanity alive by his providential guidance: he gave his Law, he spoke through the prophets. As was fitting, he made use of sharp remedies whenever necessary, as evidenced by Old Testament tales of harsh discipline and prompt punishment of evildoers. But behind the tough measures lay the constant will to restore that which man had broken down in himself and in the world around him. That was the will that finally came to unique expression in the appearance of God's Son, the "Word of Creation" in the person of Jesus, the man born of a woman: in his life of perfect love and in his sacrificial death. His resurrection from the dead meant that the "Second Adam" had restored what the first one had destroyed; and since then, the powers of renewed life had been, and would to the end of the world be, active in the church. History was, then, a unitary, coherent course of action from beginning to end, guided by *one* divine will. The God of salvation was no stranger; he "came unto his own" — that is, to a creature that had himself to thank for the mess he had made of his life.

This energetic working out in theological terms of what was presupposed, and lived, in worship became one of the most stable elements in the thinking of the ancient church. It could at times assume naive forms, as when no tree could be allowed to grow in the Old Testament without being taken to be a prophecy of the cross of Christ; and it could also be carried through with extreme subtlety, as was the case with Origen, whose logic carried him far into the beyond, resulting in reflections on the "prehistoric" fall of the blessed spirits and speculations on the restitution of all things, the devil's salvation, and even the possibility of eternal repetitions of the entire process. Regardless of such differences, the constant purpose was to formulate and defend Christianity's original assertion about the coherence of creation and salvation. At the same time, it might nevertheless occur to the reader of those writers that the original relation between "history" and "newness," such as it can be found in the apostle Paul, became somewhat blurred under the hands of his successors. They are not free of a tendency to smooth over the tension between God's demands — they are made harmless through "love" — and his forgiveness — which is made problematic through moral reservations. Consequently, a tendency can be discerned to regard the meaning of history as something unproblematically transparent instead of something that must in the last resort be a matter of faith.

The *other* instance of the phenomenon discussed here, a thinking about history provoked by an outside impulse or challenge, can be found in *On the City of God against the Pagans,* the long treatise Augustine wrote after the sack of Rome by the Goths (410) in order to refute pagan claims that the troubles of the empire were caused by its having turned Christian. This

46

thinking is relevant in later contexts too. Here there is reason to emphasize one specific element: In Augustine's view, sacred history — as well as any other kind — is a *social* history. The love with which the creature responds to the Creator's love is by its very nature a love from which a society springs, and the same goes for the self-love, the sinful pride that is the cause of the revolt against the Creator. God has willed a society of loving creatures, but from the very beginning the revolt of a group of angels, and then of the first human couple, has led to the formation of *two* societies. One is bound together by a common love of God as the source of all being and goodness; the other by that solidarity of hatred, spite, and desire that lies at the root of robber bands and of empires. From the beginning of human history the two societies have been represented by people such as Abel, the innocent victim, and Cain, the fratricide and founder of cities. From generation to generation they live on as history-shaping forces, clearly recognizable in Holy Scripture and — to the eyes of faith — in postbiblical history as well. But they are not earthly societies only. In the evil city all the fallen angels are active, conniving with evil men here and in hell, while the city of God is a community of love that unites not only men of unselfish love here and in heaven, but all the unfallen angelic powers with them. Each of the "cities" or "states" displays its own internal life and external effects, and they will continue doing so as long as the world shall endure.

We will have to return later to the perspectives opened by this line of thought on the church and on its relationship with state power.

c. The Lord

"Knowing God is knowing his merciful acts." By these words, coming from a Christian theologian of a much later age, something important is indicated about the ancient church's way of thinking about God. God is known because he is the Lord of history and because his mighty acts are experienced in worship. That is equivalent to saying that, above all, he is known as Christ and that everything said about the Father and the Holy Spirit is determined by the experience of Christ. No wonder, then, that what occurs before everything else to the ancient church when it sets about thinking about God is the series of concrete, down-to-earth biblical images of a personally active maker, lawgiver, judge, and deliverer, images that are precisely those constantly emerging, with Christ constantly in mind, in the words and gestures of worship, in Scripture reading, in sermons, and in the sacraments. Christ is present in creation, in God's speaking into chaos. He is present in Israel's king, leading the festal procession up to the temple; in the high priest entering the Holy of Holies; in the bridegroom running over the mountains; in the sun's passage across heaven as a joyful warrior. All those Old Testament images, and many others, are implied whenever the New Testament figure of Christ is under consideration — the preacher of judgment and mercy in Galilee, the crucified and risen Lord, the judge from the skies. And conversely, listening to the Old Testament can never lead to understanding without the New being implied — without, in other words, remembering him whom Augustine called *humilis Deus,* the "humble God" who has walked on the bare earth, *humus,* and given his life for his friends. It is significant that precisely this figure is discerned by the eyes of faith in the Old Testament tale about the young Isaac bowing his neck under the sacrificial knife; and about the "servant" who suffers for the people.

It is on this background of concrete, humanly recognizable images that the ancient church's more abstract forms of theological discourse — its concepts of God — must be understood.

But not on that background alone. We must add the contacts that from an early time were established between Christian theology and the religio-philosophical traditions of the surrounding culture. From there came some of the forms of speech utilized in theology and, above all, the requirement that contradictions be rationally surmounted — a requirement that was more at home in the world of philosophy than in that of the biblical narrative and metaphorical speech. That was a demand with which Christian theology sought to comply, more or less successfully. But the central impulse to conceptual thinking came from the persuasion, derived from the experience of worship, that God is met with in and by the man Jesus. "What exactly," theology asks, "does that mean? — and how does that assertion relate to other indispensable assertions?" Among such assertions is precisely the one that makes an adaptation to philosophical forms of discourse desirable; namely, that the Creator has made himself known to mankind through the power of reason with which he has endowed them, and that an appeal to this God-given ability is a necessary preliminary to the proclamation of salvation through Christ in his church.

All this flows together in the form of theological speech known as the Logos doctrine. In using *Logos,* the Greek word for "word" and "reason" alike, as a name for Christ, the ancient church served both interests: the biblical-churchly one and the philosophical one.

Logos is the Word of creation, spoken at the beginning of things, the Word by which light came where darkness had been, and order out of chaos. It was the Word that called forth living creatures, and last of all man, the thinking creature endowed with speech, capable of answering the Creator. This Word of creation, order, and communication has since then been spoken to Israel; but now it has come uniquely close to man by becoming man itself in the man Jesus Christ, the Re-creator of the damaged and wayward human creature. Consequently, when the church uses the word "Logos" about Christ, then that is an effective way of formulating the pivotal claim of Christianity: that in Christ man meets God. This cannot be more clearly expressed than by saying that he, the Re-creator, is the very Word that called the world into being. Nor can a better refutation be found to the dualist idea of Jesus as the foreign guest.

But likewise, a philosophical interest is served. By identifying the Logos with Christ the church maintains, over against the world of philosophers, that its message is the answer to *their* questions as well as to the church's own. That becomes clear when it is remembered that the central question of philosophy is precisely the question about Logos, the Universal Reason that provides the principles of order and coherence in nature and in human thought and life.

But when it was stated that the Word of creation had become incarnate in Christ, something more was evidently meant than concepts like power, reason, wisdom, speech. The deepest reason why the divine Word had throughout history been creative action and thereby endowed the world with form and order, structure and direction, was that it was itself a *person.* Logos was the person in and by whom God had always made himself known. The words and actions of the Logos were God's own words and actions, because he was "the brightness of his glory and the express image of his person" — in one word: his *Son.*

The claim that in the life and words of the mortal man Jesus God's eternal Son had lived and spoken had already been made by very early Christian writers whose works could now be read in the New Testament. Some of them had reflected on the connection between the life of Jesus and the Son's action as the one by whom the world had been created and upheld. In the prologue to his book, the author of the Gospel of John had used the very word "Logos" about Jesus.

But in such an assertion problems were implied — heavy ones that gave Christian theology more than enough to do. One was that outsiders were likely to regard the doctrine as a piece of mythology of scant explanatory value. Much more important, though, was the risk of getting into difficulties with the church's own assertion of the oneness of God.

The creed — "Hear Israel: The Lord our God, the Lord is one" — by

49

which the Jews defied a polytheistic world was confessed by the church as uncompromisingly as by Israel. But how could it be made compatible with the talk of the "other" divine Person of whom Jesus was allegedly the incarnation? But on the other hand: How could one use any lesser word than

12. This section of a mosaic showing the adoration of the Magi in the great church of St. Maria Maggiore in Rome is the earliest known representation of the child Jesus as enthroned ruler. It expresses the idea of those participants in the theological controversies of the fifth century who laid more stress on the union of Christ's divinity with his human nature than on his "normal" humanity. To that way of thinking, Christ must be called God from the very beginning of his earthly life, and Mary (not shown here) is the Mother of God. The mosaic bears witness to the strong influences from imperial court ceremonial. Behind the child stand four angels guarding the throne, and above his head the star of Jacob, and of the Magi, demonstrates his messianic dignity. The woman at his side is probably a pagan sibyl, believed to have foretold the birth of the Savior.

"God's only Son" when one knew and confessed that in Jesus God had let himself be known in a unique manner, radically otherwise than in any of his previous messengers? Especially when it was remembered that only in the light of Jesus could the full meaning of past communications from God be grasped.

This problem represented one of the two major dilemmas facing the ancient church when speaking theologically about Christ. Some thinkers tried to solve it by identifying Christ with the Father — a solution that could not help raising highly awkward questions about the incarnation, and about the death of Jesus. Others attempted to describe the Son as divine, but subordinated to the Father. He by whom God has created the world is himself created, and there has been a "time" — before time — when he was not. That, simply put, was how the fourth-century "Arians" argued, in order to avoid compromising the philosophically defined unity of God. But according to Athanasius, bishop of Alexandria (d. 373), the price paid for that unity was disastrously high. If the Son is not God in the full sense, then he is a creature, albeit a unique one; so how can it be believed that he can save the creatures? The very idea of salvation — re-creation of life through the death and resurrection of Christ — necessitates the claim that he who became man was God in the full sense of the word. Nothing less could be contemplated, and no consideration of philosophical difficulties must be allowed to get in the way. A theological and ecclesio-political controversy broke out over the question — which, incidentally, was not made any easier when the Holy Spirit, the divine power believed to make Christ present in the church and in its individual members, was drawn into the dispute. The struggle could not be brought to an end by scriptural authority, since the Bible provided arguments for the main positions as well as several intermediate ones. What must — in default of a better word — be called the solution emerged in the form of the so-called dogma of the Trinity, an elaborated version of the Athanasian position. By means of this officially sanctioned doctrine God is stated to be "One in three Persons," i.e., one divine Being manifesting itself personally as Father, Son, and Holy Spirit.

This dogma by no means answers every question that might occur to theologians. The importance of the decision for all later church history lies elsewhere. It lies, first, in the borderline it drew against what could from now on *not* be said. The Son, the agent of creation and salvation, could from now on in no sense of the word be called an intermediate being. Secondly, with this decision a space was kept open for what had from the beginning been expressed in "untheological," i.e., religious, existential, historical, metaphorical, forms of speech concerning God's revelation of himself in Christ. In other words, the trinitarian dogma is intimately connected with what is said and done in worship. Whatever the assertion about the Son's "consubstantiality" or "unity of essence" with the Father might mean "in itself" — that question has always been debatable or dismissed as meaningless — in the wider context of worship and conduct it means that the Power who is present whenever words are said or acts carried out "in remembrance of" Jesus — as an "actualization" of his words and deeds — is none less than the Author of life himself.

The *other* major dilemma for theological speech about God was one whose contours had been drawn before the official adoption of the trinitarian dogma, but naturally enough it was only after that adoption that it became the main subject of debate. The dilemma originated in the following question: How can we as rationally thinking theologians understand and explain the assertion that the Son who is God in the full sense of that word has also become fully human? That he *has* become so is unequivocally stated in the creed, it is proclaimed in preaching and teaching, and it is celebrated as a "mystery" in the eucharistic meal. But how is it to be — however imperfectly — *understood* by a Christian who is required to render a rational account of his faith?

One thing was not slow in becoming clear: no matter how a theologian might be inclined to answer the question, he would be sure to run into intolerable difficulties. If he — as did one party in the controversy — took at full value the Gospel presentation of Jesus as "one of ourselves," a complete human person, then he made it impossible for himself to explain in what sense a plausible "union" could be established between that person and the divine Son. If, on the contrary, he joined the opposite camp by taking that union as his point of departure, then it became impossible to demonstrate that what the Son had become was indeed a *man*. One of the two main "solutions" could not avoid the charge of talking about a man loosely combined with deity — and how could one be sure that such a one could be a *savior*? The other solution was painfully vulnerable to the opposite charge: that of describing a visiting deity disguised as a man — and how could such a one atone for the sins of *men*?

The dilemma got much of its cutting edge — and the controversy its bitterness — from the fact that both parties wished to uphold all three claims: full deity, full humanity, and complete union. Neither did it help the cause of theological peace that the question of Mary, the mother of Jesus, got included in the dispute. Highly sensitive religious and, incidentally, political and economic interests were involved in the celebration of Mary as the "Mother of God," but since in the last resort that title was incompatible with the first-mentioned view of Christ, it became a powerful additional cause of conflict.

No wonder, then, that here too the final solution became one better suited for "negative" than for "positive" purposes. The Council of Chalcedon (451) decided that Christ was "one person" in which "two na-tures" were united, "without division" and "without confusion." As far as the church's official attitude was concerned, that was the end of the matter, but as shall appear later, the decision caused deep divisions in Eastern Christendom.

The long controversies about the Trinity and the person of Christ constitute what could be called a fresh chapter in the story of "confession and theology." They confirmed that the two belonged together and that "theology" was in some way an extension of "confession." But from those controversies it can also be learned that the relationship had undergone a change. Among the symptoms of that were the extreme bitterness with which they were fought out, the mutual accusations of heresy, and the in-terventions on the part of political authorities. Why that was so is a ques-tion that belongs in another context.

d. Man

The acts of God in history find expression in the church's worship. But be-cause the church is an assembly of individual Christians, what happens to the "people" as an actualization of history happens also to the individual person, as becomes clear in, for instance, prebaptismal teaching. Ancient Christianity was not individualistic, but personalistic it certainly was, be-ing a message of judgment and salvation to the individual, immortal "soul" — that entity which could not be confused with anything else under the sun.

But knowing, as we do, that the Christian individual was always per-ceived in a "churchly" context, we cannot wonder at the fact that a wide web of relations connected the ideas current among Christians about indi-viduals with those about wholes. A more or less common presupposition of ancient culture — pagan and Christian alike — was the analogies drawn between the small, hierarchically ordered world of the individual or the family and the greater wholes of city, empire, and universe. The "macro-cosm" was mirrored in the "microcosm." In accordance with this influence from the surrounding culture, the questions about mental order or disor-der, harmony or disharmony between "higher" and "lower" in the soul and between soul and body were much more important in this period of Christian history than they had been in the primitive church. The church's decision against dualism was at the same time a decision not only *for* the Judeo-Christian stand on creation, but also for the Greek-Hellenistic idea of mental and social order.

It is useful to keep that in mind when considering the ancient church's view of man, in his original, his fallen, and his saved condition. And especially useful is it for understanding the answers given by Augustine, the Christian thinker most profoundly preoccupied with those questions.

His explicit and implicit watchwords when talking about the human condition are, precisely, order and disorder, harmony and disharmony, conceived analogously to what is known to be the orderly hierarchy of beings in the created world as a whole. Man has been brought into being in order to serve and love God with all his powers, but directly only with the "highest" of them, his reason-directed will. Everything else in man is meant to serve God indirectly by serving that power, just as the subhuman creatures are there to serve God by serving man. Thus, everything is destined to find its place in an order of being where every creature, each in its place, fulfills its existence by serving the respectively higher being. Ultimately, everything in creation serves and loves the One who is alone uncreated and independent, him who needs no fulfillment but whose love reaches downward.

But, Augustine continues, it is our painful knowledge, from daily experience as well as from what we are told about Adam and Eve, that this hierarchy of order and love has been damaged and warped. That has come about exactly where the highest of earthly creatures meets God, in the reasonable will of man. In that will, and not in the urges of the flesh, lies the root of the fatal revolt against God and his order. By refusing to serve, obey, and love where love is due, it has conducted itself as a being toward which everything else owes service and from which no service is due. In other words, it has usurped the place of God. But since the divine freedom and independence can never be gained and exercised by any created being, the unrightful pretension results in a catastrophe affecting the entire created order. As a consequence of the human will's refusal to serve God, man's "lower" faculties and bodily instincts refuse to serve the will, and the same goes for the whole world of lower creatures. Less mythologically spoken: the will demands of its surroundings something that it can never get because the demand is absurd: confirmation of its being something that needs no confirmation. The result is a desperate mess of frustrated desires, and of hopelessly repeated attacks on the order that — according to the Creator's will — persists through the revenge it takes on whoever seeks to break it down. Confronted with this wretched state of affairs — which reproduces itself from generation to generation, individually and collectively — the God of order and love launches his work of redemption by keeping mankind alive and counteracting its evil conceits. At last he brings the work to an unprecedented and definitive culmination by coming himself into the world in the person of the "humble God." Through Christ's example of what a human life was meant to be, through his self-sacrifice, and through his resurrection the great turn from inner and outer chaos and selfishness to a willing and joyful service in the Creator's order is made possible. The process through which the work of Christ comes to benefit the fallen individual is described by Augustine as something that is exclusively due to a divine initiative. It begins in a situation of utter powerlessness on the part of man. Man does nothing to prepare himself; he does not reach out for help from God. On the contrary, he reaches out for confirmation that he himself is God.

This is something that must be understood on the background of Augustine's own experience of conversion, as described in the *Confessions,* the great work of his middle age, in which he looks back on his wayward youth and reflects on the direction his life has taken. The central point here is found precisely in the acknowledgment that God had reached out for him long before he knew of it, and led him in the direction of something neither known nor sought by him. In the last sections of the book he connects his having been drawn out of his confused state with the events at the beginning of time when the ordered world came from out of chaos, light from darkness. This comparison serves to remind us of the interconnection of the individual and the whole. It shows also that Augustine considers his personal experience to be universally valid. But above all it testifies to his unshakable conviction that salvation, just like creation, is a divine act in the strict sense of the word. This was a tenet on which he never compromised, and it led him to trains of thought that few fellow theologians were inclined to follow. According to the logic of the initial assertion, salvation would be impossible without God's own intervention, visible in the sacrament of baptism. Consequently, infants that died before baptism would be lost forever. Further, since they had done nothing wrong, and since God condemned no one unjustly, then the sin for which they were damned to hell must be an inherited one, derived from the first man and communicated to them by the sexual union in which they had been conceived — an act which, in spite of its original goodness, now, in humankind's fallen con-

13. The creation and fall of man: a Carolingian book painting from the first half of the ninth century.

dition, represented the very quintessence of chaotic selfishness. This was a conclusion not easily swallowed by Augustine's contemporaries, although the doctrine of original or inherited sin was destined to a great future. Another product of Augustinian logic was considered even more problematic. That was the doctrine of God's eternal predestination of every human person to salvation or damnation. Here Augustine takes leave of mainstream Christian thinking, but the reasoning leading him to his conclusion proved difficult to refute, once his point of departure was accepted. Ever since then, the problem has vexed theological thinking and constituted a touchstone for the lengths to be gone or not gone by systematizing speculation.

There were, as a matter of fact, other thinkers with altogether different ideas about "the point of departure," that is, about the question of how salvation begins. Pelagius, Augustine's contemporary opponent, regarded his doctrine as absurd and contrary to the moral order uniting God and his creatures. Salvation, he said, came about by following the moral example of Christ. This was possible because sin was nothing but a mistake and a bad habit, caused by ignorance and lack of maturity. This was a line of thought for which Pelagius and his followers could count on sympathy in the Eastern Church, where the idea of salvation as a pedagogical process had long before, and with greater profundity and sophistication, been worked out by Origen. But remarkably enough, this "humanist" idea of a divine education of a human will whose powers increase in the process can also claim Augustine as an ally. According to him, the sovereign intervention of God in a human existence utterly lacking in the will to goodness and justice results in time in a gradual strengthening of such a will — one that is able to cooperate with the divine work of education and discipline, carried out through the church's sacraments and teaching as well as by means of the ups and downs of life. The distinctive mark of Augustinian "humanism" is its struggle to unite two at least partly contradictory assertions: that of man's chaotic state that can be helped by nothing but a sovereign act of God, and that of the Christian life as a process of growth toward restoration of an original order. Behind this struggle can be glimpsed not only the original Christian tension between creation, sin, and salvation, but also the problem-filled encounter between the Christian and the Greek views of man. Of that encounter, more later.

About this attempt at synthesis, considered in itself, it can with confidence be said that the question of its carrying capacity affects every other major question that can be asked by theology and the church. No wonder that in time it became a central concern of Martin Luther, for whom Augustine was in many respects the most important "interlocutor" and opponent.

14. Mosaic on a North African church wall (Tipasa). In abbreviated form the inscription runs like this: "He who believes in the resurrection of the flesh shall become similar to the angels of heaven."

As already mentioned, the Eastern tradition for dealing with these questions differed in a good many respects from the Western one, as initiated by Augustine. The Eastern guidelines were laid down by — among others — Origen of Alexandria, whose idea of a coherent history of salvation was a distinctly pedagogical one. For Origen, becoming a Christian was a movement toward what the dualists — on different premises — called *gnosis*, knowledge; and even though the ordinary church member could be sure of his salvation because of Logos's descent and his promise to the poor in spirit, the final goal for all was a higher one: personal and reflective participation in the life of divine reason. As the psalmist said: "Ye are gods; and all of you are children of the Most High." That was to be a form of existence in which theory and practice were different aspects of one and the same thing. The intellectual insight in the exalted truths about a higher world, an insight that lay hidden behind the simple words of the Bible, presupposed — and grew in step with — a purity of conduct in the person striving to gain insight. He was to become a man exercised in every virtue, a complete master of his bodily urges. Intellectually and morally, the movement was the same: from appearance to reality, from fleshly enslavement to spiritual freedom.

This view of man and his salvation was not without an inner affinity with the doctrine developed by one of the main parties in the controversy

58

about the person of Christ. Their emphasis on the Savior's human nature being completely suffused by the divine — "like a piece of iron glowing with the fire that heats it" — accorded well with a doctrine which regarded man's main goal as "participation in divine nature," conformity with the will of the Logos. The ties that connect this teaching with a doctrine of the church are to be considered in a later context.

Up till now we have been looking at the Christian individual in his capacity as a subject of reflection and debate among theologians. He has occupied us through a filter of the ideas that members of the church's intellectual and social elite formulated on the basis of their experiences in the wider context of specific cultural patterns. Those ideas do not lack reality; their influence on all later history is anything but accidental or undeserved. But they must definitely *not* be taken as descriptions of the life and outlook of Mediterranean Christians in general. The ancient church was full of men and women whose understanding of the human condition, we can confidently say, was not that of Origen or Augustine. What, then, was it?

This is where the surviving texts disappoint us. Though they deliver some information on ordinary church members' way of living in an outward sense, they remain, on the whole, silent when asked about what ordinary people were *thinking*.

Indirectly, something can be gained from the writings of theologians and church leaders and from the popular sermons in which they often vent their dissatisfaction with humbler brethren and sisters. The information that can be obtained in this way about, for instance, the widespread belief in astrology — or, as Augustine reported, the notion that Christ was useful for the next world and the stars for this one — can be relied on to express a part of popular reality. But only a part. Christianity would hardly have won over so many ordinary people if its message of liberation had remained without response — a liberation, that is, from the "powers" through God's personal presence in him who had been followed and obeyed by the star of Bethlehem and who had taken all the demonic powers captive.

One thing is, however, clear: much of what the preachers said to and about the people contains valuable information about *their own* view of man and his salvation. From their popular teaching do we in fact often learn more than can be learned elsewhere about the uncertainties and contradictions inherent in their outlook. Not without reason can it be said that it reveals their difficulties with rendering a clear account of Christian liberty. Certainly the Christian is liberated from the Law — that is what Paul has taught us — and that liberation is an act of undeserved grace. But can that truly and really mean that nothing is required of man if he is to be wholly

59

and definitely free, and safe? Can one really become glad without being reasonably assured of one's goodness? And that joy — does it not forsake you if you fail to experience the goodness that — according to Jesus — flows from joy? In practical teaching, reflections like those often resulted in a wobbly compromise between gift and demand, between "gospel" and "law." This uncertainty made it painfully difficult for ordinary Christians to make sure in what manner they were allowed to conduct their daily lives as Christians. The dilemma was exacerbated by the way in which the evil "world" out of which they had been "taken" tended to be understood by the experts. It was often interpreted as if what had to be shunned was everyday existence with its constraints and its pleasures, its bodily needs, its requirements of family and work, city and commonwealth. Theologians were — to be sure — fully aware that dualism was the heresy of heresies: a denial of the God of creation. In theory, they knew that Christians had been set free to live without fear in a world that in spite of sin and death remained the handiwork of God's love. But when required to give practical advice, they dared not face the consequences of that knowledge.

Perhaps the teaching about marriage and sex is where this becomes especially clear. In that teaching, hardly an affirmation of the goodness of marriage is considered feasible without a hastily added warning against its dangers and about the preferability of (the preacher's own) celibacy. According to that view, ordinary married people's main task — apart from the production and rearing of offspring — is to control themselves and cultivate a guilty conscience about sexual pleasure. In such a teaching, the foundations were being laid for one of the great "constants" of official European Christianity. It did not make Christian living any easier, especially if it was taken at full value. About how far that was the case, little can be known — apart from the indirect information that can perhaps be gained from the fact that the admonitions needed constant repetition.

e. The Church

Worship was carried out by the church, and the practice of worship as well as the ideas that "produced" worship or were produced by it reflect the nature of the church as an idea and an institution. And conversely, church organization as well as ideas about the church presuppose worship and the

15. Bishop's throne and clerical bench in the apse of St. Maria delle Grazie in Grado, Northern Italy (fifth century). (Courtesy of Osvaldo Bohm.)

notions of God, history, and humankind that found expression in worship. Moreover, in its capacity as a way of organizing social life, the church interacted in a special manner with the surrounding world. Thus, in a sense it can be said that all the threads of ancient Christianity ran together in that practical and theoretical concept: church.

When the church manifested itself as a community of worship, it did so under the leadership of its bishop. In the church buildings that were erected in the wake of the "Constantinian peace," the bishop's seat was placed in the center of the semicircle at the eastern end. There he sat, surrounded by his clergy; from there he preached to the standing people; and from there he stepped forward to celebrate the Eucharist at a freestanding table, around which were every year the newly baptized in their white clothes during the week after Easter. Everything not done by himself in the course of divine service was done on his responsibility and under his control.

His function as the leader of worship reflects his role as the central figure in the life of the church. The "people of God," the "royal priesthood" whose initially rather loose notions and practice of leadership were considered above, had by the third century assumed the character of a collection of monarchically governed urban congregations whose legitimacy as Christian communities depended on the presence everywhere of a duly elected and consecrated "successor of the apostles." Before anything else, the bishop was regarded as such a successor. That historically attested dignity was believed to guarantee the purity of the true message and the continuity of the original, God-willed ways of living. The bishop was the mediator and interpreter of the message; he was judge and arbiter in disputes between Christians; he controlled his church's financial resources; and he administered its daily life, assisted by the priests and deacons who owed their livelihood to him. In brief, he was king and priest of the royal priesthood, endowed with the apostolic authority to "teach them to observe all things whatsoever I have commanded you," to "feed my sheep," to "bind and loose" in heaven as on earth.

This last-mentioned prerogative came to be of particular importance. Many impulses from within and without contributed to the formation of the episcopal system, but the decisive working out and consolidation of the system was due to a problem with which the churches were confronted after the great persecutions in the middle of the third century. The problem originated in the wish of a great many Christians to rejoin the church after succumbing to pressure during the terror and sacrificing to the pagan gods. The decision was a difficult one. On the one hand, these people's sin

16. This wooden relief in the church of St. Sabina, Rome (fifth century), shows Christ's prediction to Peter: "this night, before the cock crows, thou shalt deny me thrice." Like the Gospel story itself, it is a remarkable testimony — centrally placed in the very city of Peter's successor — to the church's determination to stick to the uncomfortable truth that "there is none righteous, no, not one." The episode also provides solace to troubled consciences. Centuries later, the motif was used in European art as a reminder of the meaning of the sacrament of penance, and Peter was shown in company with David, the royal sinner, with the penitent Magdalen, and with the converted robber on the cross.

was the worst imaginable: worship of the devil. In principle, no separation from the saving community could be more definitive. On the other hand, had not Christ died for sinners, and would he not listen to the cry of a contrite heart? But was the heart in fact contrite? Who could tell that with certainty? What *could* be said with certainty, however, was that eternal damnation awaited the "lapsed" if they remained outside the community that God had entrusted with his work of salvation. Besides, in many cases the sinners could point at mitigating circumstances to which a just God, adjudicating justly, would have to pay attention. And finally, there was a risk that other people than the church's lawful leaders could take the cases in hand and decide on them independently.

The problem — which is primarily known from the letters and other writings of Cyprian, bishop of Carthage — was not a new one, insofar as it had already become common opinion that the words of Jesus to his apostles about their power of "loosing and binding," i.e., remitting sins or refusing to do so, were equally valid as far as their successors were concerned. But the situation — a universal persecution — was new, and the number of Christians involved was so great that an authoritative decision must entail far-reaching consequences. The decision, when it was finally made, was to the effect that the bishop, and no one else, was authorized to decide each individual case after examining the circumstances, and that his authority extended to full readmittance. This was in itself sure to enhance the practical weight of the episcopal office. But to that must be added that readmittance by the bishop's laying on of hands could take place only after a period of probation — its length dependent on the bishop's judgment — during which the sinner in search of peace with God and his church had to give public proof of his repentance by prayer, fasting, and almsgiving. Such efforts were, of course, standard expressions of Christian piety; they were expected of everybody; but the sinner who had been shut out and wanted in again had to cultivate them with particular zeal. It must hurt badly in order to help. This development led to a further strengthening of the bishop's position as mediator to the people of God's will. More and more he came to be seen as a lord of souls and bodies, a leader and a father figure on whose yes or no the sinner's destiny depended. It goes without saying that this position became even more solidly fixed from the following century on, when the powers of the state could be invoked in its support.

As for its organization, the ancient church can be said to have found its final form through the practical consolidation of episcopal monarchy. Everything that happened from then on happened with episcopal power as its point of departure and key element. In a later chapter we shall reflect on the originality of this form of leadership as seen from outside; here we shall content ourselves with looking at two further aspects.

One concerns something that leaps to the eye of the observer of episcopal types of later periods; namely, that in the Mediterranean church preaching and writing were in large measure a matter for bishops. The Sunday sermon was a normal episcopal activity, and so was the endeavor to clarify the contents and consequences of the faith through the writing of biblical commentaries, dogmatic or ethical treatises, apologies and polemics. It is, of course, not true of all bishops, many of whom were, indeed, singularly ill equipped for such tasks, but it is true of so many that it can be singled out as a characteristic feature in the idea of an ancient bishop. The fact that such men were active as preachers, directors of souls, and theologians was not without its effects on their way of carrying out their administrative and judicial obligations. And conversely do their preaching, their moral instruction, and their theological reasoning bear the impress of their experience as men of affairs, as leaders and decision makers. Accordingly, the process we ventured to regard as the "moralization" of the Christian message must be seen in connection with the development of an episcopal office whose responsibilities were precisely in large measure educational and moral. How does a genuine contrition look? That was one of the questions a bishop had to ask himself. Others might be: How is the repentant's way toward an acceptable status to be mapped out? Under what circumstances is the declaration "Your sins are forgiven" feasible? In how bad a shape must a Christian marriage be before something will have to be done? Is throwing a grain of incense on the sacrificial fire in front of the emperor's image worse than bribing an official to write a false attestation that such a sacrifice has been carried out? If yes, what effect must it have on the meting out of penance?

Secondly, on the basis of the locally limited monarchical office, a supralocal organization slowly began to take shape during our period. From earliest times it had been a common conviction that "church" was a word that covered both the individual congregation and the community of all Christians everywhere: the catholic, i.e., the universal, church. But not until the consolidation of episcopal authority did this conviction begin to acquire an institutional expression. It happened along several different lines.

One derived from the — often decisive — influence exerted by neighboring bishops on a local congregation's election of a bishop. Another can be discerned in the meetings held by the bishops of a specific region in order to hammer out a common attitude to some crisis or other. A third one was caused by the highly unequal resources at the disposal of individual bishops. Every town had its own bishop, and every bishop was endowed with full apostolic authority. But it was not unimportant whether he was leader of a big-city congregation like that of Carthage or Alexandria, not to speak of Rome, or of a small backwater church. Inevitably, therefore, small-town bishops came to be more or less subordinated to big-city ones, who were consequently enabled to speak on behalf of a great many colleagues. Such concentrations of power served to remind people that the church was something more than the local congregation, but they also encouraged tendencies toward disunity, as when, for instance, two theological parties were connected, each with a great episcopal see. In such cases political rivalry, municipal patriotism, and theological differences inter-

17. This icon (sixth century) from the monastery of St. Catherine, Sinai, shows the apostle Peter with the keys to heaven and a cruciform staff. (Courtesy of G. A. Sotériou.)

acted in a number of unholy ways. A special case of one bishop's supremacy over colleagues is presented by the see of Rome. Not only had the capital's bishop natural opportunities for dominance in Italy. He also claimed
supremacy over the church as a whole. On the grounds of the apostle Peter's special position, he argued that he himself was heir to the authority
with which Peter had been endowed in the Gospel of Matthew. If Jesus
would "build" his church on Peter, and if Peter had received the power to
"bind and loose in heaven and on earth" before anyone else, then that must
not be without consequences for Peter's successor. The claim did not meet
with approval in other great centers, and that is putting it mildly. Cyprian
of Carthage, for one, resisted it passionately, arguing that Peter had received his powers as a representative of the entire apostolic college, united
in fraternal solidarity. The ancient church was and remained an episcopal
church, or — if you like — one with several popes. But the practical deft-
ness with which a number of Roman bishops championed broadly acceptable solutions to disputed issues prepared the ground for what was much
later — under much altered circumstances — to develop into a Roman
leadership of the Western part of the universal church.

All those instances of supralocality were motivated from "within."
Others were caused by the alliance with the state — of that, more later.

The episcopal church was a clerical church, in the sense that the monarchical government of each congregation — including episcopal control
over the appointment of priests and other assistant personnel — had resulted in a thoroughgoing distinction between two separate groups: clergy
and laypeople.

As we have seen (above, p. 29), such a division was anything but easily compatible with the original view of the people as the "royal priesthood" who had received the Holy Spirit in their baptism. "The spiritual
man," Paul had said, meaning every single Christian, "judges all things, yet
he himself is judged by no man." It is well worth stressing that this was a
claim that was never waived as a guiding principle of Christian behavior.
Precisely as "kings," as just rulers of themselves; as "priests," sacrificing
themselves for their neighbor; as, in short, spiritual beings was how Christians had to conduct their lives. But in ecclesiastical practice, another way
of thinking won through, one according to which the consecrated clerics
were in a special sense entrusted with the Holy Spirit, and consequently
the sole wielders of initiative in the church. The bishop, and under his orders the other clergy, is sole mediator of the gifts with which Christ comes
to his people. He is the people's shepherd, their lovingly solicitous *pastor;*
and no one else is that. The "sheep" are required to let themselves be

guarded and nursed by him; he is neither nursed nor guarded by them. In principle, they are his sisters and brothers, but in practice he deals with them as does a father with his children, carefully weighing firmness against mildness, reward against punishment, gift against demand. As succinctly put by Gregory I, bishop of Rome from 590 to 604: "The Holy Church mixes hope and fear for her faithful."

As hinted at above, this pastoral-paternalist way of thinking went along with the acknowledgment that every single Christian has been called to be king of his own soul, priest in giving himself up in sacrifice to God and neighbor, and capable of a "spiritual" understanding of his own situation in front of God and in a context of cosmic and historical order. The far from unproblematic synthesis between these elements and the concept of a clerically organized church constitutes much of the originality of ancient Christianity as compared to its contemporary rivals. It is also one of the causes of its social and political effects.

But the synthesis was not inevitable. It had not from the first been the only construction possible, and even at the height of its influence it was contested by forces of resistance from within as well as from without. During the period under review, the Christian prophet, the Christian martyr, the Christian ascetic, and the Christian sage said and did things that explicitly or by implication, fully or half consciously, were in a state of tension or conflict with catholic normality. It is highly significant that prophecy, martyrdom, asceticism, and wisdom were to a large extent assimilable with that normality, but it is no less important to realize how much explosive material they contained.

Prophecy, the authoritative communication from above, uttered by someone whom the Spirit has taken hold of and chosen as its instrument, could of course, in a sense, be said to function in the church's normal ministry of proclamation and teaching. But it could also rise in protest against it and assume the character of a *new* expression of God's will and purpose. That was what happened in the Montanist movement from the middle years of the second century, in which the imminent end of the world was predicted and where the precept of absolute personal holiness was proclaimed by female as well as male prophets who claimed to be under direct inspiration from Christ, independently of the normal clerical leadership.

18. Mosaic from the apse of St. Apollinare in Classe near Ravenna, Italy (first half of the sixth century). St. Apollinaris is shown adoring the cross, surrounded by twelve sheep, symbolizing the apostles. (Courtesy of the Danish National Art Library, Copenhagen.)

The Christian martyr or confessor willing to face death for his faith during the persecutions appears to constitute tacit criticism of a bishop who was not himself in prison and did not — as did Stephen, the first martyr — see "the heavens opened, and the Son of Man standing on the right hand of God." Cyprian of Carthage, at any rate, met with difficulties of that order during the disputes about readmission of defectors. A signpost was, so to speak, raised in the history of episcopacy when it was finally decided that in such cases only the bishop had the authority to go further than a recommendation.

Indirectly, that decision contributed to a better-defined incorporation of the martyrs in the life of the church — after their deaths, of course. As generally recognized saints, they — and gradually also other deceased Christians of steadfast faith and holy life — came to be regarded as a distinct group in the wider context of the "communion of saints," living and dead. As such a group, they fulfilled several special functions. They were models for imitation, but above all they had powers of intercession, more effective than those of ordinary Christians. Their souls dwelt with God and were able to come before his throne with the prayers of the church and of individual Christians. In their graves, upon which the Eucharist was celebrated in their honor, the beyond was considered in a special sense present: there rested, full of supernatural power, the martyrs' remains — the bodies, or parts of bodies, that were known to belong in heaven where, after the general resurrection at the end of time, they were to be united with the souls that had given them life and whose earthly life they had provided with shape and context.

Martyrdom came to play an important role in the Donatist movement in western North Africa during the fourth and fifth centuries. Here the claim was raised that only "worthy" priests could act validly as mediators of God's saving grace. The sanctity which God had promised his people could only be communicated by men who were themselves holy and pure. When the Christian state took action against the Donatists, their opposition was intensified and deepened; with mounting bitterness and defiance they described themselves as the church of the martyrs, heirs to the victims of pagan persecutions, and to the Maccabees, Israel's martyrs who had given their lives fighting the "abomination in the holy places."

What was contested here was nothing less than a crucial point in catholic teaching; i.e., the assertion that *God* is the one who acts in the saving work of the church, and that he will let nothing and no one stand in his way. Augustine, who to his other pursuits had to add the pastoral and literary struggle against Donatism — the movement constituted a serious threat in his own episcopal city as well as in the area as a whole — commented sarcastically on the gap between the Donatists' moral claims and their actual conduct; but more importantly, he formulated in classical terms the catholic doctrine of the objectivity of sacramental action. As he said, the beams of the sun can go unsullied through a sewer; an unworthy priest brings damnation on himself in the day of judgment, but he is and remains a medium of salvation toward anyone who receives and makes use of his priestly actions in faith.

In the Christian ascetic, in his aspirations and his conduct of life, similar problems and challenges were involved — challenges that, in the long run, were more dangerous, considering that, whereas martyrdom proved a temporary phenomenon in the church, asceticism did not. In the Greek vocabulary of sports, *askesis* is the word for training. Accordingly, the ascetic is a person who exercises and shapes his bodily and spiritual existence with a goal in mind: the perfect life with God according to God's will and purpose, in obedience, sacrifice of self, and constant prayer. The ascetic ad-

19. Syrian reliquary (sixth-seventh centuries) shown in shut and open positions. By means of a canal system, oil poured into an external hollow could come into contact with the martyr's relics contained in the shrine; then the oil could be used by worshipers who dipped their fingers in the outer receptacle. (Courtesy of the National Museum of Denmark, inv. no. 15091.)

venture is one of unconditional engagement to obey the words uttered by Jesus to the young man in the Gospel: "If thou wilt be perfect, go and sell that thou hast, and give to the poor, and thou shalt have treasure in heaven: and come and follow me."

That was by no means a new idea among Christians, but not until around the turn of the fourth century did it find expression in complete and formal self-separation through renunciation, not only of marriage, property, and work, but of all other normal human bonds, including the ordinary life of the church. That could lead — as it often did in Egypt, Syria, and Asia Minor — to a purely eremitical existence, engaged in constant struggle with the demons of the desert. But it could also result in the establishment of hermit colonies or — much more important — monasteries with a regulated common life of prayer and manual work.

What was realized in the various forms of ascetic life was something that could be found enjoined or recommended in the church's Scriptures. But in the isolation from the ordinary church, and in the pretension to reach perfection through renunciation, self-discipline, and individual prayer, a threat was implied against the church's fundamental claim to communicate salvation by means of priestly teaching, discipline, cure of souls, and above all, priestly celebration of the sacraments. Of course, radical ascetics who showed open indifference toward the normal means of salvation made that threat particularly obvious, not least when they performed spectacular feats such as standing for years on top of a column, thereby arousing the people's imagination and admiration and gaining a prestige which in special situations could be exploited for politico-theological purposes. But the problem was a general one. The church could neither take leave of people whose "evangelical" striving for perfection benefited less advanced Christians, nor could it renounce its monopoly of administering the salvific acts on the basis of which every attempt at perfection had to begin and by recourse to which it must again and again renew its strength, namely: the apostolic preaching and the sacramental communication of grace, administered by the successors of the apostles. The "solution" to the problem — which nevertheless in a deeper sense refused to go away (we shall meet it again) — was found by decision of the same council that settled the dispute about the "natures" of Christ, in a ruling that all monasteries must agree to let themselves be regularly visited and inspected by their bishops. More importantly, however, ascetic thinking and practices began gaining ground in the ordinary church, most visibly among its clergy. That can be learned from Augustine's attempt at organizing the priests of his cathedral in Hippo monastically; but above all does it become clear in the priestly celibacy which came into use gradually in the Western Church from the fourth century onward. The rule of sexual renunciation for priests seems to have had something to do with the church's Eucharist having begun to be envisaged as a definitely sacrificial act, an act that involved the priest in something like a repetition of the sacrifice carried out by Christ on the cross of Golgotha. In the context of that kind of thinking, the notion and the demand of "cultic purity" must have appeared as a natural consequence, in analogy to what was known from other religions, Judaism not least. But the general movement in the direction of the ascetic life must have been a powerful factor too. At all events, the rule of celibacy contributed to the "domestication" of the movement, its partial incorporation in the life of the church. At the same time, the isolation implied by the priest's celibacy was of considerable importance for strengthening the general tendency toward a steadily deepening gap between the clergy and ordinary Christians.

Finally, the phenomenon of the Christian sage could give rise to reflections on internal tensions and contrasts in the life of the ancient church. It is, at any rate, worthy of note that Christian intellectuals such as Origen of Alexandria reveal, more or less explicitly, a tendency to regard a person who by means of speculation and self-discipline has come closer to the divine life than other Christians as worthy of wielding an authority superior to that of the bishops. This does not, however, seem to have grown to be a serious threat — perhaps because quite a number of bishops were theologically active: members, as it were, of the church's academic intelligentsia.

Be that as it may. Such a series of — often interconnected — phenomena is instructive for understanding the ability displayed by the ancient church to make productive use of a rich variety of ideas and practices not necessarily rationally compatible. Thereby a religious and ecclesiastical "style" came into being, which was to be of great importance in subsequent centuries.

Nevertheless, the consideration of those phenomena is equally instructive as a reminder that the church's road from "primitive church" to "ancient church" went through a series of choices that might have had different results. And not less important is it by impressing on the observer that the "deviant" tendencies and persons must have been more powerful and numerous than appears at the first glance. Thus far, if not farther, does the gloomy old saying remain valid: "History is written by the victors."

3. Mediterranean Christianity — Externally

The fundamental claims, reflections, and institutions of Mediterranean Christianity were homegrown ones, in the sense that the questions it asked and the answers it came up with were all organically connected with the ideas and presuppositions it had carried out into the wider world from its country of origin.

It is, however, also true that this religion established a multitude of ties to the civilization in which it tried to make itself at home. Impulses from that milieu influenced the choice of questions and became important for the form and direction taken by the answers. Conversely, the Christian religion came gradually to assume an active role toward the civilization, first as a challenge, later as one among its shaping forces.

a. The City

The spread of ancient Christianity was from city to city, and inside the city, from citizen to citizen. Both circumstances are important for understanding its distinguishing traits as compared to the Christianity of later times.

As stated above, urban life was one of the strongest cohesive forces of Mediterranean civilization. In the city, life was conducted in a way that was instantly recognizable from one place to another. Therefore, and in consequence of the lively traffic between cities, the new religion was able to settle in and spread farther rapidly. No less important: those conditions enabled the church to preserve, even without formal instruments of coordination, its supralocal — catholic — character.

The mutual similarities between the urban societies found expression not only in their form of government but also in less official institutions that could be of use to the Christians, either directly or because they facilitated the spread in indirect ways. Most important among such institutions were the Jewish synagogal communities where the missionary preaching began and among whose loosely affiliated groups of sympathizers — the "God-fearing" pagans — some of the first conversions are likely to have taken place. But also the voluntary associations of which a large percentage of the pagan population seems to have been members — clubs and communities with a religious coloring, designed for mutual support and provision of a decent burial — became important for the mission. On such a background the church was at least initially likely to appear as something not very worthy of notice, i.e., as just another association. Something similar can be said of the cult societies proper: the "mystery" congrega-

20. The sarcophagus of Junius Bassus, city prefect of Rome (355), decorated with biblical scenes. In the center of the top row, Christ is represented as the divine teacher. He delivers the "New Law" to the apostle Peter, while Paul stands at his other side. (Courtesy of the Danish National Art Library, Copenhagen.)

tions worshiping Isis, Mithras, etc. Like the Christians, they were present all over the Mediterranean world; like them, they celebrated the deity's victory over death; and like them, they observed a rule of secrecy concerning the cultic acts by which the worshipers shared in that victory. A city population's knowledge of the many lords and saviors — *kyrioi* — present in their city must initially have meant that the arrival of yet another *kyrios* was regarded as somewhat less than sensational.

At first, the missionary work in the cities was done by professional itinerant preachers, and later on the gradually emerging clergy must have been active in missionary work. But everything points at the nonprofessional mission having played a decisive role: in other words, "preaching" inside a family — the wife to her husband, the master to the slaves — or informal contacts among members of a tightly knit neighborhood. The knowledge gained by the Christians' fellow citizens through rumors of their mutual support and care of widows and orphans, and also by occasional visits to the "open" part of Sunday worship, must in many cases have resulted in some sort of loose affiliation, and later in full conversion, confession, and baptism.

The joiners comprised all sorts of people. In that respect the Christian communities differed from most other religious associations. From an early time the Christians covered most of the social gamut, from affluent citizens down to and including slaves. This breadth of recruitment — and not least the phenomenon of lower-class men in leading positions — could at times lead to internal tensions or downright schism, as in the case of Calixtus, a former slave who was bishop of Rome from 217 to 222. But such difficulties are of less interest than the social comprehensiveness itself. More than most other things, it has prepared the ground for the church's establishing itself as an "alternative society."

An interesting relation — on which the sources throw much less light than could be desired — is that between the social breadth on the one hand and the Christian religion's status as an "antisocial" movement on the other. The social breadth was a cause of scandal. It is no accident that pagan authors who from the latter half of the second century began to attack Christianity made much of the Christians' lack of regard for social distinctions in the internal affairs of the congregations. By emphasizing the new religion's openness toward humble folk and slaves, those writers probably aimed at opening the eyes of well-to-do Christians and making clear to them the dangers presented by the situation.

This was, however, neither the only nor the most serious ground of attack from high as well as low in the surrounding society. Worse than the acceptance of all sorts of people; worse than what was supposed or suspected concerning Jesus' shameful descent, his failure, and his ignominious death; worse than what was rumored to take place behind the closed doors of the house churches when the body and blood of the Lord was distributed to brothers and sisters, united during the banquet of love — worse than all that were the crimes summed up under the name of atheism. What was meant by that was the Christians' rejection of all the acts and words that from time immemorial had given expression to the mutual solidarity of the city populations, their common engagement in urban peace and prosperity — in other words, the official cult of the city's gods. That was where the Christians offended, and where they — because of the religious character inherent in all public festivals and manifestations of loyalty — were clearly *seen* to offend. This conflict on the grassroots level constitutes the most important precondition for the persecutions that came to be launched on higher levels.

But still, despite that fundamental clash of interests, it remained evident that the church encompassed a broad segment of respectable citizens from whom no other antisocial acts could reasonably be expected. In the last resort, that came to carry greater weight than the material of conflict.

As a result, Christianity ended up becoming the city's religion as well as the empire's. Its God became the god of the city, its festivals those of the city, just as its saints became the city's heavenly protectors and intercessors.

Two significant reservations are, however, called for. One has to do with the old cults' power of resistance, or rather, the strength of ideas inherent in them: conceptions that proved influential in shaping the use to which people put their Christianity. Astrological and magical worldviews and practices, polytheistic interpretations of the concept of saints — such things can render it difficult to make out how the common people's Christianity related to that of the theologians and the higher clergy.

To that must be added that the traditional forms of urban life were being undermined during the "late antique" period. Economic crises, imperial centralization, tax burdens, civil war, barbarian invasions, and epidemics threatened the traditional stability of the city societies, especially in the West where they had always been weaker than in the East. In this, then, is an additional reason why the new religion cannot unreservedly be said to have taken over the old one's function of strengthening social bonds and legitimizing the powers of leadership.

By stating that, however, we have touched upon matters that concern more than the cities. The emergence of Christianity and the church as powers in society can be fully understood only on the background of what happened on the imperial level as well as in the context of elite culture.

b. The Empire

"The world," Cicero had said, "is the common *civitas* of gods and men." It is an illuminating statement, not only because it reminds us that the state in antiquity drew its origins from the city society, but also because it helps us understand the connection between empire and religion.

That connection was a multifarious one. It had what could be called a philosophico-juridical side — hinted at in the saying just quoted, containing, as it does, a statement about the universe as an ordered whole in which rational powers work together, playing their several roles. Here laws are understood and obeyed; here boundaries are set between meaning and meaninglessness; here everyone is held responsible for upholding the order.

Also, that order has a historical dimension, in that the empire has become consonant with cosmic order as a result of a divinely ordained series of temporal events: from the fall of Troy until the present, from Aeneas's storm-tossed voyage, through the wars of conquest, to dominion of the entire "inhabited world." This final result is final in the absolute sense, according to the supreme god's promise in the *Aeneid,* Rome's national epic: "I have ordained a never-ending empire." And its principal expression is peace: a Roman peace, Pax Romana, guaranteed by the *pax deorum,* peace of the gods and peace with the gods.

The peace is upheld by correct religious behavior: cult and piety. The pious performing of sacrifices to the gods of city and empire is meant to ensure continuing peace and prosperity, as becomes clear, for instance, at the emperors' jubilees, where the promises made to the gods at the previous feast are redeemed by sacrifices, and fresh promises are made for the following period. On such occasions the harmonious interplay of cosmic forces, discerned in their fashion by the philosophers, is experienced by ordinary citizens when they observe how the sacrifices of men and the blessings of gods cooperate in the service of peace.

It was a warlike peace, imposed by military power in the face of a hostile world of barbarians beyond the borders and a dangerous world of peoples within. And it was a totalitarian peace, in the sense that each and every deviation from the peace-preserving cult was in principle tantamount to a breach of the laws of universal order.

When this notion of the empire as a religious quantity and the corresponding idea of the individual city encounter the Christian religion, conflict must, in theory, be the obvious result. In the light of the "political theology" of Rome, the Christians must necessarily appear as atheists in the full sense of that word: rebels against the gods and their order, against peace, security, and prosperity. As atheists they were accordingly denounced by pagan writers who also did not neglect pointing out how despicably they acted in benefiting from the blessings of imperial peace while at the same time refusing to contribute to the costs of peace — by military service, for instance.

They were similarly branded by the imperial government during the great persecutions. About those empirewide measures — one under Decius in the middle years of the third century and another under Diocletian just after the turn of the fourth — it can with justice be said that they were carried out in logical application of the tenets of "political theology." The emperor Decius ordained a general celebration of sacrifices to the gods; he ordered everyone who complied with the order to be put on record; and he cracked down, with executions or deportations to the mines, on those who refused. Because of the emperor's death in battle, the persecution was of short duration, but it was a determined and ruthless one, achieving what could be achieved within the technical possibilities available. That goes for the — tactically more skillful — Diocletianic persecution as well, beginning, as it did, with limited pressure and the purging of specified groups, and culminating in downright terror.

The success proved considerable, insofar as many steadfast Christians were put to death and many congregations torn apart, not least on account of a great many defections among clergy as well as laypeople. Moreover, there were cases of demoralization when well-to-do Christians took care of themselves at the expense of less-favored ones. Nevertheless, both persecutions came to nothing in the long run, and they were highly unrepresentative as far as the imperial government's practical behavior toward the Christians was concerned. Both factors call for an explanation.

As for the first one, the Christian writers provided an explanation — beyond the one which they of course considered most important, i.e., that God protected his church. It was implied in the statement: "The martyrs' blood is the seed of the church." That is to say, the martyrs' steadfastness in the face of death attracted pagans as well as encouraged fellow Christians.

This explanation is not altogether implausible. When the rhetorical bombast and the legendary frills provided by contemporary and later theologians is discounted, something remains that cannot have been wholly without effect on the pagan surroundings — to say nothing of the Christian ones. The great figures in the history of ancient martyrdom resemble our own time's martyrs for freedom and justice by being free of presumption and vanity. Perpetua, a young, literate, and well-to-do matron who just after the year 200 was convicted of Christianity and thrown to the wild beasts in the arena of Carthage, and who is known at first hand from one of the most remarkable documents of ancient church history, would if possible have preferred to stay with her child and family; and the way she stuck to her faith when offered the chance to go free by renouncing it was totally undemonstrative and devoid of theatrical gestures. But she was also utterly convinced of the road she had to take once the confession was required of her.

There is, then, something to be said for that explanation. But it can by no means stand alone. Leaving out of account the inherent attractions of the Christian faith and behavior described elsewhere in this book, one has to think of the Roman state's relatively loose and decentralized character as well as its lack of the technical means of oppression cherished by twentieth-century tyrannies. The police forces, and officials in general, were few in number and highly corruptible; the prisons were messy establishments, with guests entering and leaving all the time; the news media were never fully supervisable; and so forth. A persecuting government's chances of doing away with Christianity for good were, in fact, limited, granted that the church had been allowed to grow strong in relative peace before any other persecutions than more or less casual local ones had been launched.

Why, then, had it been thus allowed? That is the other question requiring an answer. Here, too, the looseness of the "machinery" of state and the lack of technical means must be taken into account. But apart from that, the immediate answer must be the somewhat banal one that the Romans were as disinclined as later empire builders to implement each and every principle, be it ever so honestly held. As long as things went reasonably well, that is, until signs of serious crisis began to appear in the third century, it was not deemed advisable to saddle oneself with more difficulties than strictly necessary. As put by the English many centuries later: "Let sleeping dogs lie."

But the relative passivity of the government must have been considerably strengthened by the demonstrable fact that the Christian church was on the whole a gathering of honest, hardworking, and thus useful citizens coming from many layers of society. And to that must be added a circumstance repeatedly stressed by Christian apologists; namely, that the Christians regarded the peace and order created and enforced by the Roman state as an authentic expression of God's will, and consequently recognized an obligation to pray for emperor and empire. Tertullian of Carthage (ca. 200), who — with more forthrightness than diplomatic tact — pointed out that the Christians were numerous enough to become a danger to the existing order if they decided to rise up against it, was at the same time eager to emphasize that the prayers for lawful authority which their faith required of them were the only useful ones, considering that they were directed not to demonic illusions, but to the one true God, Lord of heaven and earth. And a little later, Origen of Alexandria ruminated on a future in which empire and church were to become aspects of one reality: God's people. Also, the Christian concept of a divine plan for history was brought into play by means of reflections on the coincidence in time between the birth of Jesus and the unifying and pacific reign of the emperor Augustus. Church and Rome belonged together; if only Rome would understand it!

No wonder, then, that the last of the great persecutions ended with an order issued on his deathbed (311) by Galerius, the most savage of the persecuting emperors. It contained two main points. One, that the persecution had been a just and proper measure of government. The other, that since it had proved unsuccessful, it should be ended on the condition that the Christians prayed for the state in return for their freedom of worship.

This step — in many ways typical of the Roman version of Realpolitik — did, however, not become the final one. And it may be added: it could not become so in a cultural situation like that of late antiquity. The next step, the decisive one, was taken by the emperor Constantine, known ever since as "the Great" (306-37).

This ruler's conversion to Christianity and his incorporation of the church among the established public authorities — a policy that was somewhat later rounded off by the recognition of Christianity as sole official religion — was perhaps not quite so decisively important for the church as has sometimes been claimed. Christianity as defined by the "catholic" church was already a fundamentally completed religion, and the church was already a power in society when the alliance with the state came into being. Those were, indeed, some of the reasons why the state sought the alliance. But it is, of course, self-evident that church life underwent considerable changes in the following time; and even more important: the sheer fact of the alliance, and its consequences, throws an indispensable light on the peculiar nature of ancient Christianity.

The question of the emperor's "personal motives" for becoming a

21. Fragment of a colossal statue (ca. 315) of the emperor Constantine the Great. The upward stare signifies the ruler's relationship with the heavenly world. (Photo by Jens Fleischer.)

Christian is — in our context at least — of minor importance. Probably the question is an anachronistic one. It is, at any rate, of greater interest that he regarded the religion of the church as something from which he could expect a vitally important help in his — religious as well as political — endeavors to, as he put it, "renew the body of the world" after social crises and civil wars. That is exactly what enables us to place ancient Christianity in a clearer light, facilitating as it does a deeper understanding of the point on which it differs from all the other powers and movements in Mediterranean society, namely, the unique manner in which it combined a religious view of life with a form of social organization.

Christianity was, of course, not alone in the "market" of worldviews. On the contrary, a salient feature of Mediterranean civilization was that a great many articulate philosophies addressed people's needs for intellectual explanation, just as many religious cults appealed to other layers of the human person. Neither was it unheard of — it was, on the contrary, quite common — that those strivings were combined in a religious philosophy or a philosophical religion. The "mysteries" were envisaged in a framework of rationality, and philosophical reasoning concluded frequently in a pious awe of the mystery.

The Christian church was, also, only one of many forms of social organization. And it is worth noting that the coercive apparatus of the late Roman state itself was being developed during those years: a determined effort was made to come to terms with the empire's crisis by means of centralization and control.

But Christianity was — with the partial exception of Judaism — alone in combining all that. Here institutionalized "mysteries" were on offer, intimately connected with an attempt at rational explanation of universal order and of the course of history. And on top of that a demand was made on everybody, high or low, cultivated or not, to make this view of things his or her own, consciously and clearly. And all was inextricably bound up with a concrete form of statelike social organization, identical from place to place, with clear principles of legislation, administration, jurisdiction, and teaching. And conversely, here one could find not only an efficient apparatus of order, but one that practiced ideas about the goal of human life and about how to reach it. An organization, in short, that aimed at influencing and making claims on souls as well as bodies, and one with a clear knowledge of why it did so.

That such an institution might contribute usefully to a society in crisis and a state without any other common religious basis than the cult of emperor and empire was not unthinkable beforehand. As a matter of fact, the idea had already been aired by Christian thinkers. But it did not gain its real historical impact until the moment Emperor Constantine inserted himself into the "system" by claiming to be the chosen instrument of the God of the Christians.

Nor was that idea an unthinkable one, especially when one remembered the use both Christians and pagans made of the concept of Logos. If the God of the Christians was identical with the heavenly power that many pagans regarded as the unifying principle behind and above the pantheon of gods, then the position as earthly image of universal reason in which pagan political philosophers had placed the ruler was accessible for a Christian interpretation. Those are the lines along which Constantine seems to have thought, and contemporary Christian theologians such as Eusebius, bishop of Caesarea, did so too.

The new policy can, then, be understood as an attempt at incorporating Christianity and church into the theory and practice of the late Roman state, with the emperor as, in both respects, the key figure. He does on earth what the Logos does in the universe at large, making use of the church, which interprets the work of the Logos and collaborates in it through education and celebration of the saving mysteries.

Something of that is reflected in the practical forms of church-state collaboration. Constantine granted privileges to the clergy, similar to those enjoyed by the pagan priests. He endowed the episcopal tribunal with official jurisdiction in secular cases. He supplemented the "constitution" of the church in order to make it amenable to the needs of the state. And he interfered in the church's internal affairs when its unity was endangered by theological and political quarrels. The last two measures are particularly instructive.

For the first time the church was provided with a common agency, namely, the so-called ecumenical council: the meeting of bishops from all over the empire. Here binding decisions in cases of common concern were made under the presidency of the emperor. This instrument of imperial influence was usefully supplemented when it was decided to let all bishops of an imperial province be led and supervised by the bishop of the provincial capital — a step being thus taken toward coordinating ecclesiastical and secular administration.

As for the cases of interference in internal disputes, they occurred not only because the emperor wanted to keep control of where the imperial money grants went, but especially because of his wish to ensure theological and practical coherence and uniformity in a community whose task it was to be his partner in healing the "body of the world."

Christian reactions to the changes — so shortly after a long and severe persecution — covered a wide scale, from relief mixed with confusion at one end to enthusiastic acceptance at the other. Some were mostly interested in exploiting the material chances made available by the new situation. The clerical function now became a career in a wider sense, rich in possibilities for talented and ambitious men. The clerical courtier — a constant type in subsequent church history — entered the stage. Others went into opposition or at least formed critical views of the new order of things, once its wider perspectives had dawned on them. Two instructive examples can be cited, one practical, one theoretical.

The first originated in an act of terrorism committed by the emperor Theodosius (378-95) against the city of Thessalonica, when he ordered his troops to massacre a large number of citizens in the local amphitheater as a reprisal for the murder of an imperial official. Confronted by this breach of the law of God and the church, Ambrose, bishop of Milan, the imperial residence at the time, declared that the emperor had forfeited his right to the church's means of grace and that it could only be regained by an act of humble penitence at the discretion of the bishop. This was accepted and acted upon by the emperor — who, by the way, had tried to withdraw his fatal order, but too late — whereupon he was readmitted, all with as little loss of face as possible. It is hard to imagine Constantine the Great — not to speak of Diocletian — in a similar situation! The episode reveals, although only in a flash, that catholic Christianity contained ingredients that were difficult to bring into harmony with Roman-style political theology.

The other example, the theoretical one, can be found in Augustine. When the great theologian was elected bishop, the "Constantinian" order was the established condition of the church, and he accepted it in his episcopal practice. We see this partially from his consenting to police action against the Donatist schismatics after making a series of fruitless attempts to persuade them through peaceful discussion. As a theological and political thinker in a wider sense, his attitude was somewhat more critical. In contradistinction to fellow theologians of an "imperialist" turn of mind, he argued that there was no direct way to conclude from earthly success or failure to an understanding of God's will and purpose for humankind. The inhabitants of the "city of God," he maintained, are men and women who follow the "humble God" through sacrifice of self and love of God and neighbor. And their identity is known only to him who looks into the hearts. But one thing is certain: they who seek religious proof in earthly success do not belong — or at least not yet.

Those ideas are important because of their long-term consequences,

84

22. *(left)* This portrait of Bishop Ambrose in St. Ambrogio, Milan, Italy, seems to be close to an authentic likeness. It was made relatively shortly after the bishop's death, and an examination of his remains has confirmed the somewhat peculiar appearance of the eyes. (Courtesy of Scala/Art Resource, NY.)

23. *(below)* On one side of this silver medallion, dating from the time of the Gothic sack of Rome in 410, the emperor Priscus Attalus is shown with the ruler's heavenward glance. On the other side, he sits enthroned while the goddess of victory presents him with the victor's garland. A few years before, the Christian clergy, led by Ambrose of Milan, had succeeded in having the goddess's statue removed from the Senate chamber of the Roman forum. (Courtesy of the British Museum.)

but also because they reveal a weakness inherent in the synthesis of religion and politics represented by the Constantinian arrangement. In the last resort, the Christian clergy did not engage in the cause of imperial coherence and prosperity as wholeheartedly as Constantine had hoped. They exploited the situation's possibilities in the service of their own, more or less respectable, purposes: economic consolidation and social prestige, church building and poor relief, mission and indoctrination. But the well-being of the empire did not constitute a purpose in its own right. The church was already a sort of complete "state" in itself. Just as the empire, it had its own purposes, its own traditional methods of coordinating theory and practice. On such a background, the possibilities of mutually shaping influences were limited. The result was — roughly speaking — a mixture of three things. The church was active in social shoring up, for instance by providing ambulance services of several kinds. Further, the church acted as a parasite by placing landed property under the "dead hand," by attracting administrative talent to its own leadership staffs, and by preventing its Western clergy from producing offspring. And in some cases the church was a directly undermining factor because of the destructive forces released by theological and ecclesio-political controversies.

This description — which of course takes account of neither the longer-term perspectives of the change nor the pressures exerted by the multifarious crises of late Roman civilization — calls for qualification. That can to some extent be provided when we consider the Byzantine afterlife of the Constantinian system. For the moment, we leave such questions on one side and turn our attention to the third and last of ancient Christianity's "external" fields of contact: the one that connected it with elite culture.

c. Culture

Culture was one of the great forces for unity in Mediterranean civilization, not only because it was diffused over the entire area, but because it was a governing influence on the outlook on life that was the common heritage of the municipal and imperial power elites. The words and deeds of those elites in their capacity as dominant groups in society were strongly codetermined by what they had made their own of the literary standard culture.

A literary culture it was, above all. Throughout the entire school curriculum the classic writers, especially the poets, were the all-important basis for teaching. The task of the pupils consisted of learning to understand

and imitate the works of those normative writers. Here they could find not only models for expression and style, but also guidelines for ethical conduct and intellectual understanding of the world. Here, then, all the treasures of practical wisdom lay ready to be lifted — everything that a free man who did not have to work for his living needed to fill his position as a citizen and as a private person. By reading Virgil, a Latin-speaking member of the elite, for instance, became acquainted with the task committed to the chosen people of the Romans through the divine promise to Aeneas, the common ancestor.

That general culture could, of course, be supplemented by specialized studies if required, but general culture was the main thing. Because of his background in that culture, a member of the ruling elite that guided the destinies of cities and empire could be expected to have acquired a more or less thought-out notion of the divinely governed order of things and of how to find and fill his place in it.

The relation to this upper-class culture presented no problem for primitive Christianity. From time to time the apostle Paul refers to religious truths that can be grasped by the power of reason shared by all men, but his most important point is conveyed by his proclamation of the "foolishness of God" that has put all earthly wisdom to shame through the sacrifice of Christ. This way of thinking — later echoed by Tertullian's question: "What has Athens to do with Jerusalem?" — remained central to Christian theology, but the question of the attitude to be taken by Christians toward the "wisdom of the world" did nevertheless become a problem, as early as Tertullian's time, and indeed earlier still.

It was not always a fully perceived problem, partly because, when joining the church, members of the cultured classes brought the "truisms" of their culture with them as a matter of course. Anyhow, standard culture began influencing Christian life and thinking in a substantial as well as formal sense, with results that did not fail to reveal more or less serious tensions with original Christian points of view.

It was of relatively small significance that Christians rejected the elements of literary culture that were directly connected with pagan deities and their cults. By doing so they only did something similar to what many representatives of non-Christian culture itself had already done when they interpreted the gods as metaphorical expressions of deeper, abstract truths. Here, in fact, one of the main points of affinity is to be found, considering that Jews, Christians, and pagans were confronted by a common problem, that of having to work with texts that were by common consent normative for thought and conduct while at the same time being manifestly shaped by much earlier ways of thinking and practice. That problem, felt by Jews and Christians when reading the Old Testament not less than by pagan readers of Homer, was solved in mutually similar ways, namely, by allegorical interpretation, one that uncovered hidden meanings behind the literal one in cases where it must in all honesty be called naive, primitive, or downright false.

It is, of course, highly significant that Christian theologians did not generally abandon the literal — "historical" — sense of the holy text, irrespective of the deeper meaning it might also contain. It is no less important that the deeper meanings they found were mostly determined by the fundamental understanding of God's historical plan and purpose for the people, expressing itself in the intimate mutual links between Old and New Testament phenomena. Isaac was Isaac, but he "was also" Christ.

But another form of allegorical interpretation was also in use, one that deliberately lifted the text out of the limitations of history and tried to found it in an ideal world of timeless truths. Here Christian theologians could go along with Alexandrian readers of Homer or with Greco-Jewish Bible interpreters such as Philo (d. ca. 50), thereby weakening the view of salvation history cherished by primitive Christianity. Another consequence could be a "putting in" of meanings that were as foreign to the text as they were consonant with the social or cultural prejudices of the interpreter. This was what happened, for instance, when Origen not only interpreted Pharaoh's killing of Israelite boys as the devil's permanent attack on the human soul, but also pointed out that the target principally aimed at was the highest faculties of the soul, symbolized as a matter of course by the male sex.

Such tendencies are perhaps partly to be understood on the background of a practice similar to that of the teachers of classical literature, namely, the interpretation word by word, at the expense of the context. On both sides of the religious divide great subtlety was deployed in making use of that technique. Each single word was, so to speak, lifted up against the light in order to let it sparkle in innumerable facets, as if to demonstrate that the holy text's bottomless wisdom, its "sea of mysteries," was as deep in every smallest detail as it was in the whole.

Christian interpreters of Scripture were, then, learned in a manner highly reminiscent of that of pagan interpreters of the classics. And in the process they may have taken over more of the prejudices of the cultured world than they were fully conscious of. If so, it is by no means the last time such a thing has happened in Christian history. Modern Bible interpreta-

24. Laurentius, or Lawrence, a Roman deacon, was martyred in 258, allegedly by being roasted alive. On this mosaic from ca. 450 in the mausoleum of Galla Placidia in Ravenna, the grill is shown in the middle. The martyr carries the cross as a sign that he, like his Master, is victorious through suffering. In his left hand he holds a book; one of the functions of a deacon was that of reading the Gospel text in divine service. On the left stands the cabinet used in church buildings as a container for the four Gospels. They are in book form here; the late antique transition from scroll to book facilitated study by making it easier for the reader to look things up and to go forward and backward in the text.

tion as well as systematic theology — to say nothing of the discipline of church history — present quite a few instances.

Similar tendencies were at work when Christian writers spoke for themselves, and not only as interpreters of texts. That goes for the style, as is, for instance, apparent from passages where Cyprian of Carthage lets himself go in praise of the martyrs. Such flowers of rhetoric can hardly have grown in the church's own garden exclusively. But it goes also for content. Important elements of the theologians' worldview and of their way of looking at human life can be traced to their encounter with the standard culture of the elite. That becomes clear from their ideas about order, not least when the matter under consideration is the hierarchy of "higher" and "lower" elements of the human person. It is equally apparent in the instructions they give on how to put one's soul in order by ascetic discipline. And not least does it appear in the self-assurance with which those writers invest their intellectual status with social authority and set themselves up as a kind of mandarinate when consorting with less-favored brethren and sisters. The social and political overtones of late antique elite culture that are audible here must have contributed not a little to facilitate the transition to the status as official religion enjoyed by Christianity from the fourth century onward.

All this is a matter of general approach to problems of human existence and not so much one of philosophy in the stricter sense. Nevertheless, an encounter with pagan culture took place in that area too. By their efforts to demonstrate the identity of Jesus of Nazareth, the divine teacher of wisdom, with universal reason, a concept dear to the philosophers, the Christian theologians sought to establish a basis for some sort of understanding with their philosophical surroundings. Those efforts did perhaps not always make much of an impression on the philosophers, but it must be remembered that they were also meant to serve the Christians' own interest in arguing plausibly for their view of Jesus as someone who came from the God of ordered creation as well as their interest in bringing about a rational coherence in their beliefs. The main point in our present context, however, is the fact that the rules of the game were to some extent dictated by the philosophy in which the concept of the Logos had its origin. Something similar is valid for the speculations resulting in the doctrine of the "two natures" of Christ. If nothing else does, then the discussions of our own day make clear that the dogma in the form given to it in the fifth century is dependent on a style of thinking and a terminology that derive from Greek philosophy and do not, as it were, spring with undebatable evidence from the nature of the case. It can — by the way — perhaps be called a specifically modern insight that relations between the "nature of the case" and its terminological expression present somewhat more of a problem than is often supposed. Be that as it may, the use of the terms "divine nature" and "human nature" has at one and the same time had a clarifying and a limiting effect by having been brought into Christian discussion from outside.

By saying that, we have touched on the difficulties inherent in accounting rationally for the confession of faith uttered at baptism, in common worship, and in individual prayer. An object lesson can be had by reflecting on the definition of God as "One in three Persons." Clearly the words taken over from the philosophical tradition as designations of the common divine "essence" and the distinct "persons," respectively, had to be abused in order to be used at all. The definition was not, and could not be, acceptable to a person who had not already been convinced by other means than those of rational argumentation.

In other words, Christianity was not fully to be grasped by the methods provided by Greco-Roman culture.

Acknowledging this is tantamount to being reminded once more of a wider set of questions, those concerning the relations between Christianity and Mediterranean civilization in general.

d. Antiquity and Christianity

As always in such cases, the relationship was an interactive one. The new "world religion" made itself at home in its world and tried to adapt itself to that world, consciously and reflectedly or less so. But the attempts at adaptation often demonstrated that Christianity carried something with it that could not be fully incorporated in the existing order of things and ideas, and that, moreover, the things taken over from the surroundings were themselves changed in the process. Much of this has already been alluded to above, but a glance at the relationship under a general point of view may prove worth our while.

Crucial for understanding is the acknowledgment that the context entered into by Christianity was an ancient civilization in which both the way people related to material circumstances and their guidelines for reflecting on the meaning of life had found their forms and established a civilizational coherence long before Christianity was born. A great many "tracks of association" had, as it were, been mapped out in a permanent manner. It was, for instance, not open to discussion that civilized society comprised a category of men and women who had no civil rights: "animated things," i.e., slaves. Equally undebatable was the presupposition that people beyond the imperial borders could hardly be called fully human, considering that they were creatures devoid of real speech, unable to utter more than incomprehensible jabberings. Not without reason they bore the onomatopoeic name "barbarians." A third example: it was taken for granted not only that the goal of human life was personal happiness, but that this happiness consisted in the harmony in body and mind resulting from the predominance of the rational will and the other "higher" faculties of the person over the "lower" impulses. The wise man keeps himself under control and can benefit his fellow citizens thereby. To a greater or lesser extent, such truisms became Christian truisms as well. That is, for instance, apparent from the penance imposed by a church council on a Christian housewife, not for beating her slave girl, but for beating her to death. It is also evident in the widespread, although mostly tacit, identification of "Christian" with "Roman," and — last but not least — in the way Jesus' words about being "perfect" were understood according to the categories of personal harmony and ascetic discipline.

Above all, perhaps, the tendency can be observed in the understanding of woman's nature and role that was to remain part of conventional Christian wisdom for a millennium and a half, if not longer still. The church took over — albeit with important qualifications — the prevalent ideas about woman as the sexually and legally subordinate and dependent partner in marriage and society, and it combined those ideas with the Christian sage's contempt for her intellectual powers and the ascetic's horror of the menace she presented against his hard-won mastery over his carnal impulses. In the male world of theologians, the relationship to God tended to become a distinctly male one. "He for God only, she for God in him," as John Milton expressed the view many centuries later. There were, of course, revolutionary perspectives implicit in the Christian assertion that women were equal with men as far as their "souls" were concerned, but in daily practice that claim could hardly become realized as long as "soul" was largely defined in a context of male experience — quite apart from the fact that "soul" could be isolated from the personal unity of "soul" and "body" only at the price of abandoning original Christian convictions. This view of woman is a sign of the difficulties ancient — and European — Christianity experienced with acting on some of its own most important presuppositions.

Nevertheless, the truisms of Mediterranean civilization that were accepted were again and again accompanied by ideas that called them into question. That is for instance apparent from the — quite un-Mediterranean — assertion of the equality before God of all humankind, including women and slaves, and their full and unqualified membership of his church. And not least does it appear in Augustine of Hippo's claim that the Platonic philosophers are aware of the goal of human life but ignorant of the road leading to that goal. They know that God is pure spirit, he says, and that man's existence is meant to become a spiritual one, imbued with the love of God; but they do *not* know that the goal can only be reached because God has reached down and sacrificed himself for creatures unworthy of his love. As a matter of fact, Augustine's entire theological work can be seen as developing and analyzing such problem-laden attempts at combining Christian and non-Christian ideas. He declines to abandon any ingredient of the synthesis, but he allows it to become painfully clear that it is not an easy one to carry out.

Examples like these are apt to sharpen our eye for the interplay going on wherever Christianity encounters antiquity in theory or in practice, such as: The emperor is God's chosen instrument, and there is good sense in considering that his guardianship of law and order is an expression of God's own upholding of his creatures, *but* the emperor is also a mere man, subject to the law of sin and death, and he is a church member, exposed to priestly teaching and criticism. The Christian sage has penetrated deeper into God's wisdom than have simple folk, *but* his wisdom is empty if he fails to draw nourishment from where the simple draw their faith, hope, and charity. The dead need the community with the living and they need the family meals held on their graves, *but* the dead person is something more than a ghostly presence craving to be satisfied; he is a member of the communion of saints, united to the living through the common confession of faith.

The attitude to cultural truisms expressed in "double claims" like these could result in direct culture-shaping action, as shown for instance in the creation of the feast of Christmas. This feast has a double origin in pre-Christian religion, namely, in two cultic feasts, some of whose fundamental elements were taken over and reinterpreted by the victorious Christian church in the fourth century. One was celebrated in the East at the time of winter solstice when a virgin-born god was saluted by the cry: "The virgin has given birth, the light increases!" and where he demonstrated his divine power by turning springwater into wine. On the day of that feast — January 6 — the Eastern Church began celebrating the "epiphany" of Christ, his coming to be seen, his revealing his power, as shown in the Gospel stories about his baptism and his making wine out of water at the wedding of Cana.

The other cultic feast is the Western midwinter celebration of the sun god Sol Invictus, instituted in 274 by the emperor Aurelian as part of his endeavor to unite the inhabitants of the empire in worship of the sun as the supreme god and of the emperor as the earthly image of his life-giving and life-preserving power. On the day of that feast, December 25, the Western Church set about celebrating the birth of Jesus, the coming-to-be of him whom the Bible calls the "Sun of Justice," the "Sunrise from on high."

By instituting those feasts the church conducts a cultural struggle, and it does so by formulating a double point of view, to wit: the pagans have dreamed true although unclear dreams of him who created water, wine, and the sun, *but* only through the Christian message has it become clear who he is: that he is the Lord of nature, its Creator out of nothing; that he has made it serve humankind through a people's history; and that his image among men is the man who appeared on earth as a defenseless infant and rose from darkness to the light of a day that — unlike that of the sun — has no evening. The message proclaimed by the feasts is that God lets himself become known through sun, water, and wine, *but* in another sense than the pagans believed.

However, as we have already seen, such initiatives — whose constructive character distinguishes them from other forms of cultural aggression such as the church's collaboration in the forcible extermination of pagan cults — were by no means fully representative of Christianity's conscious and active attitude toward Mediterranean culture. Generally speaking, it did not transform or reshape that culture. Rather, it cohabited with it and took on some of its influences. But its own culture contained, as it were, the seeds of newness. Three of them merit a closer look.

The peculiarly "historical" character of Christianity was not entirely without parallels in the ancient world, as appears from the remarkable congruities between the Christian story of a people's history and the Roman national story told by Virgil. In both cases an idea about the meaning of human life is formulated by a story about a divine plan for mankind, carried out in the course of a coherent history. But the Christian version turns the idea in a new direction. God's plan is no respecter of status, personal or national. It calls earthly success and happiness into question while at the same time proclaiming the goodness of created things. This world, it says, is God's world in which he acts historically through his creatures, but the innermost meaning of the world and its history reveals itself only in the light of another world, the light that has dawned with the appearance of the "humble God." Nobody had spoken in such a way about history before, and no form of European and American thinking about history, be it Christian or non-Christian, would have been the same without it.

The Christian — and Jewish — concept of God is that of a giver of understandable laws whose action is itself unbound by laws. In this capac-

25. In this roof-mosaic, located in a sepulchral chamber beneath St. Peter's in Rome, Christ is represented as "the true sun-god." Presumably, it dates from a time close to that of the Western church's adoption of the sun-god's day as its feast of Christmas. The line of thought behind the picture had earlier found expression in Clement of Alexandria's words about Christ: "He who drives his chariot over everything, He, the Sun of Righteousness, visits all mankind."

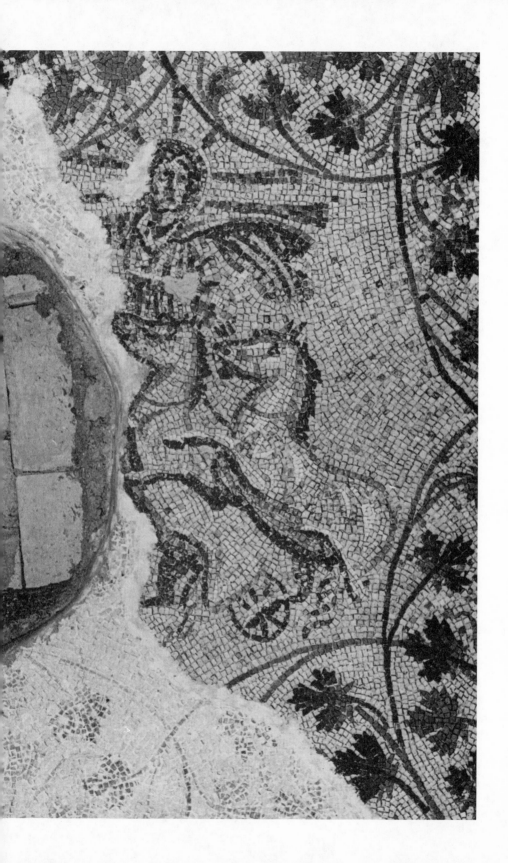

26. Clement of Alexandria (ca. 200) interpreted Orpheus, the great musician of Greek myth, as an image of Christ. The true Orpheus, to whom all nature and human life owe their harmonious coherence, is Christ. This idea is expressed in the fifth-century marble relief shown here. As Orpheus tames the animals by the strains of his lyre, Christ draws humankind to himself by his teaching. (Courtesy of the Byzantine and Christian Museum.)

ity he acts as a free personal will confronting other personal wills. In this idea a seed is hidden that was to sprout in that arch-European phenomenon, empirical science, that aims at uncovering the relation of "accidental" individual phenomena to general "laws" by way of observation and experiment.

Lastly, in the claim that the personal God is a Creator of persons and that his Son, "the express image of his person," has assumed a human personality lies the decisive precondition for a third historical novelty, pregnant with consequences. Namely, the demand made on every Christian, man or woman, rich or poor, simple or learned, to form a clear understanding of the nature and meaning of human existence and of the world in which it is conducted.

History and world order are "actualized" in every single candidate for baptism and must be understood by him or her. That is an idea that quite evidently contains explosive material, not only in a religious but also in a social and political sense. Explosive, not only in relation to the forms to which Christianity adapted itself, but also to those created by it. That was, however, something that only became clear in much later historical situations.

The problem of the mutual relations between Christianity and antiquity has been the subject of a great many highly different interpretations —

from the assertion of a total Christian "victory" to that of Christianity as the victim of "Hellenization," a quantity, in other words, without any significant connection with the teaching of Jesus. That so contradictory solutions have been more or less plausibly argued for is a telling testimony to the difficulties presented by the problem as well as to the strong element of personal and time-bound attitudes inherent in historical work. Briefly put, the debate is a never ending one; it is one of our "perpetual companions."

4. Eastern Christianity

a. Departures and Traditions in the Christian East

"Eastern Christianity" may be used as a collective term to designate the various forms assumed by ancient Christianity when, after the dissolution of Mediterranean unity, it lived on in Byzantine, Middle Eastern, and Russian lands.

Despite important changes and modifications, it was in fact ancient Christianity that lived on here, much more markedly than it did in the West. A bird's-eye glance at departures and traditions in Eastern Christianity as a whole is useful before considering its individual forms.

The first of the great departures, or epochal changes, occurred when the politico-military unity of East and West was broken in the middle years of the fifth century as a consequence of the age-old combination of external and internal pressures on the empire. The second consisted in the gradual loosening of religious and church life in the easternmost provinces from imperial "orthodox" control, with the result that independent churches of "heretical" views were established in Syria, Egypt, and elsewhere. The third was the empire's seventh-century crisis when, among other calamities, it suffered the loss of those lands to the Arab Muslim conquerors. The fourth was the weakening of imperial power from the twelfth century onward and the temporary Western occupation of the imperial capital; and the fifth: the fall of the empire to the Turks (1453) and the subsequent Russian takeover of the position of leading power in eastern Christendom.

Other changes also took place that are less easily datable, such as the gradual deepening of the empire's "Greekness" and the ever tighter linking together of Orthodox Christianity and imperial patriotism.

But the decisive thing is that none of those events and processes — except of course, in a sense, that of 1453 — resulted in anything like the transformation of the entire pattern of civilization known from the West. Vital parts of the old patterns persisted, although some underwent more or less serious interruptions and weakenings. The centralized bureaucratic state power survived to a significant extent, and the same goes for the classical lay elite culture, the supervised economy, and, not least, the Christian state religion whose forms of belief, worship, and organizational structure remained intact and in ever increasing measure determined people's outlook on life while at the same time providing the main basis of political legitimacy.

The empire's remarkable tenacity of life can to a large extent be explained by the stable pattern formed by such traditions. But it must also be

27. The magnificent church of Holy Wisdom (Hagia Sophia) in Constantinople was built by the emperor Justinian I (527-65). Its outstanding feature is the mighty dome, distended over the building as the vault of heaven, making it into an "abode of light." The four tall structures surrounding the church are minarets, built after the Turkish conquest of Constantinople in 1453 when Hagia Sophia was taken into use as a mosque.

remembered that its capital city was uniquely positioned for defense. From outside, Constantinople could only be taken by gunfire.

In short, the Roman Empire was present not as a pious fiction, but as a political and cultural reality. It kept its strong enemies at bay and dominated its weaker neighbors by military and diplomatic pressure, cultural inspiration, and Christian mission.

In those deep and enduring political, cultural, and religious influences on countries such as Bulgaria and Russia lies the precondition for the remarkable fact that not only did Roman imperial traditions survive in those lands after 1453, but the ancient Mediterranean Christianity took root and thrived in essentially its original form.

But another thing was important too — one that presumably had much to do with the power and self-confidence of the advanced imperial order: in those northern countries Christian worship was conducted in the national languages, and a vernacular Christian literature began to appear. Here we have, so to speak, a departure that made for continuity — a continuity, it may be added, that of course also exacted a price.

The other forms of Eastern Christianity — the "heretical" churches in the Middle East: in Armenia, Syria, Persia, Egypt, and Ethiopia — resulted from politico-religious disharmonies and schisms in East Roman Christendom, but they were bearers of continuity all the same. Not only were their "heretical" doctrines concerning the person of Christ deeply rooted in central dilemmas of ancient theology, but much of what they thought and said otherwise was generally acceptable to "Orthodox" Byzantines.

b. Living Orthodoxy

Byzantine Christianity, and its direct heirs in Russia and eastern Europe, call themselves Orthodox. That is not in itself a very enlightening designation, considering the well-known fact that every single form of ancient Christianity uses it about itself, just as all modern states are "democratic."

But as a point of departure for a closer look, it can be of service. Byzantines and Russians use the word in a sense that is more or less special to them. That appears from the fact that the Greek term *He orthe doxa,* and still more plainly the Russian one, *Pravoslavie,* covers not only the concept of "true and correct faith" but also that of "right worship." Such a definition is, of course, not unique in an absolute sense. As will be remembered, the intimate links between confession and worship lay close to the heart of ancient Christianity. The church's faith reaches its full expression in the practice of worship, and Christian knowledge as well as Christian confession tend toward adoration. It is inseparable from what is seen as the "exercise" of faith — *askesis* in the wider sense of that word. But in Byzantine-Greek and in Russian Orthodoxy, the combination is carried through with a wholeheartedness, an inventiveness, and a wealth of nuances as nowhere else.

Understanding that is one of the two main conditions for understanding its peculiar character. The other is the pre-Christian Greek concept of correspondence between heaven and earth — the idea that a supraterrestrial order makes itself manifest in a terrestrial one. Earthly order reflects, albeit imperfectly and problematically, the heavenly one. Their mutual relation is one of archetype and image.

In Orthodox Christianity these two lines of thought are characteristically combined with the biblical history of creation and redemption. That is what appears, more or less clearly, from all manifestations of Orthodox life.

The framework of that life was, for a thousand years, the Roman Empire in its Greek version. That empire had regarded itself as a Christian one from the time of Theodosius, but especially in its specifically Byzantine phase — from the reign of Justinian (527-65) onward — did its Christian character become constantly more marked. Gradually freeing itself of pagan traditions, the empire presented itself as God's own country, an island of correct belief and practice surrounded by an ocean of heresy and barbarism. Its ruler was installed by God in order to do what the Logos himself does in the universe as a whole: organize, enlighten, and nourish the people of God — image of the heavenly community.

That meant that he became the absolute center in the church's life as well as in that of the state. The laws of the church needed his sanction and were meant to serve the welfare of the state, just as many of the state's laws were of benefit to the church. The patriarch of Constantinople, the foremost dignitary of the church, was appointed by him and functioned in accordance with his will. All that is reflected in the ceremonies surrounding the imperial office and its bearer, the *basileus*. The ruler's coming to appear in state before his court and his people was an epiphany, a manifestation of divine power. He was no god, and neither was he a priest, but he was, in an eminent sense, the one by whom God revealed his will. He was an image of the World Ruler himself. It is not without reason when, in Byzantine art, Christ appears as a heavenly emperor.

This idea of the ruler was one of Orthodox Christianity's most durable elements. It lived on in the Russian Empire. Notwithstanding the fact that the Russian state was in most respects a somewhat more primitive quantity, its rulers were as fully convinced as were the *basileis* that theirs was *the* empire, the "third Rome," as one Russian writer called it, that is: the last universal realm before Judgment Day. In the "Holy Russia" of the czars, the patriarch of Moscow — insofar as there was one — was just as subordinate a person as his predecessor in Constantinople, the "second Rome," had been — or more so, considering that the Byzantines, more than the Russians, found it desirable that a balanced harmony, or "symphony," be in practice maintained between the powers of church and state.

This holy order, this politico-religious unity under imperial leadership, was the instrument of dissemination of Orthodox faith to the outer world. As the Logos enlightens every rational creature, so the faith of the

28. Christ, flanked by the apostles Peter and Paul, shown on the left wing of a Byzantine diptych (folding tablet). The ornamented arch over his head is taken from palace architecture, and his seat resembles that of a consul. (Staatliche Museen zu Berlin-Skulpturensammlung und Museum für Byzantinische Kunst. Photo: Jürgen Liepe.)

emperor was to radiate beyond the borders of the Byzantine Empire, out into the world of the Slavonic peoples. Not surprisingly, it happened in intimate connection with other external activities undertaken by the empire. That empire, reduced as it was in comparison to earlier times, lived in a dangerous world; in its struggle for survival it developed a wide and subtle range of foreign policy instruments. Diplomatic maneuvers, money handouts to barbarian princes, display of imperial splendor, cultural propaganda, and war were among those instruments; and so was Christian mission. It was conducted with courage and a spirit of self-sacrifice, and sometimes with a touch of genius. No lesser word is appropriate for Constantine (also known as Cyril, d. 869), who, together with his brother Methodius, worked among the western Slavs of Moravia and, above all, created the basis for all later Orthodox mission: the written Slavonic language without which Christianity's popular impact upon Bulgarians and Russians is as unaccountable as it is without the importance they attach to the act of common worship.

By saying that, we have touched on the one thing that characterizes Orthodox Christianity more than anything else: the preponderance of worship and the influence it has exerted on all other manifestations of Christian life. In worship the heavenly world becomes visible on earth; past and future are gathered into the present; the meaning of theoretical assertions is revealed in pictorial as well as verbal proclamation and adoration. This attitude, known of course from other premodern forms of Christianity too, has reached its classical perfection in Orthodoxy. According to Byzantine and Russian Christians, there is nothing problematical about *he orthe doxa,* considered in its capacity as a set of creedal assertions about the meaning of life. That faith has been defined and confirmed by the "seven ecumenical councils," and it is not a matter for dispute. Its meaning and implications are revealed not by means of discussion, but in the acts of worship where the other meaning of *orthe doxa* becomes apparent: the right way of adoration and praise.

Worship reaches its culmination in the Eucharist, where the people's response to Christ's act of liberation takes shape in a "reproduction" of his self-sacrifice. That, however, can be said of ancient Christianity or of Western Catholicism as well. The distinctive marks of Orthodoxy are to be sought elsewhere — for instance, in the message of the Orthodox church building. Its space is crowned by a dome, as a sign that heaven becomes present here. And above all, the wall that separates the area of the altar from that of the congregation is filled with the holy images that actualize salvation history and represent the celestial life.

The use of pictures — icons — in worship is one of the most characteristic methods by which Orthodoxy demonstrates the "mysterious" union of heaven and earth, brought about by the Logos when he appeared
among men as Jesus of Nazareth. The holy image is one of the expressions,
and one of the consequences, of the incarnation. According to common
conviction — be it supported by Platonizing profundities or not — the
icons are earthly expressions of a heavenly reality. In them the persons depicted are present: Christ, his mother, his saints. Consistently enough,
some icons are said to be "not made by human hands"; they are believed to
have come into existence by heavenly intervention without a human artist

29. Schematic delineation of a Greek *ikonostasis*. The picture wall separates the people's
congregation from the choir where the eucharistic mystery is performed. To the left of the
main, or "royal," entrance the Mother of God is seen carrying the infant Jesus; to the right,
Christ is shown as the *pantokrator*, universal ruler. The upper row of icons present the
twelve most important events in the life and passion of Christ, corresponding with the
twelve great feasts of the Orthodox church year. (Staatliche Museen zu Berlin-
Skulpturensammlung und Museum für Byzantinische Kunst. Photo: Jürgen Liepe.)

being active. And when he *is* active, it is in a "priestly" capacity. He pre-
pares himself by prayer and fasting, and engages his entire artistic ability in
the attempt at reproducing the image's standard type as faithfully as possible.

These ideas and usages did not always go uncontested. The Old Testament ban on images; the propaganda effect emanating from Islam;
intra-Byzantine conflicts between the monks, who produced and worshiped icons, and those in church and state who feared the monks' influence — all led in the eighth and ninth centuries to several bouts of reac-
tion against the practice. "Iconoclastic" emperors introduced drastic
measures: destruction of images and persecution of their worshipers. But
that policy came in the end to nothing; the cult of icons proved to be too
firmly rooted in the people's as well as theologians' hearts and minds.
Since then, nothing could shake it. Just how centrally placed it is appears
from the awe with which the icons are greeted by believers entering and
leaving the church; but above all does it appear from the way the images of
a church building "work together" in pointing to Christian faith as a
whole. Patriarchs and prophets who announced the Savior before his
coming, Mary who conceived and bore him, apostles and martyrs who
bore witness to him through the history of the church, Mary and John the
Baptist who on the last day shall pray to him on behalf of all humankind
— all appear in an ordered series of images. In their entirety the icons constitute something like a compendium of sacred history, the meaningful sequence of events to which the congregation and its individual members
themselves belong. And at the same time they, together with the icons representing the angelic powers, refer to the "heavenly church" — the tran-
scendent community of adoration that the acts of worship bring close to
the congregation on earth.

The endeavor to make past and future merge into the present and to
concretize the beyond, forms the leitmotif, as it were, of Orthodox liturgy.
That comes to light also in the liturgical processions. In the first of those,
the priest and his assistants carry the Book of Gospels out of the altar
room into the nave as a sign of the coming of Christ to the world. In the
other the eucharistic elements, bread and wine, are carried out to the people and then back to the sacrificial altar while the choir sings the "Cherubic
Hymn" that helps the people understand the meaning of the act. It is meant
to signify both Christ's coming to the people in the shape of "flesh and
blood" — Jesus the man who offers himself in sacrifice — and his divine
coming as king and judge on the last day, accompanied by the heavenly
hosts. A final example can demonstrate how the Orthodox view of things

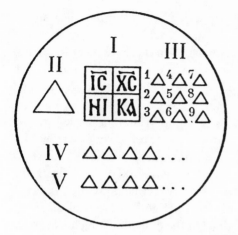

30. Schematic representation of how the pieces of eucharistic bread are placed on the *patena* (plate). The symbol under I stands for the Christ-piece, stamped with the sign of the cross and the words: "Jesus Christ is victor." The piece under II represents the Mother of God, while the pieces under III stand for prophets, apostles, and saints. The groups IV and V symbolize the living and the departed faithful respectively.

is worked out in the tiniest detail. The piece of bread that is destined to become the body of Christ has been cut out of a larger loaf and then placed on a dish surrounded by other pieces, representing Mary, the saints, the congregation's dead, and the congregation itself. They are all present at the sacrifice, the act of liberation that is aimed at them all.

It will be seen, then, that the "divine liturgy," as it is called, conveys the impression of one long attempt at reproducing and concretizing the Orthodox faith. That is, of course, an impression that finds a further confirmation in the Bible texts and prayers which now, as before, changed with the phases and feasts of the liturgical year.

All that serves to throw a clearer light on the distinctive marks of Orthodox political attitudes. Orthodox Christianity was highly political in the sense that emperor and empire, the organizing and coercive power of the state, were centrally placed in its notions of God's action in the world. At the same time, though, it was highly *un*political, not only because the emperor's leadership prevented an independent priestly initiative as far as political and social matters were concerned, but also because of the very concentration of interest on the act of worship. Both these things must be kept in mind when one tries to understand Orthodox church law and theology. In the West those pursuits became politically relevant and provided material for controversy, because of the growing independence of the clergy. Not so in Byzantine and Russian lands. That becomes apparent, above all, from the fact that Orthodox theology shows few signs of the critical and disputation-prone spirit that became a hallmark of Western thinking. Another pointer in the same direction may be found in the modest role played by the sermon. Interestingly enough, by the way, it seems to have gained ground much later, in the Soviet period, when a militantly atheistic state prohibited all other forms of Christian teaching.

All this tells us something about what — in these respects — Orthodoxy was *not,* when compared to the West. If, on the other hand, we ask what it *was,* we shall have to turn, above all, to Orthodox mysticism and monasticism.

When theology is understood as "worship in another mode," it is no wonder that it tends to merge into mysticism, the thinker's personal involvement in the divine, his striving toward intellectual and emotional experience of God's presence with him and his with God. In the liturgy, the coming of the God-man is celebrated — the event that aims at turning the faithful into "gods, . . . children of the Most High." In mystical theology, what is experienced is the "divinization" of the individual. Such words are deeply rooted in Greek philosophy and philosophical religion as well as in earlier Christian theology and monastic piety. Their intention was not to abolish the distinction between Creator and creature, but to make clear just how much more than ordinary human beings the God-man's coming could make of men and women of faith. Simeon, known as "the New Theologian" (around the year 1000), and Gregory Palamas (fourteenth century), the two great practitioners and interpreters of Orthodox mysticism, thought along such lines. It is worth noting that — according to Simeon — the experience of "God's light," the moment of blessed vision, is to be understood in the light of ordinary liturgical experience. It is equally significant that the hymns in which he gave expression to what he had seen were put to use in the normal congregational cult.

The "place in life" of mystical theology was the monastery. Orthodox monasticism can indeed be said to have the mystic experience of liberation and illumination as its principal and ultimate objective. That can, for instance, be seen in the division of monks into different degrees of perfection. The ascetics who attain to the highest degree do of course take part in common worship, but apart from that they are free of any occupation other than solitary contemplation and prayer. Monastic *askesis,* the "training" in self-discipline, is ultimately not there for outward action, but for upward devotion of self.

That has, however, not prevented the monks from playing a part in the "world." That is what appears, for instance, from two distinctive institutions or usages. One is the Orthodox tradition of recruiting bishops from the ranks of the monks. That, in its turn, has to do with another tradition, namely, married clergy, which was preserved in the East in connection with eucharistic practices current there. Unbroken cultic "purity" was not required of Eastern priests because the sacrifice was not, as in the West, celebrated daily. Bishops, on the other hand, were expected to possess the higher quality that was unthinkable without sexual abstinence. That is one of the reasons why only monks became bishops. The other institution that expresses an involvement in the world outside the cloister or the hermit's cave was the confessional and counseling activity ascetics exercised among local people. One example is provided by the Russian startsy, immortalized by Dostoyevsky: men who were consulted by men and women from all ranks of society. During an earlier phase of Orthodox history such "spiritual fathers" might hear confession and give absolution without being ordained priests. A remarkable testimony to the tenacity of a suppressed idea, that of a necessary connection between personal sanctity and ecclesiastical authority, as well as to the strength of the Orthodox notion of individual "divinization"! Nevertheless, in the long run such practices could not be tolerated by a church based on the claim of "apostolic succession" and the principle of exclusively priestly authority.

Orthodox cultic piety and Orthodox monastic asceticism were in some respects conducive to a greater closeness between church and people than was the case in the West. Common worship in the native language provided a broad inspiration for popular piety, and the monk- and hermit-counselors helped make the ascetic ideals known and appreciated. At the same time, however, the distinction between the church's conception of worship and magical superstition could on that background easily become blurred, considering that the central assertion or claim in both was that of a mysterious power by which things and words were suffused. It is, of course, true that when formulated by the church, this idea of a depth of mystery in and behind the sacred words and gestures and objects was understood in a context that was anything but magical. But open to magical interpretation in popular practice it certainly was.

The overwhelming preponderance of the holy rites was revealed with special force in the conflicts that shook Russian Christendom as a consequence of liturgical reforms, initiated by a seventeenth-century patriarch of Moscow. As a matter of fact, the changes he decreed were quite modest, and their purpose, ironically enough, was to maintain original liturgical forms over against distortions. But in the people and among the lower clergy they aroused a resistance of unprecedented force and tenacity. World history tells of few parallels to the ferocious passion of the "Old Believers" in defending the sacred traditions on which, to their minds, the very idea of a meaningful human life depended. The cruel persecution launched against them by the state was unable to shake their determina-

31. By means of the motif of Christ's descent to the dead and his liberation of the Old Testament faithful, the art of the Orthodox church gave expression to its conviction of the inner relations between Christ's death, his resurrection, and the salvation of humankind. In this eleventh-century painting in the monastery of St. Catherine, Sinai, Adam and Eve are shown to the left of Christ, and other Old Testament persons to his right. At the bottom are the broken gates of the underworld and their scattered keys.

tion. Many died a martyr's death on the stake; others would rather burn themselves and their families than give in. The monument of this struggle is the autobiography of Avvakum, a priest and resistance leader who, together with his heroic wife, stands as an embodiment, so to speak, of suffering Russian dissidents through the ages. He perished on the stake in 1682. A special interest attaches to such groups of Old Believers as were unable to get hold of a priest to provide them with the sacraments. "The

4. Eastern Christianity

Priestless," as they were called, tried to make do with prayer services and with the worship of holy images — to whom some confessed their sins — but they also took the decisive further step by electing lay priests and basing their right to do so on primitive Christian usage.

c. Christianity in Asia

The idea which ancient Mediterranean Christianity formed of itself was to a large extent determined by the fact that it belonged to the Roman Empire. That is one of the reasons why it was slow in adapting to the new surroundings created by the Germanic invasions in the West. The empire and civilized humanity were seen as more or less identical quantities. That outlook was shared by Byzantine and, in modified form, Russian Christians, and it has also strongly influenced Western views of the Christian past.

It is true that rumors were heard about a Christian empire in Asia, governed by "John, the priest-king" who would come to the rescue of hard-pressed Christendom in its struggle with Islam. But real knowledge of — not to speak of regard for — the existing forms of Christianity beyond the old imperial borders has been lacking until quite recent times.

There were reasons why that was so, quite apart from the instinctive "empire piety" hinted at above. Foremost among them was that those Christians were heretics, dry branches, so to speak, cut off from the living tree of the church.

Such a metaphor does no justice at all to Oriental Christianity. Christianity was originally an Oriental religion, even if the Hellenistic cultural elite had difficulty accepting that fact. The new religion expanded eastward as early as it went westward, and from the second century on, it won a following among Syrian speakers across the border. There an indigenous church life of great vitality came into being, and from there Christianity spread into the Sassanian Persian Empire — Rome's most dangerous rival. Farther north, where the Armenians led a precarious life between the two giants, a national church began taking shape as early as the closing years of the third century, the conversion of king and magnates leading to that of the people at large.

As to the charge of heresy, it is a fact that Armenian, Syrian, and Persian Christians, and in equal measure the Copts of Egypt and the Ethiopians, described the person of Christ in theological terms that, after long, drawn-out controversies, had been declared heretical by the imperial establishment. Also, the local Christian populations were in many cases reinforced by fugitives, expelled from imperial lands for theological reasons.

109

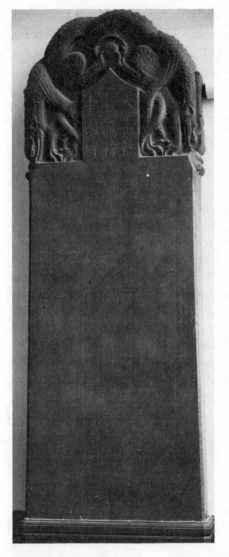

32. *(facing page)* As early as the third century, Christianity became the official religion of Armenia, and a Christian culture flourished there despite constant pressure from powerful neighbors. An impressive amount of church building was carried out from the sixth century to the fourteenth. This picture shows the church of Aght'amar (early tenth century).

33. *(left)* The "Nestorian stone," from Sianfu in northwestern China (the picture shows a plaster cast), was erected in the year 781. Its inscription relates the arrival (635) and subsequent work of Nestorian missionaries in China under the Tang dynasty. (Courtesy of The Royal Library, Copenhagen, Department of Maps, Prints, and Photographs.)

But heresy is a wide-ranging concept indeed. It can with justice be said that the christological heresies of the fifth century, for example — considered in their theological aspects — to some extent originated in terminological differences and linguistic misunderstanding. Moreover, the theological school disputes quite often merged with rivalries between episcopal sees as well as with ethnic and social tensions in the Eastern provinces. That meant that they generated more extensive consequences than they otherwise would have; the situation was not helped by the inevitable involvement of the government and its police. Last, and most important, the practical church life that — even in the eyes of some theologians — counted for more than did theological niceties remained largely untouched by what was proclaimed by the contending parties about "person" and "nature" when defining the God-man. Just how untouched is apparent, for instance, from two hymns for Christmas, one from the East Syrian church and one from the Armenian. They express themselves in identical terms about the Savior whose birth is celebrated on the day of the feast. But the two churches had been condemned for two diametrically opposed christological heresies.

In short, all those churches had good cause to use the title "orthodox church." All are worth studying, not least because of the way national and cultural contexts contribute to their respective versions of Orthodoxy. Nevertheless, one is especially important in a long-term perspective. East Syrian — also known as Chaldean, Persian, Nestorian — Christianity spread over a larger area than any other ancient form of Christian religion: to Arabia, to the oasis cities of central Asia and farther away, to China as well as to southern India. During this process — which culminated in no fewer than two hundred episcopal sees in the thirteenth century — Nestorian Christianity entered into contact with other great religions and contributed to cultural interchange both under Islamic and Mongol rule. One instance of that was the part played by Nestorians in communicating Greek science to the Arabs — something that later on was to become of vital importance in Western intellectual life. At a moment in time a decisive Christian influence on the Mongol rulers seemed to be within reach, but this momentous possibility remained unrealized, and the Nestorian church went into decline under the pressure of persecution and other difficulties. Consequently the sources for its history are far scarcer than its importance for a centuries-long period of Asian history would lead one to expect.

d. East and West

The two halves of Mediterranean Christianity had been moving away from each other for a long time, and the process was hastened by the collapse of imperial unity during the fifth and sixth centuries. Admittedly, many Western Christians went on regarding Constantinople as the center of their world, but the mounting degree of separation — organizationally and liturgically as well as linguistically — was and remained an established fact. As time went by, Eastern and Western Christians became ever more inclined to regard divergences and disagreements as manifestations of a fundamental difference between truth and falsehood, correct belief and heresy. From an Eastern viewpoint, an additional aspect of the difference was that between civilization and barbarism — a claim that one can perhaps find indirectly acknowledged by Western attitudes of fascination and resentment toward the Byzantines.

When the situation is viewed from a twenty-first-century perspective, cultural differences, broadly defined, bear the main responsibility for the separation growing irrevocable. The new cultural milieu to which Western Christianity was now obliged to adapt itself — and which we shall have to consider in a moment — was a foreign world to the Byzantines, and conversely, it added to the strangeness of Eastern ways in Western eyes.

The distinctive character of Western Christianity, such as it evolved gradually after the separation, is something we can only hope to identify in

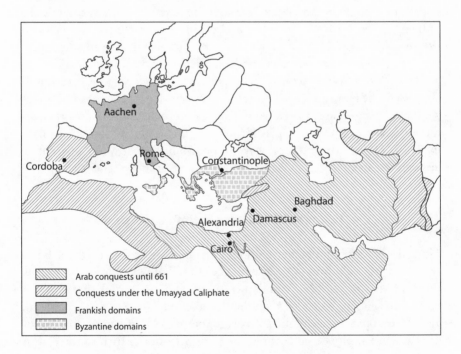

34. The map shows the three empires of the European–Near Eastern world in the year 800: Charlemagne's Frankish empire, the Byzantine Roman empire, and the Islamic empire. The Frankish empire was the earliest big power of Catholic Europe.

any detail later in this book, but a preliminary hint at the decisive long-term differences between East and West may be useful.

Above all, two differences compel our attention. One is the theological difference between Eastern worship-orientation and mysticism on one side and Western tradition-critique and discussion-orientation on the other. The other is the political difference between imperial unity in the East and papal-royal duality in the West — in other words, the difference between an unchallenged unitary control on one hand and a tension-laden two-power competition on the other. Both differences are connected with initial overall cultural differences, and both are coresponsible for innumerable small divergencies between East and West.

The differences are also mutually connected by a great many threads. One of them can be glimpsed in Eastern theologians' inclination to regard the empire as some sort of church. Another one comes to view in the Western analogy between political competition and theological discussion — two tendencies that stimulated and strengthened each other.

There can be no doubt that such differences between two forms of Christian thought and practice have been important for the further development of the respective cultural and political character of Eastern and Western life up to this day. They have been coresponsible for the emergence of two more or less irreconcilable forms of social organization.

That is, however, by no means tantamount to a *religious* irreconcilability. On the contrary, it is important to emphasize that every single main characteristic of one of the two Christianities is to be found in the other, although less prominently displayed; and that this is due to both forms having realized — in their several ways — possibilities that were apparent or implicit in their common origin: ancient Mediterranean Christianity.

5. From the Mediterranean to Europe

The old Western half of Christendom went another way than did the Eastern one, with wide-ranging consequences for all of later cultural as well as religious history. In order to understand how and why it took that separate direction, it is necessary to keep the vast complex of economic, political, and cultural processes in mind that resulted in — and from — "the fall of the Roman Empire," and covered the period from the fifth to the eighth centuries — and, indeed, longer than that.

As we have already seen, the Roman Empire did not by any means "fall" in the absolute sense of the word, but it is a certain fact that there can be no talk of a common political organization of the Mediterranean countries after the fifth century, and that no economic and cultural homogeneity can be discerned in the area after the eighth. West became separated from East in all those respects, and the West was split up internally because of the Germanic invasions; the decay or disappearance of urban life, the money-based economy, and the traditional educational system; and the transposition of economic and political power to the class of military landowners that emerged from the meeting of native and foreign — Roman and Germanic — elites. The breakdown of traditional factors of cohesion was a process during which the various disruptive forces stimulated each other mutually. As a consequence of all this, the civilizational interplay of economy, politics, and culture assumed an entirely different character as far as the Western part of the old empire was concerned. Increasingly, that area "turned its back on" the sea and found its centers of gravity farther inland.

Naturally, the Christian religion that had adapted itself to Mediterranean civilization and profited by its forces of cohesion was drawn into this great process of transformation.

That became clear not least in the matter of church organization. The "ecumenical council" could no longer be summoned to discuss and decide on common, supraregional problems; and it goes also without saying that the coordinating activity of the imperial government went down the drain as well.

Both circumstances hastened the separation of the Latin half of the church from the Greek one. But the internal Western cohesion was also seriously damaged. The position — vindicated by the bishop of Rome since the late fourth century — as supreme Western judge of appeals in church disputes could no longer be maintained in the absence of a supporting imperial authority. The new rulers — Germanic warlords — considered themselves the natural governors of "their" churches and tolerated no papal interference. In this situation the groundwork was laid for the form of intermingling between political and ecclesiastical power that was to become so marked a characteristic of European history.

But gradually the transformation process began to release even more fatal consequences on the "grassroots" level. Here the distinctive mark of the old church order had been the concentration of governing authority in the hands of the bishop. Mediterranean Christianity's homogeneity and power of resistance depended above all on his position as "successor of the apostles" and his power to draw conclusions — material and spiritual — from that position in relation to the people. Therefore the breach of epis-

35. Wars and migrations left their marks on early Europe — it was a time of upheaval. This seventh-century funerary stele shows a horseman armed for war.

copal unity inaugurated by the landed aristocracy's building of churches on their estates constituted a more serious threat than did the collapse of imperial and papal authority. The phenomenon of "private churches" not only enabled the squire to treat the church in the same way he treated the mill or the winepress, which all his subjects were compelled to use for payment. It also made it possible for him to treat the local priest as his functionary, thus adding power over his dependents' souls to the material one he already possessed. This state of things became of course especially glaring when the priest was legally "unfree," subject to his master's corporal punishment, but from the viewpoint of traditional Christianity the milder cases were more than bad enough. When it is also remembered that the episcopal sees began to be filled with men from the selfsame governing elite; when it is kept in mind how isolated the lesser units of social life tended to become; and when the decay of formal education is taken into consideration, then it becomes abundantly clear how broad and deep went the impoverishment of Western church life.

That is, however, by no means the whole truth about the centuries of transition. Not only were old forms and contexts broken down; new ones emerged and established themselves. They did so on the premises of the new situation, but — noteworthy enough — also on those of the old one inasmuch as vitally essential elements of the Mediterranean heritage were maintained and transmitted to the nascent European world.

Most important of those surviving elements was the catholic faith itself, such as it was confessed at baptism and in Sunday worship. Its fundamental tenets, and the interpretation of world order and history implied by them, were seriously contested by no one, notwithstanding the fact that only a minority of the clergy, to say nothing of the laity, were able to account for them in any kind of detail or depth. In a time without original theological questioning and discussion, spiritual and intellectual nourishment had to be drawn exclusively from the complete and coherent conception of history and destiny inherited from Christian antiquity.

That became important in a situation where no comparable conceptions had survived. In the Mediterranean context catholic Christianity had been only one among several rationally articulated interpretations of world order and history, and it had by no means been alone in offering a coherent set of moral precepts, built on a foundation of sacred texts. Now, it was of course not the only way to relate to human existence, but it was the only one of its kind. Its book; its sacred acts of worship in which the events of the book were "made present"; its authoritative teaching about an obscure past and a problematical future — all that must have been of extraordinary impact in the new surroundings.

A special role was played by the priestly office, inasmuch as its fundamental characteristics remained unaffected by the crisis of institutional coherence and the decay of literacy. It was never open to doubt that the priest alone — be he ever so subjugated socially — was endowed with certain powers. He could administer the means of salvation by virtue of his ordination at the hands of the "successor of the apostles," and the defects in his formal education were counterbalanced by his monopoly of such training.

In the new situation the clerical skills at reading and writing became vastly more important than in the old world.

The result was that those two "monopolies" supported and strengthened each other mutually, endowing the clergy with a new form of prestige. In this connection it must also be remembered that the Christian mission in the West — unlike the Eastern one — retained the old language in the liturgy. The new Christians in the West had no direct access to the Latin words of the Mass; as for the vernacular sermon, it was of decreasing importance. No wonder the arts of reading and writing became enveloped in mystery and awe — as witnessed by the fact that the English word "glamor," magical power, is etymologically identical with "grammar."

The work of mission in the Germanic-speaking lands inside and outside the old imperial frontiers was another factor of cohesion — naturally enough, because now, with people no longer living closely together in big cities, the mission had to be carried out by full-time professionals who were able to cover great distances and relate to multitudes of people, but also because conversion to Christianity generally took the form of a collective act: common acceptance of the new *sidr* (as the Norsemen called it), the new way of life that was believed to safeguard human society more effectively than the old one.

Yet another force for unity was provided by the new Western forms of the "perfect" life: monasticism in its Benedictine and other versions. That was not due to any organizational coherence — which indeed it conspicuously lacked — but because it propagated something rarely seen in early Europe: the idea of a regulated life with a rationally defined purpose and aim. It was also due to the circumstance that many monks worked as missionaries.

Two more factors contributed importantly to the preparing of a new form of ecclesiastical unity. One was the papacy. It is a remarkable aspect of early Europe that the bishop of Rome — quite regardless of the limitations of his practical powers of leadership — enjoyed religious prestige in his capacity as successor of Peter, the heavenly "gatekeeper," and as guardian of the apostle's tomb: the center of spiritual and magical power, goal of pilgrimages from as far away as Anglo-Saxon England. As was to become clear later, this robust, theologically unreflected, but warm and earthy attitude of awe provided one of the bases for a renewed growth of governing influence on the part of the papacy — just as the respect for priestly ordination implied the possibility of development in the direction of practical leadership for the clergy.

Last but not least, the cooperation between secular and clerical pow-

36. Harald "Bluetooth," the first king of united Denmark to become Christian, was baptized ca. 960. The event is shown on an altar-plate from a church not far from the ancient royal seat of Jelling in Jutland. (Courtesy of the National Museum of Denmark.)

ers acquired a new importance. In the new situation, beset with obstacles to the establishment of supralocal authority, kings and bishops were — so to speak — thrown upon each other much more than before. The bishops needed support from an effective supralocal force for peace and unity if they were to uphold the catholic character of the church and secure their own position in it. And early European kings needed not only the technical help that the literate clergy could provide, but also the legitimacy that could be derived from the support of the sole communicators of the powers of salvation.

The lack of a firm supralocal authority of the kind that had existed earlier necessitated a tighter alliance between church and state than before. Here, as well as when speaking of the other forces of unity, it can be said that a new situation caused an old idea to be realized in a new way.

All the tendencies summed up here — and indeed, several more — conditioned a sequence of momentous events around the middle of the eighth century, events that, not without justice, can be said to signify a crucial beginning of a European ecclesiastical unity.

At the center of those events stood the alliance concluded between the pope and the Frankish king — the most powerful Western ruler. The accord implied that the pope got the king's help against his Italian and Byzantine enemies and, conversely, that the pope helped the king — a usurper of the throne — to gain legitimacy by means of the sacramental anointing, thereby putting him on a level with the kings of Israel. Quite apart from being the outcome of an obvious community of political interest, the alliance represented a confluence of all the forces for unity — epitomized, so to speak, by the man who stood sponsor to the alliance, Boniface (d. 754), the Anglo-Saxon monk, missionary, archbishop, and church organizer, a passionate champion of Peter, the heavenly gatekeeper, and of his vicar on earth.

This alliance stands for the Roman see's farewell to Mediterranean unity and its engagement in the new Western world, and for that new world's engagement in the ecclesiastical and cultural idea of unity, which the successor of Peter brought with him from the old world. In a very real sense, western Europe can be said to come into being at this moment. Its definitive separation from the East is foreshadowed, and the outlines of its distinctive characteristics can be, however dimly, discerned.

part three

Christianity as a
European Religion

1. Old Europe

The course of events considered in the previous chapter reveals that a new pattern of civilization began to appear: a pattern that was to determine life on the European peninsula and its adjacent islands for more than a thousand years.

The word "pattern" is of course somewhat misleading, inasmuch as the civilization of old Europe was a dynamic one, evolving into ever more complicated forms, with many shifts in emphasis from one element in the "pattern" to another. It is nevertheless necessary to use some such metaphor, however unsatisfactory, to make clear that we are dealing from the eighth to the eighteenth century with something that "resembles itself" more than what went before and what came afterward.

In contradistinction to its modern successor, old Europe was an agrarian civilization insofar as the overwhelming majority of its inhabitants lived in the countryside, working the land. It is true that this situation underwent modifications through the growing importance of urban life, but it was not decisively changed before the Industrial Revolution.

Both the continuity and the modifications are important for understanding what distinguished old Europe in general and its form of Christianity in particular. In a religious as well as a cultural context, tradition — the practical wisdom, handed down through the generations by people whose life was subject to the "will" of land and climate — certainly underwent questioning and criticism from individuals and groups for whom the wisdom of the fathers was not incontestably sacrosanct. But on the other hand, again and again new ideas and new ways of living ended up inserting themselves in strong traditional structures, putting them under critical scrutiny without tearing them apart. And behind such fruitful tensions between old and new one can, more often than not, discern the fundamental tension between town and country.

In the same way, social and political organization can only be understood on the background of the preponderance of agrarian life. Notwithstanding all differences, the landowning aristocracy's predominance among the ruling powers was a common feature of the old European centuries. That is true of the early centuries, when supralocal communications were scarce and a money-based economy was more or less absent. But it is also true of the period after the changes in that situation. No state power, no national monarchy could function without some sort of understanding with the landowning aristocrats — the king was such a one himself. No form of bourgeois life in old Europe is fully understandable with-

out considering its element of "gentility" and of admiration for the aristocratic lifestyle. And the general outlook on life and the theoretical approach to the world retained to the last a number of ideas and sentiments about rights and duties in relation to neighbor, society, and God that cannot be explained without reference to the "feudal" past.

But here again, it is a distinctive mark of old European civilization that the dominant and fundamental forces never escaped tensions and criticism. In many disguises, aristocratic culture demonstrated its wearing quality and its power of endowing society with continuity and a sense of tradition; but it was by no means alone on the old European stage. The monarchical state's gradually stronger grip on society; the urban citizenry's spirit of economic innovation; and the attempts by the "intelligentsia" to construct systematically coherent images of physical and social order — in all those things tendencies were active that were finally to disrupt and overthrow the old world, but until then they introduced an element of fruitful fermentation and unrest into that world.

The agricultural roots of society and the aristocratic character of its leading groups both, to some extent, bear witness to the links that tie old European civilization to its Mediterranean predecessor. But those links are much stronger as far as intellectual culture is concerned. Not only did the Latin language reign supreme or predominate in academic communication through the entire period, but the images that old Europe formed of the world and of mankind were profoundly stamped with the ideas of Greek and Hellenistic philosophy about a hierarchy of things, a "great chain of being" connecting the stone on the beach with the heavenly spirits, and an analogous hierarchy of soul and body, reason, will, sentiments, and urges in the microcosm that is man. And one of the governing concepts of old European thinking about society is to be found in the ancient idea that the patriarchal household, the monarchical state, and the divine government of the cosmos were mutually illuminating manifestations of one and the same principle of order.

More than a few old European "constants" connect this period with the preceding one — and separate it from its successor. But the period is in no respect simply a continuation of antiquity. It has its own face, as a con-

37. The construction of the great gothic cathedral of Cologne, Germany, was long under way. Its foundation stone was laid in 1248, but it was finished only in 1880. It was designed to be a gigantic shrine for the relics of the Three Magi, brought from Milan to Cologne in 1164. (Courtesy of the Danish National Art Library, Copenhagen.)

sequence of new geographic and climatic conditions, the collapse of Mediterranean unity — that "awful revolution" (Gibbon) — and last but not least, the role played in it by Christianity and the Christian church.

We are thus returning to our central theme. Old European Christianity differed from the earlier form because of the shaping influences exerted by the new context. But conversely, that context underwent an influence from Christianity that went immeasurably deeper than had been the case earlier.

In ancient times Christianity had inserted itself into a civilization that had developed and been completed on its own premises. But in Europe it became cocreator of a civilization. We have already noticed some of its creative effects in the seminal events of the eighth century, but the process was much deeper and wider reaching than that.

In the lands and peoples that came into contact with Christianity in the earliest European centuries, all institutions and cultural links that exceeded the narrowly local sphere were weakly developed, of scant efficiency, and vulnerable to crises. As strong a unit as was the village and the great landowner's household, just as weak was the state — if that word can be meaningfully used at all. The same observation is valid for a national, an economic, or a legal unity, and something similar can be stated about the "theoretical" aspects of life. The lack of a literary culture based on writing, and of a formal education, constituted a decisive obstacle to coherent and articulate interpretations of history, world order, and society, to say nothing of an internal critique of things as they are and the powers that be.

This is exactly the state of affairs in which the distinctive mark of the Christianity of the church — appreciated by the late Roman emperors — namely, its unique combination of an interpretation of human existence and a social organization, could gain its full weight and power of impact. The church arrived with a rationally coherent explanation of things and an instruction about salvation, based upon Bible and creed. It communicated its message through a clerical organization regulated by law, and it worked under monopolistic conditions. Naturally, such a body came to occupy a much more important position in the landscape of civilization than had been possible under earlier circumstances. It provided impulses toward a new form of legitimation of royal power as well as some of the technical means for such power to be exercised. From it issued the first rudiments of

38. The interior of Cologne Cathedral represents the ideal gothic sacred space, with soaring pillars and high pointed arches letting in the light. (Courtesy of the Danish National Art Library, Copenhagen.)

universally valid systems of law and important incentives to supranational economic communications. And above all, from it came the decisive concept of Christendom — a collective term for a supralocal and supranational human community, with a common history in Israel's and the church's past; a common lawbook in the Bible; common means of salvation in sacraments, preaching, and catechetical instruction; and a common hope for the future.

Conversely, it is worth noticing that Christianity itself underwent changes that issued from its new social role and from the pattern of culture it helped create. Increasingly it became defined in legalistic, moralistic, and political terms, and its clericalization gained speed accordingly. Individually and collectively, those processes released consequences — for the message, for the organization, and for their interplay — that can be felt to this day.

Because the Christianity of the church was so crucially active in establishing institutional and cultural links that exceeded the elementary and locally limited sphere, it could not avoid influencing the form of those links. That is why institutions and ideas that were not Christian by origin came to assume shapes that were decisively stamped with Christianity and differed more or less widely from those taken in the Mediterranean context. Royal monarchy became a "kingship by the grace of God"; the aristocracy became imbued with the ideas and lifestyle of Christian chivalry; social experimenting became a matter for monks and nuns; the inherited ideology of order was turned in another direction by the notion of a personally acting God being welded into it; rational philosophical reflection came to be seen as finding its necessary completion in the "supernatural" revelation. Last but not least, from now on human society came to be viewed in a dual perspective: beside the Christian state stood the Christian church, as its collaborator and its critic and rival.

As already hinted at, the old European interplay was marked by a characteristic relationship between, on the one hand, a number of remarkably long-lived "constants": the agricultural base, the aristocratic predominance, the idea of order, and on the other, the tendencies and forces that criticized while at the same time enriching them — and ended up destroying them: the bureaucratic state, commercial and industrial capitalism, empirical science, and liberal individualism. By considering the Christianity of the church, we can gain a deeper insight into this relationship. That religion is of course in itself one of the great constants, as an institution and as a set of ideas, and it sets an unmistakable mark on the rest of them. But it is also — in a more or less direct sense — one of the forces for change and disruption, and as such influences the others. Many other causes can be pointed at for the coming into being of the centralized state, the capitalistic economy, and liberal individualism, but all were *also* expressions of Christian attitudes toward the question of how to define and practice the Christian message and the tradition of the church.

The preceding considerations give occasion to the concluding reflection that no single complex of events and ideas like "the Renaissance" or "the Reformation" can be said to constitute a decisive breach in the unity of old European civilization. The reorientations and tensions expressed by those movements have in some way or another been present long before them, and conversely, the great constants are present and alive long after them, serving as important ingredients in the working out of their shapes and their consequences.

That is not tantamount to denying a meaning to the traditional way of treating the Reformation as epochal, but it is worth trying to look at it as an epochal event *inside* the history of old European civilization and religion. Therefore, in what follows, the period from the eighth to the eighteenth centuries will be considered under two main headlines: "Old European Christianity: The Time of the Church" and "Old European Christianity: The Time of the Churches."

2. Old European Christianity: The Time of the Church

a. The Course of Events

Old European Christianity was historically coherent; it resembled itself through the centuries, but it was not a static phenomenon, and it did not spring into being at once.

As we have seen, the middle period of the eighth century was a seminal one. During those years the links to the Greek Church were decisively loosened; the idea of a Christian kingship, consecrated by the "Israelite" anointing, broke through; and an alliance was concluded between the Roman see and the strongest power in the new West, the kingdom of the Franks. By no means did those events create a "finished" European Christianity, but vitally important bases were laid for institutions and conditions that could provide the inherited Christianity with possibilities of growth and gradually turn it into something different from what it had been before.

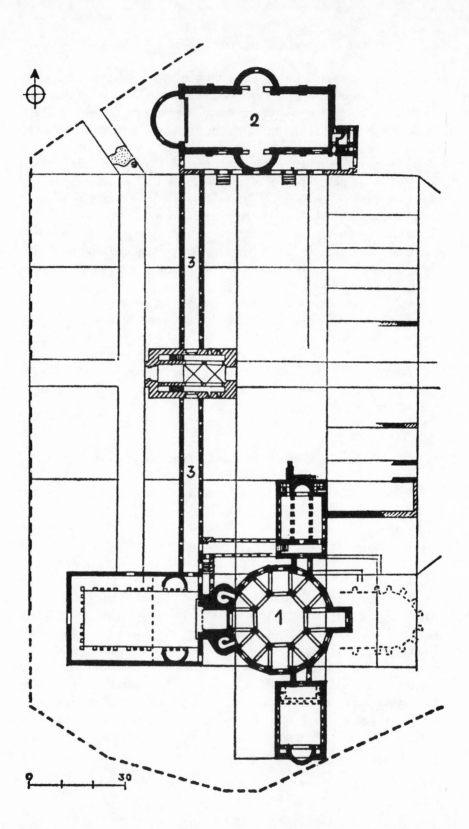

2

3

3

1

0   30

2. Old European Christianity: The Time of the Church

The importance of those seminal events was confirmed by the consolidating and enlarging work done during the short flowering of a supranational Western unity under Charles the Great, or Charlemagne (768-814). Here the alliance between state and church was deepened by incorporation of the higher clergy in the system of personal links, tenancy of crown property, and parceling out of state authority known as feudalism. In a longer perspective, that was tantamount to a consolidation of the aristocratic influence on church government as well as a widening of the gap between high and low clergy — an ominous heritage to later centuries. At the same time, the organs of ecclesiastical unity were reformed and strengthened in order to make them serve the royal church government more efficiently, but also to make them better able to resist local encroachments of property and rights. No less important was that Charles, the very same ruler that terrorized thousands of vanquished Saxons by forced baptism, was also the organizer of a large-scale attempt at popular education by an empirewide system of schools and preaching to the people. It came to nothing shortly after his death, but it was a portent of things to come and of the inherent possibilities of European Christianity.

When the typical traits of the early old European situation are considered, it is not surprising that the centrifugal forces regained their prevalence almost immediately after the great ruler's death. Political disruption set in, and ecclesiastical and cultural life was impoverished. But toward the middle of the tenth century a new political and ecclesiastical unity was established farther east, with its center of gravity in what later became Germany. From there missionary campaigns were organized toward the east as well as the north of Europe, and politico-military interference in Italy resulted in the papacy becoming inserted into a new imperial structure of a feudal cast. During the same period a reform and coordination of Benedictine monasticism was initiated in eastern France, the very wide repercussions of which were felt all over Europe. And the new Western unity of

39. Charlemagne's imperial chapel in Aachen/Aix-la-Chapelle (western Germany) is only scantily preserved, but the original appearance must have been highly impressive. A contemporary court poet called it the "Second Rome." In accordance with Byzantine tradition, the chapel (1) was connected with the palace (2) by means of a corridor (3), so that the emperor could move directly from the secular sphere to his exalted seat in the chapel to attend the celebration of mass. The court of Aachen also drew inspiration from the Old Testament. Charlemagne was likened to King David, the arch-chaplain Hildebold was Aaron the high priest, and the chapel symbolized Solomon's temple.

faith was rounded off through the conversion of the peoples of Hungary, Poland, and Scandinavia.

This unity of faith was very far from a full unity of church organization, and the steps taken in that direction were under firm royal control and served the interests of royal power — a Christianized power, but one totally foreign to the idea of the church as an independent and self-governing institution.

That is the background for the rise of the ecclesiastical liberation movement, which from the middle years of the eleventh century took hold of the Roman see. Here a coherent set of clericalist conclusions were drawn from common Christian premises. The Roman reformers claimed that the sacramental transmission of heavenly power, by which not only the church but the human community as such was upheld, had to be independent of any other control than the one exercised by Saint Peter's successor on earth. Every other form of church government constituted a sacrilegious rebellion against God's plan and purpose for his people.

40. During "the time of the church" the cult of relics became increasingly important and found expression in, among other things, a great number of pilgrimages. The reliquary shown here, containing the head of Pope Alexander I, dates from the first half of the twelfth century. (Courtesy of Musées royaux d'Art et d'Histoire.)

Furthermore, the pope's pastoral duty to answer for Christian souls on Judgment Day must necessarily imply a right and a duty to interfere in the royal government of Christian bodies whenever it offended against God's law — the law of which the pope was sole interpreter. Saint Peter's vicar must have the power of deposing a recalcitrant ruler and sanctioning the election of his successor. And in order to carry out his will, he must not only be able to close down the churches in the ruler's domain but also to call on military means — his own or others' — against him.

If the breakthrough of "complete" old European Christianity is to be placed historically at any particular point in time, it must be here. That is so not only because the Roman reform drew one of the most important conclusions to which the fundamental Christian assertions were open, but because the ensuing success of the movement presupposes — and makes clear to us — a higher degree of Christianizing than had hitherto been in evidence. Christian claims and tenets must have gained broader ground and struck deeper roots among the peoples of Christendom than before.

Also, the papal program could be implemented only under a number of "secular" conditions, like the fact that short-term interests could tempt lesser rulers to go along with the program against greater ones. But above all, the general economic and cultural "takeoff" must be kept in mind: from about the turn of the millennium, a complex of growth and expansion, in population, in agriculture, in urban trades, in commerce and the use of money, and in supralocal communications, was discernible across Europe. It is hard to imagine any kind of supranational concentration of ecclesiastical power being successful in practice without that background and incentive.

When using the word "success," we must remember that papal monarchy was never totally realized. Even at the height of Roman power and prestige, lay control of churches continued to a wide extent all over Christendom, often in more or less unofficial shapes and disguises. But compared to the previous situation, the success was remarkable. A reform of church law on Roman principles and with a universal scope was initiated. A considerably widened control of episcopal appointments was established. International church councils were held under papal control. Monastic reform movements and an internationally recruited body of university teachers as well as of heresy hunters were put to service for the unity of the universal church. Last, but by no means least, the presence of Saint Peter's successor everywhere in Christendom was secured by means of a network of correspondence, legations, gifts and benefices, and judicial appeals to the papal courts.

From circa 1300 to circa 1500 — the concluding period of the old European "time of the church" — two tendencies met and struggled for supremacy. One was a continuation and radicalizing of the papal system; the other, a deep-reaching criticism and a partial undermining of that system. Some of the forces contesting the traditional order were familiar ones: royal and municipal endeavors to exploit the weaknesses of the system. Others were more or less new: popular religious mass movements that turned the papal church's weapons against itself by attacking its alleged abuses of Bible and creed, its immersion in politics and warfare, in short: its way of adapting to "the world." Independent experiments in individual devotion and new forms of communal life; a proud and responsible urban citizenry's gradual undermining of episcopal power; attempts at a collective government of the universal church by ecumenical councils; preaching about an imminent overthrow of all earthly things, conceived as the breakthrough of the millennium or as social revolution, or both — all were portents of change in the old structures of life and thought.

b. The "Common Faith"

Use of the term "catholic" — in the sense of common and general, all-encompassing — is debatable when applied to European Christianity in our period. First, the Christian faith appeared in many socially and culturally conditioned variants; second, the sources that make it known to us are overwhelmingly clerical in origin; and third, the Christian religion had fully prevailed only in comparatively small segments of the European peoples. Much of what passed for religion in the population at large — especially in the countryside — was hardly Christian at all, and much that was in fact Christian cannot without severe qualifications be called anything like a complete and coherent interpretation of the world and of human existence.

The term must nevertheless be retained, considering that a fully elaborated system of thought and practice was in actual existence — keeping its identity through the entire period and enjoying a monopoly of religious teaching. Regardless of the degree of success in attempting to make it universally known and accepted, the acceptance of *that* faith was what the church proposed to bring about.

As for its fundamental assertions and their practical expressions in worship and organizational claims, the catholic faith was inherited as a "finished product" from Mediterranean antiquity. Now as before, Christian opinions and life in the church were two sides of the same coin, and now as before, both things aimed at being all-encompassing. Christianity as a theoretical and doctrinal quantity claimed to provide a full explanation of world order, past history, contemporary and future existence; and it pretended to give inerrant directions concerning the mode of life required by the explanation. Now as before, religion was anything but a private matter or an activity on the level of others. Like Christianity in the ancient world — and, be it noted, like ancient paganism — old European Christianity was what Norse people called *sidr:* sacred custom, directions for human life as a whole. That was indeed a character that became deepened in early Europe as a consequence of the new material and cultural conditions.

The all-encompassing Christian "theory" was a theory about the world. As such, it had appropriated the ancient model of an ordered cosmos: a chain or hierarchy of mutually coherent forms of being, from mere "being there" over vegetal and animal being, to the human combination of body and reason, up to pure intellect. But it had put the model to use in its own way. It had done that, first, by incorporating the creed's notion of God's nature and action: Behind the ordered cosmos stood not only an uncaused essence of being and reason, but a personal creative and salvific will, a will that had taken — and continued to take — re-creating measures against the confusion that had been brought about by man's fall into sin and selfishness. Secondly, Christian theology had seen the decisive expression of that salvific will in the Son's encounter with the fallen on their own level, his taking their lot upon himself "on the bare earth." And thirdly, the church insisted that the created order had to be grasped in its elementary outlines by everybody, insofar as it insisted on the notion that everybody had to understand himself as a created and disturbed order, a microcosm in which God's loving and re-creating will was meant to hold sway.

The inherited theory was also a theory about history, and again: one that everybody had to make his own. It was based on the claim that the divine will had manifested itself through the coherent series of experiences of a definite people and its individual members; through prophecy about what was to come; and through the explanation provided by those coming things. And furthermore, it was based on the assertion that history would come to an end, with revelation of all human acts, disclosure of the innermost concerns of human hearts, and judgment to heaven or hell.

Finally, the theory was a theory about the church as the vehicle by which the re-created order came about. During the Mediterranean centuries that theory had ended up establishing its center of gravity in the doctrine of the episcopal office, the bearer of "apostolic" authority over the entire field of church activity. Everything that God would say and do in his

people would be by means of a hierarchy of consecrated ministers under the incontestable leadership of the bishop. This hierarchical organization was seen as anything but accidental. In accordance with the Creator's will, it was meant to serve as a mirror of the general order of things as well as of the individual expressions of that order: the hierarchically ordered "choirs" of the angels and the human person's original harmony between governing and obeying faculties. Something of that is meant when Pope Gregory I, "the Great" (590-604), talks of the encounter of heaven and earth that takes place when a priest acts on behalf of Christ. At the culmination of the eucharistic service, when the sacrifice of Christ becomes present reality through the word of the officiating priest, "the heavens," Gregory writes, "are opened; the angelic choirs are present; the lower things enter into communion with the highest; the earth is connected to heaven; the visible things and the unseen become one."

Such words are genuine expressions of ancient Mediterranean Christianity, but in our context they can be regarded as alluding to something that was to become characteristic of old European catholic thinking and practice: a strong concentration on the church as sole mediator of divine energies to the world.

The institution of the church became the central religious phenomenon. The question of its right order, its conformity with the divine will to order became *the* question that determined the way all other questions were formulated and answered.

As we shall see, ideas about what was the correct order could turn out differently according to the angle from which they were formulated: a papal angle, a royal one, a monastic one, etc.; but the question was central to all, and there was broad agreement about the purpose of the institution. It was there for the sake of salvation, and it was there to help regulate life in society.

As for the first and most important of those purposes, it was a common conviction that the work of salvation first and foremost took place by

41. In salvation-historical thinking, the miracle of Pentecost, the coming of the Holy Spirit to the apostles, was the revelation of what had been mysteriously meant by the giving of the Law on Sinai. Also, it represented the restoration of the understanding between peoples that had been lost by the building of the Tower of Babel. But above all it was regarded as the birth-hour of the church: the sending down of the Spirit had enabled the apostles to go and "teach all nations." On this manuscript illustration from Cluny (twelfth century), the miracle is visualized by means of beams of light emanating from the risen Christ to the twelve apostles, with Peter in the middle.

means of the sacred acts. That was a conviction that fitted well into the general objectivism and collectivism characteristic of the Christianity of peasants and warriors — as it had been of their paganism. What God does to the world, he does through tangible things; he does it for the people rather than for individuals; and he does it everywhere in the same way. That is to say, he does it — with the ordained minister as his representative — through the formalized communication of "blessing" by sacraments and sacramentals.

Which sacred acts were sacraments and which were only sacramentals was to be determined by the theologians — and that took time. It was a given fact that some acts were more vitally important than others, but it was also certain that all the acts constituted a salvific attack on the powers that threatened to destroy the order of human life in society. Salvation took place when the newborn child was baptized, that is, when it was liberated from the consequences of Adam and Eve's sin; and also when the self-sacrifice of Christ was "repeated" in the Eucharist. But a work of salvation was also done when stables and cornfields and marriage beds were consecrated by gestures like crossing, or sprinkling with holy water, and by the accompanying prayers.

The seven acts of worship for which the name of sacrament was finally reserved were baptism, the Eucharist, confirmation, marriage, penance, last unction, and ordination. In a sense, all stood and fell with the last-named, as is confirmed by the papal understanding of the church's faith.

After infant baptism became prevalent, confirmation, which in ancient times had consisted in an anointing of the newly baptized, was a separate act performed when a child had reached the "age of discretion." Only the bishop could confirm, and the sacrament was used to draw the chil-

42, 43a, 43b. *(facing and following pages)* Rogier van der Weyden's tripartite altarpiece in Antwerp, Belgium (1450s), presents the seven sacraments of the Catholic Church. The middle part shows Christ's self-sacrifice on the cross, the fount and basis of all the sacramental acts. In the background, the priest celebrates the Eucharist, thus actualizing the sacrifice on the cross. In the left part of the painting, the sacraments of baptism, confirmation, and penance are represented, and in the right part those of ordination, matrimony, and preparation for death (extreme unction). It is worth noticing not only that these sacraments realistically take place in the church building but also that the sacrifice on the cross, the past event from which they all draw their origin, is shown taking place in the same building and thus being realized in the present. (Courtesy of the Danish National Art Library, Copenhagen.)

dren's attention to the fact that they belonged to a larger unity than the parish.

The sacrament of marriage was unique in that it was performed by the recipients themselves. The church's blessing was important, but the essence of the sacrament was the couple's bodily and spiritual union — whereby they expressed its "most holy exemplar": the union of Christ with the church.

The central element of the sacrament of penance was — now as before — the priest's communication, on behalf of Christ, of the forgiveness of sins, in accordance with the Savior's promise: "Whatsoever ye shall loose on earth shall be loosed in heaven." And now as before, the sacrament was bound up with a system of penitential acts at the priest's discretion; but penance had gradually ceased to be an entirely public sacrament. Confession of sins, judgment, and absolution took place under four eyes only — since 1215, once a year as a minimum.

The institution of the church, the maternal mediator of the gifts from heaven, was the foremost fact of religion. It can with justice be said that she herself, in her capacity as a visible tool of invisible divine power, was *the* comprehensive sacrament, epitomizing all the others. On that background it is no wonder that questions about the church's institutional order, its hierarchy of offices of varying competence, as well as the status of its personnel and property within society at large, were considered subjects of religious not less than juridical reflection. The celibacy of the clergy, for instance, their freedom from other bonds than that to the Lord of the sacraments, was a matter for theologians to reflect on and argue for; and so was the inviolability of the church's property. Also, the organizational demarcations between priestly offices were anything but unconnected with ideas about the institution as the bearer of salvation. By means of the parish priest salvation was meant to reach everybody; on the next level, the bishop and his canons took care of the catholic coherence in space and time and exercised control over what went on lower down. And above the bishop stood the successor of Peter, bishop of bishops. The questions of how this hierarchical order had to be interpreted in practice and how it had to relate to other powers in Christian society could be — and most certainly were — answered in different ways, but its existence and its religious necessity were beyond doubt.

The church institution as the great "sacrament" — that was one of the distinctive marks of the catholic faith in its new, European situation. Another was the clericalization of religion — the widening of the gap between clergy and laity. To a large extent, that was due to the breakdown of the ancient forms of lay education as well as the fact that Latin was re-tained as the liturgical language of the church. But it can also be seen as a result of the passionate interest in the church as belonging to the sphere of the "holy," rigidly demarcated from that of the "profane." Be that as it may, the dividing up of the church in an actively providing clergy and a passively receiving laity, which had been well under way in late antiquity, was carried further during this period. It was clearly expressed in the practice of wor-ship, where preaching and teaching had been radically curtailed and where the Latin language as well as the partition of the church building between choir and nave contributed to making "God's people" into a largely passive one. Admittedly, this is not the whole truth about the role of the laity. One of the fruitful tensions in old European church life is the increase in lay ini-tiatives, along unofficial as well as official channels, which constituted an ever more painful problem for the clerical way of thinking. But as far as the heart of catholic Christianity was concerned — the eucharistic service — that thinking was all-pervasive.

Yet another main feature to be kept in mind when comparing old Eu-ropean Christianity with its predecessor is its role in society at large. It was a much wider and deeper role than that of the Mediterranean church. And it was played on a theoretical as well as a practical plane: theoretical in the sense that the church's religion was the source of the commonly predomi-nant cultural and societal "myth" of old European civilization. It provided the concepts and the images needed by social and political structures, both during their building up and later on.

The "myth" was the story about God and his people as the church told it, a story that — in each and every phase, from Abraham to the pres-ent — was socially and politically relevant as a series of patterns to imitate, warning examples, and incitements to hope. What was to be understood by a well-ordered community; in what manner its functions must be regu-lated by law; how legitimate rulership had to be established and exercised; what were the criteria for unjust use of power, and how it could legiti-mately be protested against and resisted — all that could be generally learned from Israel's and the church's history, and specifically from the lives of, e.g., King David, the prophet Jeremiah, and the apostle Peter.

Something could of course also be learned from the European peo-ples' own histories and customs — the "good old rights and usages" — but nowhere was it endowed with the kind of authority that backed up the church's story, and nowhere in the rationally elaborated form in which it had been handed down by ancient theology. Social coherence and conflict; rights and duties of social groups; political institutions; principles of law, of power, and of criticism of power — all could be met with there. And — vitally important — it was met with in a form that was inextricably bound up with the church's authoritative teaching about the conditions of becoming saved from eternal perdition in hell.

In actual practice, the societal function was exercised through clerical cooperation in establishing and administering the institutions of society. One branch of this cooperation appears in the activity of members of the higher clergy as administrators in royal chanceries and as bearers of delegated authority on episcopal lands. The bishops filled an important place in the feudal system as local lessees of crown rights: jurisdiction, taxation, policing, and military conscription. Another vehicle of practical influence was the law of the church, known as canon law. That was because it could serve as a muster for state legislation, but above all because certain parts of "secular" legislation were directly administered by the church, the most important of which were the laws governing marriage; their regulation by the church had extremely wide-ranging consequences, not least the gradual weakening of family control over the contracting of marriage. Thirdly, the church's character of a "state" in its own right, gradually worked out by the papal government, served as a tool of social influence, both theoretically and practically. Only through the Rome-inspired centralization and homogenization of church life at the height of papal power did the entire political potential inherent in the catholic sacramental and doctrinal institution become actualized. That is something that will come under consideration in a later chapter. The type of Christianity that was socially active along such lines, by inspiration and by pressure, was itself something that was influenced and molded by its surroundings. Its active role could only be played because of a specific set of cultural conditions — those prevailing after the collapse of the ancient world. But to that must be added the evidence provided by the following centuries about how the society in which the active role was played charged a price, so to speak, in the form of adaptation by the church to its ways.

A hint of that can be got by reflecting on what a catholic bishop had once been and what he had now become. The authority "from above" to which a bishop laid claim had early become universally acknowledged in the context of Mediterranean Christianity, and already then it had had consequences for the way Christians regarded their relationship with God and their fellow men: a tinge of moralization and legalism is unmistakable. But it makes a difference whether the "apostolic" authority of preaching, administration of the sacraments, and cure of souls is combined with full titles to public power or not. Such a combination became a reality of Christian life in Europe when the office of bishop was inserted into the feudal system that endowed him with secular power — not only economic power, but military and police power, and power of jurisdiction — over the inhabitants of episcopal lands. Consequently, when those peasants and laborers had to deal with the bishop, they met him as someone who simultaneously controlled their access to heaven and their enjoyment of daily bread and civil reputation. Another example: when the transition from paganism to Christianity took the form of a mass conversion — either because of indigenous traditions of collectivism or because of compulsion from an expanding royal power — that must by necessity have consequences for the religion itself, notwithstanding the fact that confessionally, dogmatically, and liturgically it was the very same religion as the one that in earlier times had been accepted freely and individually. And a final example: the overwhelming majority of the population was now made up of peasants, field laborers, and — initially at least — slaves, all more or less dependent on a class of military landowners. When the church was incorporated into that system, when the bishops were drawn from the landowning aristocracy, and when theologians confirmed the system by teaching as the will of God that society consisted of "men of prayer, men of war, and men of labor" (*oratores, bellatores,* and *laboratores),* a consequence must be that the preaching of the Christian message came to constitute one of the forms of man's coercion of fellow men.

Nevertheless, the last-mentioned example indicates a characteristic dialectic of European life. The social theory just hinted at was not a mere tool of oppression. It also represented an effort to humanize the existing social structures by acknowledging the place of the oppressed in God's plan for the world, thus endowing them and their station in life with a dignity that had never been theirs before. That means that the theory — indirectly, and on a long view — can be called one of the channels for the gospel's inherent critique of things as they are.

As we have seen, old European Christianity in the "time of the church" was a religion with inner consistency and firm common features. But it had room for a great number of different conclusions in practice. To them we will turn now.

c. Royal Christianity

The first great variant of catholic belief and practice to be considered is at the same time the first important example of the mutually shaping influence between the inherited Christianity of the church and the early European culture. "Royal" Christianity — in which the king is regarded as the chief human guarantor of success for God's plan for church and people and for the right reception of his gracious gifts — is an instructive subject of study, both as a result of that encounter and because it, in a multitude of forms, became one of the most stable elements of the European religious picture for a thousand years.

When Christianity arrived in Europe, it carried with it a tradition for regarding the secular ruler as appointed by God and endowed by him with a special task. But it also bore a tradition of viewing all earthly rulership in a critical light. Both traditions ran as constant strains through its Bible, and they had both been put into use in the framework of Mediterranean civilization, even if the first one had always proved to be the strongest in the church's practical attitude toward the affairs of society.

Both ways of thinking were represented in the newly converted peoples of Europe. The first appeared in the Germanic tradition of regarding the king as mediator between the people and the gods: his was a special relationship with the powers on which the peace and well-being of human society depended. It is no accident that the conversion of the Germanic peoples was decisively conditioned by the conversion of their kings. And the other strain of thought — the critical one — is found in the Germanic "right of resistance": an idea and a practice according to which the relationship between king and people was one of reciprocal obligations, which could not be broken by the ruler without the people taking countermeasures. The "good old rights and usages" were above the king as they were above the people.

But no less important than these analogies was the practical circumstance that supralocal rule was much more difficult to establish and maintain than it had been in the ancient world, and that, consequently, the Christian clergy and the king tended to be natural allies.

All this, and more, served as impulses and driving forces for the coming into being of kingly Christianity. Its first great manifestation was the breakthrough — in the mid–eighth century — of the Israelite form of religious initiation of kings: the rite of anointing. Better than most other things, the initiation ceremonies, concentrated in the anointing, give us an idea of what this form of Christianity is all about. In the complex of rites

44. Charles II of England (1660-85) took great pains with performing the ancient royal rite of healing. Perhaps nearly a hundred thousand people were "touched" by him in the course of his reign. (In M. Bloch, Les Rois thaumaturges [Paris: Colin, 1961], plate iv.)

and insignia in use in the "Germano-Roman" empire from the tenth century, God is implored to give the king power from above to govern and defend the people, protect widows and orphans, nourish and teach the church, and shield it against visible and invisible foes, so that all men can come to a mutual accord and peace in the true faith. Performing all this, the king is bearer of the "name of Christ" as his "vicar." That is because he is *christus domini,* "the Lord's anointed," thereby resembling *the* Christ, who is himself anointed as the eternal King. In other words, what God proposes to do in his people to uphold and continue his work of creation is done by means of his consecrated servant, the king. By acting as ruler and protector, the king acts on behalf of God. In him the people encounter God's own power of bestowing order, peace, and prosperity to the world.

Similar ideas find expression in the coronation garment and the insignia. The royal cloak — embroidered with celestial signs and hung with bells — is made to resemble that of the high priest of Israel. One of the plates of the crown imitates the high priest's breastplate, beset with twelve precious stones symbolizing the twelve tribes of Israel; and another plate, also with twelve stones, points at the twelve apostles, the leaders of the new people of God. In its entirety the crown, by its form, its colors, and its numerous entities of stones and pearls, refers symbolically to the heavenly Jerusalem as described in the book of Revelation as the goal of the church's pilgrimage through history.

The impression we gain through all this of a special form of catholic Christianity is confirmed by the custom of the English and French kings acting as miracle-working healers. According to common belief, on special occasions those rulers were believed able to cure people suffering from tubercular glandular inflammation by placing their anointed hands on the sufferers' necks while invoking divine help.

In such manifestations the king simultaneously appears as God's representative to the people and the people's to God. In other words, he is some sort of priest in his capacity as king, exactly as the priest is some sort of king in his capacity as priest.

It is worth emphasizing that all this is cast in the mold of catholic sacramental theology. Christ, the King who, by his life, sacrificial death, and resurrection, has vanquished the demonic enemies of charity, order, and peace, uses his church's visible signs to send invisible power to a mortal man to enable him to execute the will of the King of heaven on earth. Thus, and not otherwise, he becomes the true and authentic leader of church and people. Not he himself is important, but that which is done to him. It is not by accident that a German chronicle — with an allusion to Saul, the first king of Israel — reminds us that the anointing has turned the king into "another man."

Important consequences follow from this insertion of kingly power into sacramental theology. In the first place, the king becomes superior to all other secular potentates. The sacrament of anointing is meant for him alone; and for all his subjects the psalmist's words are applicable: "Touch not mine anointed!" So anybody who rebels against legitimate royal power sets himself up against God himself. It is evident that this expresses what would today be called using "ideology" in the service of "social control." But it is no less important that in this way of thinking some of the seeds are sown for the concept of a sovereign state — one that is independent in relation to all citizens, irrespective of their mutual differences.

Secondly, the king's government of the national church — not least his control over its episcopal elections and its economic and military resources — acquires a convincing legitimation: such a power may rightly be wielded by a "high priest"!

But, in the third place, the king whose power has thus been incorporated in sacramental thinking and practice has by the same token become subject to God's law for the conduct of human life. What delivers the guidelines for legitimate exercise of state power is not the will of the ruler, but God's law of rulership — according to the Bible, when anointed kings of Israel broke that law, they did so with disastrous consequences for themselves. So, what is legitimized by kingly Christianity is by no means an absolute, unbounded sovereignty, but a power that is in principle defined and limited by a written law, interpreted solely by another branch of God-given authority than the ruler himself. The Bible is a sort of constitutional document, which provides room for criticism as well as for legitimation of power.

Finally, when the king is sacramentally "ordained," he becomes one of several consecrated tools of divine will on earth. God acts through his king and his priests toward a people, which is at the same time a church. Both as a people and as a church, human community is kept alive by what God does to it through his consecrated servants. The king serves the church as a kind of priest, and the priests serve the people as some sort of kings: What is indeed cure of souls if not governance of them? In this unworried welding together of priestly and royal activity on the basis of the idea of consecration, a distinctive mark of early European Christianity lies hidden. It is a significant manifestation of a situation in which order and peace were rare and fragile blessings, and in which the links with pre-Christian Germanic life were stronger than they became later on. Above

all, it testifies to how fruitful was the meeting of the two widely differing forces and tendencies that merged into that situation — as well as to the power of Christianity to mold and shape its new surroundings.

But this way of thinking was not without its latent difficulties — problems that could become virulently actual as soon as the question was radically and coherently asked about the true, divinely ordained relation between a power that could transmit heavenly benefits — namely, that of the priests — and one that, when all was said and done, could not: the kings'.

When that happened — when the question was asked and answered on the basis of the papal claims, and when, as a consequence, the kingly power became theologically "devalued" in comparison with the authority of priests — that meant that, in a theoretical sense at least, the time of kingly Christianity in its older form had run out. That was by no means tantamount to a disappearance of the thoughts and sentiments that went into that version of Christianity. They lived on, as did the social necessities that had contributed to its emergence.

It is, however, an illuminating fact that the theoretical way of arguing for the scope of Christian kingship began to assume new forms in the later centuries of our period. An attempt at getting rid of the constraints inherent in the sacramental argument can be observed, along with a corresponding tendency to readopt late antique arguments for state power. As will be remembered, the late Roman Christian emperor had appeared as a kind of "image" of the Logos on earth without having been consecrated by priestly hands and without in that sense being dependent on the church. That is one of the reasons European kings and their advisers from the twelfth century on began to take an interest in the tenets of late Roman law that expressed that idea of the authority of a Christian ruler. This phase in the history of kingly Christianity can, however, only be fully understood on the background of the theory and practice of papal Christianity. We

45. In this Danish country church, one of many founded by aristocratic families all over Europe in "the time of the church," a "squire's gallery" was built for the use of the lord of the manor. This arrangement reaches back to the cult of the Roman emperor in pagan times and reflects the awe of the ruler "by the grace of God" in Byzantium, in Charlemagne's empire, and in the Holy Roman Empire. Sitting in the west end of the church, face to face with the present Christ on the altar in the eastern end, the emperor received the liturgical homage of clergy and people. (Cf. the plan of the Aachen chapel, p. 130 above.) (Courtesy of the National Museum of Denmark.)

shall come to that presently, after a glance at the special form of old European reflection that concerns the power of an emperor.

As a factor in power politics, the empire was important only when held by a king who was powerful "at home," in his own realm. But the empire in its "Germano-Roman" shape became suffused with religious ideas and expectations that are important for the understanding of old European Christianity in its early phase. The Roman Empire, it was believed under inspiration from the prophet Daniel and the apostle Paul, was the last world empire. After its fall the end would come, the forces of the Antichrist would be let loose, and Christ would return after much suffering by the faithful. But it was a Christian's duty to keep the empire alive and call it by the name of Roman until the gospel had been preached everywhere in the world; and the emperor himself had a special obligation to support the work of mission. At last, when that task had been completed, the last Roman emperor must make the journey to Jerusalem, lay down his crown on the Mount of Olives, and await the outbreak of the "woes." Such and other ideas about the future end of history reflect much of what European Christians thought about their present.

d. Papal Christianity

In most of its predominant forms, old European Christianity was religious and political simultaneously. People, church, Christendom were viewed as referring to one and the same human community, and the earthly goals and purposes of its existence were regarded as closely connected to the heavenly ones. Therefore every religious statement was at the same time a political one, and vice versa. That goes for the papal version of catholic Christianity as well as the kingly one.

"He is the door-keeper whom I will not gainsay." In such robust terms the chronicler reports the Northumbrian king's promise of adhesion to Roman Christianity in the year 664. In other words, a man's eternal destiny hangs upon his being on right terms with Peter, the "heavenly door-keeper," and with his vicar on earth. From an early time that idea was expressed with religious ardor. But it was a political idea too, in the sense that the bonds with the apostle were conceived in terms that remind us powerfully of the way secular society described the personal relationship, with mutual rights and obligations, that must connect a "lord" and a "man" if order and peace were to reign in human affairs.

Nowhere does that become so clear as in the great way-breaker of papal Christianity, Hildebrand, known as Pope Gregory VII (1073-85). And

46. These illustrations from a manuscript of Bishop Otto of Freising's world chronicle are supposed to be copies of the ones in the book presented by Otto to his nephew, Emperor Frederick Barbarossa, in 1157. They show episodes from the life of Pope Gregory VII. Above left, the emperor Henry IV is seen together with his antipope Wibert; above right the pope is expelled from Rome. Below left, he excommunicates Henry, and below right, he dies. (University of Jena: Ms. Bos. q. 6, Bl. 79ʳ.)

his thought and actions also reveal the deeper and broader sense in which the papacy can be called a political as well as a religious entity.

In Gregory's world the apostle Peter is personally present at the pope's side with help, warning, and comfort in adversity. Under his loving care the pope lived since his childhood; he stands by his successor on his lonely post, not as the distant heavenly saint, but as a person who reads his letters over his shoulder and inspires him with answers. He himself interferes mightily in the life of the universal church and binds princes and peoples to himself as his vassals. Every rebellious and sacrilegious attack on his vicar is an attack on him, and vice versa.

This idea of vicariate, and the political actions on which it set its mark, are personally and passionately religious. It is in the light of that idea that we must understand the Gregorian, and later, program of practical papal government of the church. It is a vision of church and of human community in which far more radical conclusions are drawn from common assertions than ever before.

Being the vicar of the prince of the apostles is tantamount to being bearer of the essence of the priestly authority on which hangs the destiny of church and society. Only by priestly intervention are the heavenly benefits transmitted — or kept back — which Christ has brought into the world; every teaching about the goal of human life and about the way to the goal comes from there. But all those crucial activities are concentrated in the Petrine office, the office of him to whom it was said: "Thou art Peter, and on that rock will I build my church." With him — i.e., with the man who sits on his throne and guards his tomb — every initiative originates and all appeals end. He alone is "immediate" to the heavenly world; he alone can be judged by no one except God himself.

That is why God has decreed that that office — and consequently all priestly offices — must be totally free in order to function in accordance with their purpose. If the holy things — without which church and society fall back into darkness — are to benefit the people, then their transmitters must be independent of any other regulation than the one exercised by the holy offices themselves: by the bishop over the priests, and by the pope over everyone else.

That is tantamount to an utter and total condemnation of kingly Christianity. Gregory gives us to understand that the great divide goes, not between consecrated and nonconsecrated persons, but between those who can transmit the powers of consecration to others and those who cannot. One of those who cannot is the king. As Gregory says, "What earthly king has ever torn a soul out of the devil's hands; who can prepare the Lord's body and blood on the altar; and who has received the power to bind and to loose in heaven as on earth?" The humblest exorcist is greater than the mightiest king, for to him is given the authority to command the evil spirits; he is an "emperor of the spirits," a *spiritualis imperator.* When the king arrogates to himself the power of command over the man who makes it possible for the exorcist to exorcise — that is, the bishop — then indeed is all God-willed order turned upside down. The king is and remains a layman, and as such he is subject to the priestly power of binding and loosing. He becomes bound as a stubborn sinner through the papal sentence of exclusion from the saving community; and as a penitent sinner he becomes loosed by the absolution that can only be given by the vicar of Saint Peter. That was how Gregory acted in 1076-77 toward the German king, the Lord's anointed, to the consternation and dismay of many contemporaries; and in two other respects also did he make clear that his program was a blueprint for action.

In the first place, he interfered actively in episcopal elections in order to secure their "liberty" — the king's "crime" being his attempt at infringing that liberty. The God-willed order of priestly offices required that the bishop be independent of secular power, in respect both of his election — that must be conducted by the local clergy — and of his instatement in the rights of the office — that ceremony must be the prerogative of archbishop and pope, notwithstanding that those "rights" involved public ones, deriving from the crown. That was, of course, the point that made it impossible for the German king to remain passive when confronted with the Roman claims. The coherence and stability of the realm depended on the king's control of the episcopal sees; therefore, the Roman attack resulted in a long and bitter controversy, ending only with the pope's death in exile.

Secondly, Gregory drew an epoch-making conclusion from his idea of the church: not only did he excommunicate the German king, he deposed him on behalf of Saint Peter, absolved his vassals from their oath of fealty, and claimed the right to approve the election of a successor. In line with that measure, he aimed at making kings and princes turn their lands into fiefs of Saint Peter, and, not content with that, he tried to establish a papal military force, the *militia Sancti Petri,* designed to interfere rapidly in the cause of ecclesiastical liberty.

This complex of political measures is clear evidence that Gregory acknowledged no limits to apostolic authority. The logic of his concept of the church required him to assume an "imperial" role. If it was true that the heavenly benefits administered by him were vitally necessary for human life in society, and if the pope was to render account on Judgment Day for his administration of those divine gifts, then he must by necessity be able to interfere on all planes and in every sphere. Thus Pope Gregory gave the general old European reluctance to distinguish between church and people, religion and politics a far more consistent expression than had been possible for kingly Christianity. The consequences that resulted became important far beyond the context of church history.

The words and actions of Gregory VII represent a spectacular breakthrough for the idea of papal Christianity. But he did not by any means see his visions triumph. The radical, "imperial" pretensions remained largely in the sphere of ideological ambition. But quite apart from that, the claims that strictly concerned the church, its order and its liberty, could only be carried into reality by his cooler-headed successors. Greatest among those was Innocent III (1198-1216).

From his hand a text has been preserved that once again illuminates the papal way of looking at church and society. But in addition to that, it gives a downright classical expression to common Christian presuppositions. In his opening sermon, or keynote speech, at the opening of the "ecumenical" council in the Lateran at Rome in 1215, the pope points at two main tasks for the contemporary church: reforming itself in order to make its practice correspond with its essence, and liberating the Holy Land from the hands of the infidels. Those tasks are bound up with each other in their common character of transition, a movement toward a God-willed goal. And as such, they are inextricably connected with the individual Christian's personal reform of his life and with the church's final passage from this world to the eternal.

Here, in an utterly typical way, cure of souls, church law, political and military action are viewed as a unity whose individual ingredients illuminate and color each other. Such a mode of thinking was current in Europe for a thousand years, in faithful imitation and continuation of the ancient church. But the decisive point of the speech is a papal one. The entire complex of actions and interpretations is bound together by the idea that the pope is the one with whom every initiative originates and who guarantees its realization. He acts on behalf of Christ as his authorized vicar on earth. It is no accident that Innocent takes his point of departure for the sermon in the concept of Easter as Passover with a sequence of words that, in any other context than that of papal Christianity, would have been considered blasphemous: "With desire I have desired to eat this Passover with you before I suffer."

The use of such words in such a context tells us something about the impact inherent in the papal version of common Christianity. They could be used and accepted only because papal ambition met with such practical success during the four or five generations after Gregory VII.

In the last resort, that success was due to no individual person. Rather, it might with justice be called a result of the workings of a "spirit of the times." Papal Christianity had the "logic" of common Christian assertions working for it — notwithstanding the fact that many contemporaries found it to be wrong to draw conclusions of such rigidity in matters like these. But to that must be added that the papacy was the institution that was best qualified — and needed more than any — to make an international institutional use of the general cultural "takeoff." The more urban

47. A small section of the altarpiece of the "Adoration of the Lamb," painted in 1432 by the brothers Hubert and Jan van Eyck for the cathedral of Ghent, Belgium. According to some scholars, the enthroned person is Christ, while others identify him with God the Father. Regardless of the choice of identification, it is worth noticing that the divine person wears the dress and crown of a pope.

culture, moneyed economy, and commercial intercourse revived and flourished, the better practical possibilities for the papal government to concentrate resources and exercise control across great distances. And conversely, the more Rome's need of consolidating its network grew, the more possibilities appeared for the new intercourse across frontiers and for the general differentiation of European life.

One element in that process of differentiation became particularly important for papal Christianity. That was the emergence of schools and universities in the new urban communities. From there the theoretical and practical champions of the universal church were recruited: lawyers, theologians, administrators — men with talents for abstract reasoning, calculation, and conclusion drawing, men with a passion for homogeneity and consistency. But the ferment that was brought about in European societies by the economic recovery benefited papal Christianity in more than one way. It did so through the military expansion that, in the form of crusades, was exploited for the purposes of the church, but also in the social conflicts that — initially at least — provided Rome with useful allies in its struggle against traditional powers.

The result of the process as a whole was the phenomenon that much later became known as *societas perfecta,* the "perfect society." That was how the universal church could be considered, because it possessed everything required by a complete human order of society, and because it possessed it by divine will and prescription. Here was a "constitution" prescribing general rules of action. Here were rationally coherent provisions for behavior in special cases. Here was a hierarchical order of government with well-defined demarcations of competence. Here were resources — spiritual ones such as sacramental grace, the merits of the saints, religious and moral teachings; material ones like church lands, buildings, and tithes. Here were schooling, propaganda, hospitals, and asylums, as well as tribunals and prisons. First and last, here was "the servant of the servants of God," the "vicar of Christ," the authorized interpreter of past, present, and future. Here was, in sum, the leader whose position is described with admirable succinctness by Pope Boniface VIII (1294-1303) with the words used by the apostle Paul as valid for every baptized Christian: "He that is spiritual judgeth all things, yet he himself is judged of no man."

Theoretically speaking, this whole complex provides one of the historically important models for the absolutist monarchies of later times, and indeed for the totalitarian state — the twentieth century's gift to humanity. There are, however, very good theoretical reasons for not carrying this comparison too far. For one thing, the papal "state" itself bore the key to criticism and protest against it in its very "constitution," the Bible and the creeds.

And as far as practice was concerned, this *societas* was anything but *perfecta.* The international organization with a common system of law, with a centralized administration, with control of lower offices, and with powers of taxation was unique for its time, and it turned out to wear sufficiently well to surmount all crises until the present day. But measured by its theory — and with modern European practice — its efficiency was limited.

That was due to technical difficulties, such as the slowness of communications. Even more was it due to powers with divergent interests, the national monarchies and the municipal councils, who were in a great number of cases strong enough to have their own way or force through a compromise. Kings and princes were also apt to form alliances with bishops whose aristocratic background and interests often caused them to be highly unsatisfactory tools of Roman policies. Another important limiting factor was bureaucratic inertia and corruption, one of the secondary effects of centralization.

But one thing above all cries out for consideration: the inevitable disillusionment in a Christendom that had contributed to the papacy's success by regarding it as the place where justice could be sought and found against traditional rulers and ancient tyrannies. That enthusiasm turned gradually into disappointment — cynical or sorrowful — in ever wider circles under the impression of how the papacy itself became an established power by its constantly deepened engagement in political, military, and financial pursuits.

It is true that this disappointment can be exaggerated. Old Europe was very well aware of the distinction to be drawn between the divinely sanctioned office and the reprobate sinner that might possess himself of it. Such was, after all, the way of the world under the conditions of original sin. But the disillusionment was real enough, and it came to have far-reaching consequences, both in old European times and later.

e. Monastic Christianity

One of the most important decisions Mediterranean Christianity made was binding the religious elite of monks and nuns to the church of ordinary people. It was not carried out without the strong tensions inherent in the relationship becoming clearly visible from time to time. But carried out it was. Not only was the principle never seriously contested, but monasticism came to be connected with the rest of the church by a thousand practical links. That can for example be seen in the fact that European monks soon received the priestly ordination as a matter of course, as well as in their involvement in nonmonastic activities such as missionary and educational work.

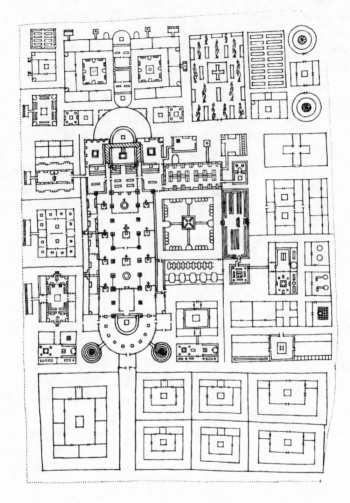

48. Large and well-run monasteries were among the pillars of the state in the Carolingian empire. The plan designed for the monastery of St. Gallen, Switzerland, in the 820s was not realized, but it offers an idea of how many administrative, technical, and economic functions could be performed by a Benedictine house in this period. The middle of the drawing is occupied by the church, a basilica with two apses. To the left are the abbot's residence, the school, and a guest house provided with kitchen and bakery for the guests' use. To the right: dining hall, baths, kitchen, workshops, mill, barn, and stable. In the lower part, there are fenced-in areas for sheep, goats, cows, pigs, and horses. The upper part is occupied by the sick-ward, vegetable garden, cemetery, and chicken-run.

Monastic Christianity was and remained a variant of catholic Christianity. Although the fundamental ideas of the common faith of the church were held by monks and nuns as well as by the people at large, just as in ancient monasticism those common premises were supplemented by a special one: the claim to realize a Christian "perfection" in freedom from "worldly" ties and in total devotion to God. Thereby the common ground inevitably appeared in a different light, so that monastic Christianity became a specially profiled variant of the catholic faith.

The claim of a perfect life, in "imitation of Christ," assumed a multitude of shapes in European Christendom; the same is true of the ways of meeting it. But only one difference stands out as decisive: that between Benedictines and Mendicants.

The adherents of the first-named form acknowledged the sixth-century rule of Benedict of Nursia as the guiding norm of endeavor. That rule had long-term effects in two respects: Firstly through the demand that the striving for perfection had to be molded in practice by a lifelong commitment to a monastic community, renunciation of all rights and obligations outside the monastery, and total obedience toward the elected leader of the house, the abbot or abbess who stood in Christ's stead in relation to the "brethren" or "sisters." The monk or nun was required to bind himself or herself by a solemn vow to observe lifelong poverty, chastity, and obedience within the walls of one defined place.

Secondly, the Benedictine rule was epoch-making by prescribing a balanced division between three main activities by which the daily life of the monastery was to be governed. These were "the work of God," i.e., liturgical prayer in common at fixed times of day and night; "the work of the hands," manual work in the building and on its lands; and "the divine reading," individual immersion in the Bible, the works of the Fathers, and devotional texts. Those were the works the monk engaged himself to pursue when — after a trial period — he took his vows face-to-face with the abbot. Those activities constituted the "positive" aspect of what was "negatively" defined as renunciation of property, family, and personal autonomy. They were the tracks along which "perfection" was to be reached; in other words, they were the way in which commitment of self to God was to take concrete shape. Thereby a set of general principles was pointed out for one of the two main forms of monastic Christianity.

The rule proved, however, to be treated as a point of departure for further development in several directions. One of them came to light in an increased emphasis on the "work of God," at the expense of the two other pursuits. That tendency was probably not unconnected with the landed aristocracy's growing infiltration of monasticism — in such a social context the "work of the hands" was inevitably regarded with less favor than intended by the rule. However, it must be remembered that early old Europe's "collectivistic" style of thinking made it natural to lay a special emphasis on liturgical prayer, in the interest of society as a whole, and that this development can also be regarded as an expression of genuine conformity to Benedictine intentions: the founder had been in no doubt of the superior importance of communal prayer as compared to the other two activities. Anyhow, in the Cluniac version of Benedictinism (from the tenth century on), liturgical prayer and eucharistic worship were overwhelmingly emphasized. In Cluny (Burgundy) and her daughter houses, the singing of the biblical psalms — the traditional nucleus of communal prayer — was regarded as a foreshadowing of the goal of human history. In its capacity as anticipation of the eternal song of praise in heaven, it began to fill most of the monks' day: in Cluny, the 150 psalms were sung through in little more than one day in spite of the rule foreseeing a full week for that purpose. Such a state of things gave rise to criticism, in the name of ascetic strictness as well as Benedictine balance. The liturgical and artistic splendor, and the substantial meals that were deemed necessary to provide the monks with stamina for the long services, were condemned in purist circles as an offense against genuine ascetic principles. This is one of the causes of the Cistercian reform movement's attempt (from the beginning of the twelfth century) at observing all three "tracks" in equal measure far from the dwellings of men.

Yet another development consisted in a series of experiments with organizational coordination of monasteries. Here as everywhere else, organization — establishment of "right order" — was considered in the light of religion and piety as well as in that of law and politics. Naturally enough — when the ever present risk of exploitation and abuse of monastic institutions is kept in mind — coordination was seen as a necessary condition for implementing the specifically religious purposes. The Cluniacs practiced a system of subordination of a great many houses under Cluny as their "mother" and its abbot as their common "father." The Cistercian solution was markedly more hard-wearing, inasmuch as it did not depend on the moral and intellectual qualities of one man, but on a system of institutional and collective supervision, decision making, and exchange of ideas. All Cistercian abbots met in conference once a year, and each monastery was obliged to undergo an annual visitation by its mother house.

Such organizational initiatives open important perspectives for the relations between monks and society and the consequences of those rela-

49. Model of the eastern part of the monastery church of Cluny, according to historical and archeological estimates of its appearance in its final shape (early eleventh century) when its size could compete with that of St. Peter's in Rome. The church was destroyed during the French Revolution.

tions in European history. Before considering them, let us look at the other main version of institutionalized asceticism.

Mendicant (Franciscan and Dominican) Christianity differs from the older form in one decisive respect. It regards the imitation of Christ, that is, renunciation of the world and commitment to God through ascetic training, as something that has to be practiced by means of extrovert action in the world, and not by lifelong seclusion and subjection to claustral discipline.

The inspiration that hit home to Francis of Assisi (1182-1226) came from the story of Jesus as told in the Gospels. As Francis understood it, the imitation of Christ must be a life as homeless and vagrant as that of the Master and his disciples. If the Son of Man had nowhere to rest his head, his followers, now as well as then, should lead the same sort of life. They must scrape a living together as day laborers, be content with what they were paid, and beg for bread if cheated of payment. Those were the conditions under which they must do what Jesus had done: preach the remission of sins, talk of remorse and conversion, make peace, and care for the needy. Thus Christ would come to be known to the people as a living and joyful presence.

If that train of ideas had been put into practice in its entirety, "monastic Christianity" would have been a somewhat inexact name for what was attempted here. All the same, it may be retained, not only because the general, overriding aims — liberation from worldly ties and commitment to God — united the Mendicants with the Benedictines, but above all because Francis's intentions failed to be carried out to the full in his order. His successors attempted to observe them by compromising with the traditional style. The Franciscans became ordained priests; their order became regulated by church law; they acquired houses that could serve as bases for their outward activities and as places of study, necessary for competent preaching and efficient refutation of heretics.

Nonetheless, a great change had occurred, indeed the greatest since the collectivization of the hermits some nine hundred years earlier. Even though the "follower and imitator of Christ" had his base in a sort of monastery, he was seen by the Mendicants as one whose task could by no means be exhaustively described in monastic terms.

Consistently enough, the change found expression in the organizational structure established by the Mendicants, or friars: Dominic's "Order of Preachers," or Dominicans, as well as Francis's "Friars Minor," or Franciscans. Those orders became associations of persons rather than houses. A Franciscan or a Dominican friar must by definition be able and willing to move quickly from place to place, from country to country, according to the tasks to which he was assigned; he must in the nature of the case be responsible to the worldwide community of men with similar obligations.

That is one of the things that can teach us something about the relations between the "elite of achievement" and the church at large as well as society in the wider sense.

The ascetics were meant to serve as models and intercessors for the church as a whole. They observed those evangelical "counsels of perfection" that ordinary Christians were unable to fulfill, impeded as they were by the weakness of the flesh and the obligations of the world. That endowed their intercession with special power and provided ordinary sinners with a model to imitate. Therefore they were vitally necessary to the church; they were "limbs" with a special function on the "body of Christ"; they were servants of the other "limbs" who, in return, were obliged to serve them with the physical necessities of life.

Such, in brief, was the gist of what the common faith had to say about monastic Christianity. But the importance — positive and negative — of the ascetics for the rest of Christendom was of course further reaching than that. The question will turn up again in connection with the religion of the theologians, the common people, and the heretics, because professional asceticism set its stamp on all those forms of Christian life. As for now, our main interest must be on the inspiration flowing from the very existence of a "regular" life, out into the wider world.

Such an inspiration must already have been provided by the Benedictine house living on its own, without links to other houses. The regular and well-ordered prayer and praise, engaging body and soul, that went on in the monastery as a community of brotherly love could be regarded not only as in some way a restoration of the original state of humanity and church, and as an anticipation of the heavenly life. It could also — by virtue of its practical details, e.g., its fixed divisions of time — deliver a model of disciplined life in society, not least in a situation where rational and purposeful planning was far from the everyday phenomenon that it became in later European centuries.

But to that must be added the perspectives opened by the coordination of houses or individuals in an order or congregation. The Cluniac association of monasteries under one leader is — in practice as distinct from theory — the first European example of international ecclesiastical unity. As such, it was a precursor of the papal unity at least partially established in the twelfth and thirteenth centuries, but also of similar endeavors in the secular sphere. It is significant that — in a text by one Cluniac monk — the organization is called *res publica nostra:* "our state." And it is no accident that the Cistercians and the Mendicants, with their international structures, came to be vitally important partners to the international papacy.

As becomes clear in the Cistercian reform, the "regular" life had economic consequences too. Aiming at a stricter observation of the rule and all three activities prescribed by it, the Cistercians placed their houses on remote or previously uncultivated land. As a consequence, the monks not only contributed to the ongoing pan-European work of clearing and cultivating land; they also, by ridding themselves of the obligations attendant on older agricultural structures, became able to engage in big-scale planning, involving profitable changing of crops, sheep farming, and wool export. Thus the Cistercians' struggle against the flesh resulted in their becoming pioneer producers of meat. That is something that, not without justice, can be called the first great European example of a special interplay of religion and economics. It is by no means the last.

The Cistercian attempt at setting the monastic life free from the strictures of traditional feudal conditions reminds us that the older monasteries were subject to those conditions. That means that the relationship to the external world was anything but a one-way affair. The older monasteries were integral parts of aristocratic society. Like the bishops, the abbots were big landowners, rulers of dependent peasants and laborers, and the recipients of large-scale gifts of land and money donated by secular potentates in return for their prayers of intercession before and after the benefactors' death. In the course of time the Cistercians came to assume a similar position. But with the Mendicants the situation changed, not in the sense that the renunciation of property, preached and practiced by Francis of Assisi, was observed in its severity by his successors — far from it — but in the sense that their houses were placed in the flourishing urban communities, as well as because their lack of landed property constrained them to seek support by accidental earnings from collections or from sale of burial places in their churches. The Mendicant orders were one of the expressions of the new urban culture, and their members satisfied some of the special needs of that culture, both by the services they could provide in competition with the normal clerical apparatus and because the friars were active as neutral conflict-solvers in feud-infested communes. Their originality is perhaps most apparent in their activity as open-air preachers to an urban mass audience. Here something new was emerging, as compared to old European Christianity in its earlier phase — strong at sacraments and poor at sermons as we know that religion to have been. At the same time as

50. Francis of Assisi, as painted by
Margaritone d'Arezzo.

the city culture was resuscitated, the Mediterranean church's appeal to the rationality of the common man (as well as to his need of entertainment) began to reemerge by means of the teaching conveyed by sermons in the city squares.

Such a phenomenon opens a glimpse into an important trend in old

European life — the rationalizing tendency. One of its roots is in what we shall be looking at in a moment — the Christianity of theologians. But we cannot end our consideration of monasticism without glancing at a problem that is — so to speak — incarnate in the great inspirer of the Mendicants, Francis of Assisi: the question about the place of the original personality in Christian history. The problem is, of course, a general one, but Francis makes it appear more clearly than is normally the case.

There can be no doubt that Francis was the *one* man without whom the Mendicant movement cannot be understood — quite apart from all the external circumstances that contributed to its emergence. But it is equally clear that his highly personal, free, and sovereign conduct as "God's fool" was of limited importance for the lifestyle of his successors, and also that his conception of the Christian life was far from reigning supreme in his order. That order was an organization which — like the papacy, its sponsor and collaborator — was very well aware of a need to take care of tomorrow and provide itself with the wherewithal against which to lean its head.

If the student of Franciscanism wants to take both sides of this doubleness seriously, then he has serious work on his hands and his results will always remain contested. It is no wonder that research on this subject is apt to remind the reader of what he knows about the exploration of the life of Jesus, considered in relation to the Christian church. He will, for that matter, be reminded of the difficulties inherent in determining the place of *any* individual in a course of events that in the last resort consists of the choices and destinies of individual men and women.

f. The Christianity of Theologians

Monks and Mendicants were also linked to the church in their activity as theological teachers and writers. But that linkage between theology and church began to appear in a different light than it had in the Mediterranean civilization. While theological thinkers in those centuries had, more often than not, been men who were simultaneously active as practical church leaders, that combination was now by and large a thing of the past. The church's bishops had become administrators and politicians pure and simple, and the theologians had likewise become "intellectuals" in an exclusive sense: professional teachers and thinkers.

This process of specialization — implying that church leaders were free to command, legislate, and pass sentence without being disturbed by direct contact with the problems presented by Scripture and tradition, and that, conversely, the theologians escaped confrontation with everyday realities of life in the church — came to have far-reaching consequences for both parties, and for church and society as a whole.

The "de-theologizing" of the episcopal order, and the cultural loss it suffered as a consequence of early old European circumstances, was, however, not solely responsible for the professionalization of theological endeavor. That endeavor had from the earliest Benedictine times been an integral part of monastic life, intimately connected as it was with the form of ascetic striving prescribed by the rule under the name of "divine reading." The devout daily immersion in Bible and church fathers meant that study and reflection were inextricably united with existential engagement — perfectly in keeping with the Mediterranean heritage. The divine reading was part of the personal striving for "perfection"; it was, in short, a kind of prayer. And the men who were thus occupied were neither church leaders nor professional theologians.

The decisive change in that situation came as a consequence of the events that were partly conditioned by and partly responsible for the economic "takeoff" beginning — roughly — during the eleventh century. Most important among them was the Roman or "Gregorian" reform movement. It needed men who were able to reason and persuade by argument. More importantly, its criticism of traditional arrangements and its passion for rational homogeneity in ecclesiastical structures naturally inspired and stimulated a critical treatment of tradition on a wider front. Pope Gregory's words: "Jesus did not say, 'I am custom,' but 'I am the truth'!" could be used in other contexts than church politics — and perhaps in ways that would not have appealed to the pope. At the same time, the reemerging urban culture instigated the founding of cathedral schools and, later, universities. In this connection it is worth keeping in mind that urban culture in itself constituted a form of rebellion against tradition. Finally, the closer contact with the Islamic world led — momentously, as we shall see — to a renewed knowledge of the largely forgotten Greek tradition of philosophy.

All that, taken together, effected deep-reaching changes in the practice of theology, and indeed, in people's ideas about what theology was all about. Significantly enough, the links between theological thinking and the life of prayer and ascetic endeavor did not become severed. Those links are typical of old European Christianity in this as in all its phases. The great Mendicant theologians were "practitioners," in the sense that they saw the intellectual work as something that sprang from faith and aimed at adoration of, and indeed at mystical union with God.

Neither were the scriptural and ecclesiastical tradition, or parts thereof, thrown overboard — not consciously and voluntarily, at any rate. "That which we have received" — the sacred corpus of revelation and admonition, contained in the Bible, the creeds, and the "Fathers" — remained in its entirety the incontestable basis of all thinking.

What the changes actually meant was something else. First, the traditions were put under the searchlight of organizing reason, in an effort to explain their internal contradictions and repair their seeming lack of rational coherence. Such a process could, and indeed must, result in something not quite so harmless as was intended — not least because its practical form was shaped by the controversial debate conducted in the universities: the "disputation."

Secondly — and most important — it became consistently and systematically acknowledged that Greek pre-Christian thinking, albeit independent of the biblical revelation, contained valid information about the world and its physical workings as well as reliable directions for the process of knowledge and the logical conduct of argumentation as well as for life in civil society. Valid, that is, as far as it reached. To the knowledge thus acquired must by necessity be added what lay beyond its grasp: the divinely revealed information about the creation of the world out of nothing; about the transcendental goals of human life; about the supremacy of self-sacrificing love; and above all, about the triune nature of God and his coming to men as the Incarnate. Those ultimate truths were inaccessible to reason alone; they were transmitted by the church on the basis of its biblical revelation and actualized by it in its sacred acts. It was an event of great moment for all subsequent centuries when the Dominican theologian Thomas Aquinas (d. 1274) acknowledged a distinction between "nature" and "supernature" and argued for a rationally demonstrable connection between the two.

Thomas's "theological Christianity" — which did not remain uncontested or alone on the market, even though it exerted an enormous influence — was a version of catholic Christianity. It was one way of formulating the "common faith." It is no accident that it turned out to be an instrument of legitimation for the papacy — the institution that was believed to represent the supernatural disclosure of the ultimate meaning of nature and of human society, and which consequently claimed authority to interfere in nature and society as a formative and directive force. But Thomas and his fellow "scholastics" did nevertheless introduce an element of tension into the sphere of the common faith, an element with destructive potential, later to be actualized.

51. Thomas Aquinas, in a painting in the Dominican church of Saint Caterina in Pisa. The great thinker, dressed in the habit of his order, is seated within a halo, suggesting that he is caught up into another existence. He is struck by inspiration in the form of beams of light from Christ and from Moses, Paul, and the evangelists. He is flanked by Plato and Aristotle, his non-Christian teachers. Below him, his Dominican brethren are receiving his teaching, while vanquished Islam in the person of Averroes, the Arab philosopher, lies prostrate. (Courtesy of the Danish National Art Library, Copenhagen.)

g. Popular Christianity

It was a basic tenet of catholic Christianity that the church was there for the people's sake. It was common conviction — as a matter of principle at least — that the church was identical with the saved people of God and that, consequently, the salvation of one soul was infinitely more important than any earthly success. This immortal soul, wherever and whoever it was, must be the chief target of the church. If not, then it was no true church.

What is thus the case in the common faith is also in principle valid for all its great variants. The king is God's chosen instrument for the upholding of peace and law so that the weak and lowly can live securely and quietly in the land. The pope's and his priests' transmission of saving power from above is meant to go to the people, and each and every member of that people who thereby learns to govern his own soul rightly has, according to Pope Gregory, an immeasurably greater claim to be called king than a ruler of countries and peoples who has failed to learn. Cloistered people do their special thing because it is necessary for the people that it be done. And so on and so forth.

It is obvious that those great formalized variants of catholic Christianity have exerted a deep influence on what the common people in Europe understood by Christianity. That "the crown" — as Hans Andersen, a late and lowly born old European, put it — "has about it a flavor of sanctity"; that no earthly welfare or eternal salvation can be brought about without the powers administered by the priests; that the prayers and self-discipline of cloistered men and women protect the people from the consequences of their sins — this we can discern in the Christianity of the people. By saying this, we also imply that the strain of paternalist, one-way communication that runs through all the great religious variants was on the whole accepted, or at any rate complied with, by the people at large, just as it was in everyday social life.

If, however, we want to be more explicit, then we must stress the reservation of what we can discern from the outset. The Christianity of the people is not in itself one of the "formalized" variants. The people rarely spoke for themselves, so the access posterity can have to the people's faith is mostly indirect and invariably beset with difficulties.

It seems certain that the Christianity of the people was rather a lopsided affair and full of holes when viewed from a "correct" clerical standpoint. Anything else would indeed have been remarkable, considering that the liturgy was conducted in a foreign language; that preaching in the vernacular — to say nothing of catechetical teaching — was notoriously ne-glected in a great many places; and that the clergy with whom the people had direct contact were, more often than not, almost as slightly informed about the deeper truths of the faith as their congregations.

It is also a fact that more than a few popular religious attitudes were in reality quite pagan. That is the case when — for example — the saints' pictures were beaten as a punishment for failing to deliver what they had been asked for. The same is true of the attitude described by Pope Greg-ory VII in one of his letters: the Danes, he writes, are angry with their priests when they fail to supply them with fair weather. And it is also true — with reservations! — of the rich variety of "magic" arts whereby people tried to cope with everyday hardships, and for which Christian names or things were brought into play. "With reservations," it must be added, be-

52. Death frightening the rich man: section of a miniature by Jacques Grand, ca. 1400. (Re-printed by permission of Bibliothéque nationale de France.)

cause the possibility ought not be excluded that such usages may contain more genuine Christian thinking and feeling than a present-day reader has ways of discerning at first glance.

The claim about the ignorance of the common people does in fact call for reservations, especially when one remembers differences over time: "catholic Christianity" was not in every detail the same thing in the fifteenth century as in the eighth. Above all, it has to be kept in mind that urban life in the later part of the period, with its mass sermons, its religious theater, and its riches of pictorial imagery in the churches, provided considerably better opportunities of information than did the countryside. Of particular importance are the "mystery plays," considering that their main theme was nothing less than the whole course of sacred history and that they combined the Christian view of world order and history by letting heaven, earth, and hell materialize simultaneously in the city square and by making the lives, choices, and destinies of their respective inhabitants spring to life before the eyes of Everyman and Everywoman.

In view of the comparative scarcity of sources, however, it is advisable to concentrate on those features of religious life that can with reasonable certainty tell us something about how the people *used* their Christianity.

One of the first things that springs to view is their passionate interest in a "good death." The sources testify to the importance attached to having children baptized as quickly as possible after birth. In view of the towering mortality of infants, it was essential thus to protect them from the risk of eternal perdition. Instructive are the stories about mothers who, with prayers to the Mother of God, lay their dead infants on her altar and are granted the favor of having the child called back to life long enough to be hastily baptized. Even more were people concerned about an unprepared death later in life. A quick and unexpected death, the object of hope for many moderns, was one of desperate fear for the inhabitants of old Europe. The prospect of such a death was, as a matter of fact, highly realistic, especially during the great epidemics in the second half of the fourteenth

53. Woodcut (ca. 1450) from "The Poor People's Bible," *Biblia Pauperum*. The baptism of Christ occupies the middle space. To the left, Israel is saved "through water," passing through the Red Sea while the Egyptian pursuers perish. To the right, the men sent "to spy out the land" cross the Jordan River carrying the proof of the Promised Land's glorious fertility. Both Old Testament events refer to the baptism of Christ and of Christians for their deeper meaning, as do the accompanying texts. Demonstrating the meaningful unity of sacred history was a main purpose of this widely read book of devotion and also inspired many church paintings. (Reprinted by permission of G. E. C. Gad Publishers, Copenhagen.)

century — the Black Death — when more people died than the survivors could manage to bury. Remedies against sudden death were: individual preparation in the form of reflection and prayer; frequent use of the church's collective means of grace; taking care that a priest would be present in the hour of death; joining a "fraternity" whose members would commemorate its dead and pray for them during their sufferings in purgatory.

Between the two critical mileposts, birth and death, a rich variety of pious acts aimed at safeguarding life in family and society. Material prosperity must be made possible by the priest's benedictional acts; but above all other goods to be strived for was the social peace without which nothing else could be accomplished, and which was always a highly problematical and uncertain quantity in the suffocatingly close and shortage-ridden village communities. Peace was the supreme concern: the priest's role as a conflict-solver was important; the church's blessing of marriages was an instrument of conciliation between families; and during the Sunday service in church, prayers were said for the peace and the "peace tablet" was handed round and kissed by everybody as a sign of their willingness to preserve elementary civil solidarity. A similar function was fulfilled by the feast of Corpus Christi, from the thirteenth century. Several purposes were served by the procession of the consecrated eucharistic bread through the cities, but inculcating the sense of social coherence between all "limbs on Christ's body" was not the least important.

One other, highly significant religious symbol of social solidarity — which of course meant a great many other things besides — was provided by the cult of the saints — those of the nation, the city, the trade, or the fraternity. Most all-embracing, most "catholic" among them was Mary, "the Mother of God." The forms under which she was worshiped could, and often did, let her character as a created being among other creatures appear in a problematical light, making her cult into a paradigm of the difference between theological theory and religious practice. That has something to do with the cult's social functions, not least that of making the subjection of women, in law and in daily life, somewhat more tolerable. But the tendency toward polytheism, or at least toward blurring the official claim

54. A German fifteenth-century wood carving of the Virgin Mary. This manner of presenting the mother of Christ — as the compassionate and merciful protectress of humankind — was widely used in Europe from the thirteenth century onward, not least in the religious fraternities. (Staatliche Museen zu Berlin-Skulpturensammlung und Museum für Byzantinische Kunst. Photo: Jürgen Liepe.)

about Christ as the unique manifestation of divine action in the world, was a current feature in the cult of saints as a whole. That is an illuminating fact, not only about popular catholicism as a force for social cohesion, but also about the tensions inherent in that same popular religion: the latent threats against a church unity that presupposed the monotheistic creed, as well as against the social coherence guaranteed by the church.

Everything touched on above concerns the people as a whole — i.e., those who did not express themselves in clerical parlance. But at a closer look, this "people" is, of course, a much more varied quantity. The word covers a lot of differences: for instance, that between town and countryside and that between rich and poor. The religio-historical significance of the last-mentioned difference becomes clear in the Crusades, a movement that expressed not only some religious aspirations that were common to all but also some that were conditioned by station in life. Among the "regular troops" of the Crusades, consisting mainly of mounted professionals, members of the knighthood, ideas seem to have been current about a Christian behavior specially to be cultivated by warriors. Christ was regarded as the great feudal lord whose land had been taken and who could lay claim to his vassals' armed help in recovering what was his. By acting thus they were to fulfill the obligation they had taken upon themselves by becoming his "men." He on his part had the feudal lord's equally self-evident duty to protect his faithful with every means at his disposal.

Such more or less articulate notions are in one text carried so far as to motivate a group of crusading knights, who hear a rumor that the main army has been defeated, to withdraw their allegiance from Christ by suspending divine service and prayer. There are grounds for doubting the universal validity of such an attitude, but the story is instructive of a real tendency to use the categories of the feudal contract — a self-evident presupposition of well-ordered society in everyday European life — when describing the Christian's relation to God. To be sure, the story represents a palpable distortion of catholic Christianity, but it is historically more significant that it delivers one testimony among many about an emergent aspiration among laypeople who want to be Christians on their own premises, based on their own experiences and needs.

Something similar can be discerned in the distinctive features of the crusading movement of the poor, and the children. Such "irregular troops" were no doubt motivated by greed, lust for adventure, hatred of Jews, to say nothing about famine and other forms of misery at home — just as similar profane motives spurred on the knights. But other emotions were in play as well, based on the Pauline words about God's power that is "made perfect in weakness." In other words, God who has revealed himself in the despised shape of the Son of Man will enable the weak and lowly to succeed where the strong and mighty have failed. The sufferings of the poor, especially the woes to be endured in Jerusalem at the end of time, when the Antichrist shall set up his reign in the holy place, are necessary for the final breakthrough of Christ's kingdom.

It is impossible to establish exactly how widespread were those and similar notions, but they are in keeping not only with general ideas about the salvific effects of suffering — ideas of which no Christian could be ignorant — but also with the popular annual church feast where everything was turned upside down — the choirboys, for instance, elected a bishop from their midst — as a sign of God's grace resting on what was small and despised in the eyes of the world. It is no accident that the feast was held on the day when the church's very earliest martyrs were commemorated: the quintessentially powerless "innocent children" murdered by King Herod in Bethlehem.

Irrespective of the difficulties of interpretation attendant to the details of such occurrences, they testify to stirrings behind the smooth facade of clerical religion: tensions caused by a more or less articulate wish to be Christian on one's own account in accordance with one's station in life. Such aspirations must have asserted themselves on a broader front than is immediately discernible; they must have been among the active motives whenever laypeople exerted influence contrary to strict clerical theory, for instance when state or city authorities took initiatives to control elections or interfere in property administration, or when fraternities, the voluntary religious associations, made independent arrangements. We need the priest — such was the implied viewpoint — but he is *our* priest!

The striving for independence could, however, express itself in more radical ways.

h. Deviant Christianity

It is a distinctive mark of old European Christianity that — at a closer look — "orthodoxy" is a more dubious quantity than it appears on the surface. All the old European forms we have been considering are variants inside a framework of broad catholic unanimity. But variants they are, and the features that give each a special face contain elements of tension threatening to make the very concept of a "common Christian faith" appear in a problematical light. That is of course most apparent in popular Christianity, but it is also, in varying degrees, true of each of the great formalized types — a fact we must keep in mind to understand the dynamics and practical possibilities of change in what was by and large acknowledged to be the common faith. No less important is it when talking of the "heresies" proper: they can only be understood if it is remembered that they are rooted in the common faith and present a case of the release of explosive possibilities inherent in that faith — and if at the same time it is remembered that the explosive matter might very well turn out to actualize itself in the practical behavior of people who were not called heretics and whose theory was considered blameless. Such considerations are least valid in the most "authentic" of all heresies, the Cathar movement, disseminated in northern Italy, southern France, and the Rhineland in the eleventh and twelfth centuries. In continuance of ancient dualism and under inspiration from its Near Eastern offshoots, the Cathars — the "Pure Ones" — yet again proclaimed the "Foreign God," the liberator from the world of the evil Creator. But even Catharism makes use of fundamental Christian assertions at the same time it neglects or falsifies others.

So much the more have the other heresies — so to speak — grown up in the church's own garden. That becomes apparent in the dominant place taken in those movements by the church's Bible. Christian faith and Christian living are exclusively defined as a result of man's encounter with the Bible. What is not found that way is not Christianity, and everything done on any other basis than the literally understood Bible is not a Christian life. In a catholic perspective such a way of thinking becomes heretical, first, because of the claim that nobody can call himself Christian without meeting the word of God without intermediaries; secondly, because the priestly administration of the sacraments is made dependent on the priest's living in accordance with the Bible — the church being a community of the holy and the pure; and thirdly, because "Scripture" is in practice treated as identical with the Gospel stories of Christ's life of poverty and the precepts contained in the Sermon on the Mount about imitation of that life.

This idea, which forms the leitmotif of the deviant movements from Waldensianism in the eleventh via Wycliffism in the fourteenth to Hussitism in the fifteenth century, is a Christian idea, and it has sprung from motives and tendencies central to catholic faith. But the movements that cherish it no longer belong to catholic Christianity because essential elements of that faith are thrown overboard.

Those movements are historically interesting as witnesses to social conflicts in a society under transformation. Several of them became temporarily mass movements in which national and social aspirations mingled with the religious ones — sometimes on the basis of an expectation of the imminent end of the world. And they do shed light on the extremes to which the church — that *societas perfecta* — was willing to let its tribunals of inquisition and its anointed kings go in suppressing and terrorizing the deviants. But in the perspective of the history of Christianity, two things are more important than those. One has already been mentioned: the movements tell us indirectly something about the multifariousness, complications, and vitality of the common faith. The other lies in the pointers they contain about coming things. They are distant omens of the choices made by modern European Christianity in its clash of ideas with the old.

i. From the Church to the Churches

There are good reasons to call the period we have been considering the "time of the church." That is not because the question about the "holy order" is one of central religious interest for men and women of those centuries — a question that subsumes most of the other questions that can be asked about religion. In that respect the period is not essentially different from the following centuries until around the year 1800. The main reason is rather that the question was answered in a way — namely, the papal, Roman one — that came to dominate other answers. That had consequences for Christianity as a whole, because papal Christianity, the variant that became fateful for the church in its capacity as institution, also succeeded in setting a decisive stamp on the "common faith." Because of that, the official face of that faith came to appear as something highly homogeneous, rounded and finished.

The religious reality, however, was less homogeneous and finished than all that. That is true about the institution — where quite a few unpapal goings-on can be discerned behind the façade — but it is especially true about the religious aspect. We have seen this already in our consideration of the other great variants. Kingly — and knightly — Christianity's explicit and implicit premises in regard to the way God's power becomes visible in his people; monastic Christianity's latent or open tensions between sacramental religion and striving for personal perfection; the ways popular Christianity testifies to the difficulties of letting the supernatural become active in everyday life without in practice turning that action into something like magic; the problems encountered by the theologians when attempting to prove the correspondence between revelation and reason — all that could be more or less easily "explained" by the competent authorities, but that did not by any means explain it away.

But the fact that catholic Christianity was not in all respects intrinsi-

55. *Above:* Judgment Day — a relief above the west portal of the pilgrimage church in Conques, southwestern France (twelfth century). In the center, Christ is shown as universal judge. With his right hand he calls to the saved to come forward, while with his left he rejects the doomed. Below and to the left: the saved in Abraham's bosom; to the right: the gap of hell and Satan with devils and the doomed. *Facing page:* Detail of the Conques judgment relief. Below: an angel receives the saved and a devil the doomed. Above: another angel stares down a devil, across the great divide between salvation and perdition. (Courtesy of the Danish National Art Library, Copenhagen.)

cally uniform meant it was not finished either. The tensions that rocked its uniformity contributed to releasing the forces of change that led old European Christianity from the time of the church to that of the churches. Three mutually connected tendencies became centrally important in that process. All were rooted in common Christian tradition while at the same time giving expression to movements in the general cultural picture — the theoretical and practical worldview that influenced religion at the same time as religion contributed to shaping it.

One tendency, the "nationalizing" one, meant that institutional control was gradually gathered in by the state, by means of bans on appeals to "foreign" tribunals, control over movements of capital out of the country, and agreements concerning supervision of elections to higher offices in the national church. That tendency — which was active in municipal contexts as well — had much to do with the general strengthening of the national monarchies. That was a process which, especially in Spain, France, and England, was favored by economic and social developments. But it was also in accord with important elements of Christian tradition, not least of course being kingly Christianity.

The papal government sought — not without some success — to profit from the trend by entering into agreements with the princes. But it was unable to prevent things going in a direction that in important respects resembled that of the early phases, before the breakthrough of papal Christianity. That is true not only in church politics and organizational structure, but also in religious reform. Initiatives that, for a couple of centuries from the mid-eleventh on, had been taken by Rome or supported from there were now undertaken elsewhere, on a national, regional, or municipal level, and they succeeded — or failed — without Rome entering seriously into the picture.

The second tendency was individualization. It was active both in practical devotional life and in "academic" thinking. Like the first trend, it was rooted in age-old ways of thought while at the same time corresponding with salient features in general cultural developments. The relative freedom from traditions in the urban communities was an important factor, and the same is true of the professional and educational differentiation favored by urban life. As for its rootedness in Christian tradition, that religion had always — even in its most collectivistic versions — aimed at the individual soul. But more recently a way of thinking had emerged, especially in monastic circles, that found the very essence of Christianity in the individual soul's lifelong labor to conform itself to Christ. The innermost meaning of Christ's passion and death, said Peter Abelard, the Parisian theologian (d. 1142), was to be found in the love and passion for others it called into being in the Christian soul. Consequently the Christian life must be seen as a life of cultivation of that reciprocating love. This was, of course, an idea that could — and mostly did — enter into combination with the more "objectivistic" elements of catholic Christianity, but perspectives had been opened toward an individualism that did away with such elements: the sacraments, doctrinal authority, the institutional framework of religion.

Something like that can be met with in isolated Christian mystics. But more important was that the devotional practice of educated church members became increasingly colored by the tendency, as can be discerned from the enormous popularity of a book of devotion called *On the Imitation of Christ* by Thomas à Kempis (d. 1471). A pointer in the same direction is the custom of meditating during divine service: a devout concentration of thought disconnected to the public actualization up at the altar of the objective salvific events. Thus, one could be tempted to say, did Christians take their revenge on the clericalization of worship. Of course, public worship went on as before, with pomp and magnificence, and nobody dreamed of abolishing it, but as far as religious initiative was concerned, the main emphasis was to an increasing extent laid elsewhere. Significantly enough, something vaguely similar took place on the more primitive level of devotion, such as when the mere sight of the consecrated eucharistic bread, elevated by the priest as a sign of Christ's presence in his people, was considered religiously beneficent, quite independently of any further participation in worship. As a logical consequence, the more elevations one could manage to see during the day by looking in at several services, the better.

This emerging tendency of loosening the individual person from the churchly unity was also active in formalized Christian thought, especially in cases where inspiration was sought in ancient Greek and Roman moral philosophy, in such a way that the idea current in that philosophy about a well-rounded moral personality with firm control over its "lower" urges tended to become paradigmatic for a life in conformity with Christ and love of God and neighbor. When Christian humanists such as Erasmus of Rotterdam (d. 1536) called the teaching of Jesus a "philosophy," purer and more elevated than that of the pagans, what they saw in it was a set of prescriptions for the rational shaping of individual life rather than something that went on in the church by means of its dispensation of objective divine gifts.

Yet another tendency of change, rationalization, is present in just that striving for a calculated buildup of a well-ordered moral personality that was hinted at above. Not only in academic and monastic circles, people began to define a Christian as someone who works at himself by means of regular prayer and reading, meditating on the state of his soul, and more or less using his participation in the public celebration of the "mysteries" as a tool in that personal endeavor.

No wonder people like Erasmus had great fun depreciating and scoffing at phenomena like pilgrimages, the cult of relics, etc. True, the theology of the church had always acknowledged a duty to prune popular piety of its more extravagant excrescences, but it had done so in the reverent conviction that the people's faith expressed a genuine consciousness of God's wondrous intervention in human affairs. That conviction is conspicuously absent in a humanistic critique that by and large regarded popular religion as a bundle of noxious aberrations of insufficiently organized minds.

In such phenomena, an increasingly influential "bourgeois" lifestyle can be discerned. Those phenomena form counterparts to the rational calculation, the awareness of clock time, the keeping of books that was a condition of survival for the leading people of urban societies. But they also originate in much older religious traditions which lay behind the bourgeois style itself, things like the orderly division of time and activities customary in monastic houses, as well as the theologians' polemical way of distinguishing between "truth" and "custom" and their attempts at rendering a rational account of the church's message. But what must above all be kept in mind is the general Christian tradition of holding every single believer to account as to his place in world order and history and his handling of the life given him by God. That was a tradition which had in a good many respects been weakened during the earlier centuries of old European Christianity, but it had never become extinct, and it was strengthened in step with the slow, quiet — and sorely incompletely documented — process by which Christianity "oozed down" among the peoples of Europe during the centuries following its formal acceptance. In other words, the process of "internal mission" — a phenomenon to which we shall have to return.

This "mission" in an increasingly differentiated society was a presupposition for, and gives us material for understanding, the changes in outlook and practice. Another motivating force was provided by the common targets of criticism: the so-called abuses for which the papal establishment was — not without justice — held responsible. This establishment must in any case, even when operating efficiently, present a challenge to independent-minded people such as royal officials and city councilors, as well as theologians wishing for a personal encounter with the Bible, and educated burghers, jealous of their right to be the judges of their own devotional needs.

But much more must resistance and criticism make themselves felt when — from about 1300 — the papal establishment did *not* function efficiently and showed neither the will nor the ability to reform itself. Financial exploitation; bureaucratic centralization without safeguards against corruption and sleaze; abuse of the office of "heavenly doorkeeper" by waging holy war against Christians and by excommunicating debtors — such occurrences, which, ironically enough, resulted indirectly from the original prestige enjoyed by the papacy in its capacity as guardian of justice and mercy, stimulated and supported the forces for change by provoking a criticism that, notably enough, was put forward on premises provided by the Christian message itself and by a genuinely Christian idea of the church. Even more important were the weaknesses of the institution on the grassroots level. Irresponsible use of badly educated vicars in the parishes while the incumbents enjoyed the fruits of office elsewhere; mass production of eucharistic services for living and dead, performed by underpaid "altarists" — such things deepened the gap between high and low clergy, weakened institutional coherence, and left in the lurch the people for whose sake the institution existed. When — summarily expressed — bishops were unwilling and priests unable to satisfy the popular needs awakened by the Chris-

56. Erasmus of Rotterdam, the renowned humanist writer, advocated religious and ecclesiastical reform along lines he found in what he called the "philosophy of Christ." That caused him difficulties with influential fellow Catholics as well as with Luther, whose ideas and actions he had initially welcomed. Engraving by Albrecht Dürer, 1526. (In Erwin Panofsky, *Life and Art of Albrecht Dürer*, © 1955 renewed 1983 by P.U.P. Reprinted by permission of Princeton University Press.)

tianization of the people, and when — in consequence of that — skepticism and resistance against the papal leadership became more than a concern of a very narrow elite, then it is no wonder that the forces for change were stimulated and became more and more sharply articulated.

The movement in old European Christianity from *church* to *churches* cannot, however, be exhaustively explained by analysis of those tendencies and their presuppositions alone. Decisive for understanding the form and direction taken by that old movement up until the breakthrough of modernity in the eighteenth and nineteenth centuries is an insight into the new departures in Christian thought and life that took place in the first half of the sixteenth century.

3. Old European Christianity: The Time of the Churches

a. Luther's Christianity — and Calvin's

Consideration of the forms assumed by old European Christianity during the last three centuries of its history will make us recognize its two great overriding features: Christianity as the sole and final explanation of human existence, and Christianity as the dominant societal "myth," carried into institutional practice by an all-encompassing church with power of compulsion over its members. Those are characteristics which — on the background of earlier development in Mediterranean times — began to appear in specifically European forms in the eighth century and have been in process of dissolution since the eighteenth. In another respect as well, the three centuries we shall presently consider must be regarded as belonging to a coherent course of events lasting a thousand years, in that the internal critique went on through the old European period as a whole: the permanent mutual criticism between the individual and the collective, between Bible and church, between clergy and laity, between nation and Christendom, between state and church, between otherworldliness and social action, between "mysteries" and reason, and above all between the idea of God's being distant as ruler and judge and his being close as servant and brother. We shall have occasion to identify the same basic tensions when we now turn to the last phase of old Europe.

It is, however, not a matter of things merely repeating themselves. Far from it. Even though fundamental patterns can be recognized, the picture of Christian Europe cannot be drawn in the same way after the middle of the sixteenth century as before. That is due to a strengthening and deepening of old forces for change: nationalization, individualization, rationalization. But above all it is due to a religious and ecclesiastical reorientation with its point of departure in the experiences of one European, the Saxon friar and academic Martin Luther (1483-1546).

Those two things are in some ways interdependent, both because the Lutheran reform movement acquired its mass effect from the old forces

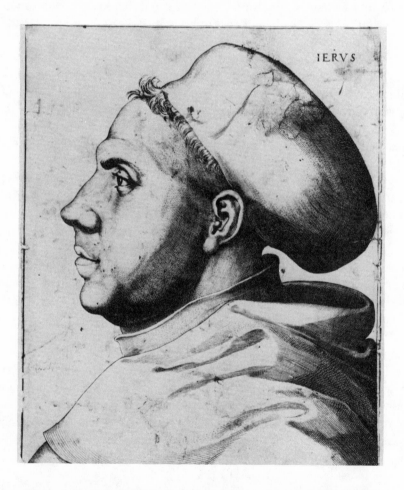

57. This portrait of Martin Luther was drawn by Lukas Cranach in 1521, the year in which he defended his cause at the Diet of Worms and declared his readiness to let himself be persuaded by "the word of God and clear reasons." (Courtesy of The Royal Library, Copenhagen, Department of Maps, Prints, and Photographs.)

for change and because Luther himself was to some extent one of their exponents. But if ever there has been a case in European religious history where a course of events has been decisively determined by one man's highly personal experience, reflection, choices, and actions, then the Protestant Reformation can confidently be claimed as it. One may indeed with reason go further and state that no individual Christian since the apostle Paul has been so broadly and deeply influential as Luther. No wonder he was celebrated as the infallible founding father and prophet in what came to be called the "Lutheran" churches, and that his image in the Roman Church became that of the arch-heretic, the tool of the devil, or Antichrist himself.

Personally, Luther protested angrily whenever he heard talk about "Lutherans." Christians had to call themselves by the name of Christ alone, not by that of Doctor Martin, that "sack of maggots," a frail and mortal fellow human. And his persistent claim was that not he but the pope was responsible for novelties, fabrications, and falsehoods. He himself preached what Peter and Paul had preached: the message of the one holy catholic church.

Luther's was a rebellion in the church's name against the church. That had been attempted before, but never in the way it was done here; that is, on the basis of a radical rethinking and reformulation of the central claim of the Christian tradition. What was protested against here was neither that the church was rich whereas its Lord had been poor nor that it made use of thought forms and customs that were not expressly documented in the Gospels. What was protested against was its falsification of *the* message in comparison with which everything else was secondary: the teaching about how goodness and joy come into being.

God comes to his fallen creatures as one who at the same time pronounces judgment on their selfish laying waste of goodness and joy and offers himself in sacrifice for their sake, thereby liberating them to joy, and to the goodness that comes from joy and from joy only. Such, according to Luther, was the message entrusted to the church and falsified by it. It had perverted it by making goodness — in the sense of moral striving and subjection to the precepts of the church — into a condition for liberty and joy, thus demonstrating that it had understood the meaning neither of perdition *in* nor of liberation *from* selfishness.

At the time when Luther — on the basis of his monastic experience and his reading of the Pauline letters — came to understand that "getting a gracious God" had nothing to do with "merit," he had no notion of this being something other than what his church truly and really meant. That happened only gradually, not without assistance from the authorities of the church who believed Luther's to be a case to be handled as a normal disciplinary one, without proper discussion. Step by step he became convinced that the entire system of authority, the entire way of viewing and treating Bible, sacraments, worship, and social life, constituted one all-encompassing manifestation of confusion as to the central meaning of the message. Or, as Luther expressed it, an unholy mix of law and gospel, of God's demands and his promise, a confusion that inevitably resulted in despair whenever the demand was taken at full value. Step by step he was led to discern the effects of the falsification everywhere in the church's life — not only in the administration of the sacrament of penance, but also in the doctrine of the Eucharist as a sacrifice offered by the church, in the pope's and his hierarchy's use of pseudopolitical coercion in spiritual matters, and in the last resort in the understanding of the priestly office as a ruling and regulating intermediary between God and humankind.

Thus Luther's ideas about what happens when God meets an individual person with unconditional judgment and equally unconditional grace led to conclusions about the church. The church is not what the pope has made of it; but neither is it a mere association of individuals who have experienced judgment and grace. Christ has willed a people to come into being, a people where his sacraments — baptism and the Eucharist — are administered and where mutual love expresses itself in mutual service. It is a central conviction of Luther that such care of human needs can be taken only by those who have been liberated by grace, and not on the basis of their own goodness or merits. The church, conceived as a people, is nothing but the community of men and women who live by grace; it is not the society of those who are busy saving themselves and making themselves good in order to become happy.

Another conclusion is expressed by Luther in the claim that "everyone who has crept out of baptism becomes, by that alone, a priest, a bishop, and a pope." In God's people all "worldly" distinctions vanish. In the interest of elementary peace and order, it is of course desirable for the church to have specially educated and qualified ministers, but in principle they are there only because of appointment by the people — the "royal priesthood." Yet a third conclusion is the demand that worship be conducted in the people's language, on the basis of an idiomatic translation of the Bible, and with the people participating actively by singing hymns of prayer and praise.

Behind all this lies the assertion about how liberation comes to the individual person. But it is worth noting that the mutual solidarity in the church also comes from what Luther presupposes as the permanent condition of fallen and redeemed man, namely, that liberation happens anew every day. As long as the Christian is in the world, he is not only "entirely justified" but also "entirely a sinner." He has met God with empty hands, and that is how he keeps meeting him. "The old Adam," who has been "drowned" in baptism, has to be drowned daily "in repentance and penance." From that, the church community as a whole derives its distinctive mark; and that is why Luther rejects each and every notion of special status such as a religious elite, an order of specially meritorious Christians, monks, nuns, and friars.

Thus Luther's ideas about the salvation of the undeserving — ideas that had sprung from solitary experiences in cloistered isolation — opened wide-ranging perspectives for life in the church.

But also for social life in a wider sense. Luther's definition of the church as the realm of freedom, a community without coercion, implied a total rejection of any attempt by the church to lord it over the state. In other words, it made it possible for Christians to ascribe sovereignty to the secular order. Certainly Luther was no theoretician of sovereignty. He viewed the independence of the state in the light of the obligation imposed on it by God to keep down the powers of wickedness so that confusion and chaos could be to some minimal degree averted during the short time left to the world. In that sense, secular authority wielded the sword on behalf of God, but its exercise of that power must be judged in the light of God's will as known from the Bible. Last but not least, it was a Christian's duty to refuse obedience to "ungodly" commands.

Another great social reorientation to which Luther's theology gave rise was the new form of Christian legitimization of ordinary work — the station in life to which God had called you. There, and not in any kind of illusory search for perfection, was the place where your neighbor was to be served and the cross of Christ carried. Whatever a Christian's state in life may be — merchant or soldier, peasant, lord, laborer, housewife, hangman, or pastor — he or she is free to perform its tasks joyfully. Confident of having been unconditionally released from the duty of "deserving" anything, he or she is "servant of all and free lord of all things." Certainly Luther was under no illusion here. The joy he spoke of had nothing to do with the euphoria of progress, and what he had in mind when using the word "freedom" was neither democracy nor cultural advancement. Freedom meant being free to stand where Christ himself had stood and continued to stand, namely, with the needy neighbor. Here again Luther proves his closeness to Paul, and his distance from many others who had pleaded the apostle's teaching and example.

58. Luther at his dinner table in company with friends and associates. Together with the listening young people to the right, this family atmosphere reveals something characteristic about Luther's reformation. His contributions to the daily conversations at meals were written down by table companions, collected, and published as *Tischreden*. This picture is taken from such a collection.

Yet another new departure concerning life in society was Luther's revitalization of the "appeal to the rationality of the common man," something that can be discerned in his call for personal appropriation of what he considered the central message of the Bible. The instrument for that appropriation was Luther's *Lesser Catechism,* a short book designed to be the place where men and women encountered the meaning of existence directly and at their own risk. Hereby, evidently, perspectives were opened in other directions than the religious one. But again, such perspectives were of scant interest to Luther himself. He had no time for large-scale cultural planning, and he accepted — here as elsewhere — the patriarchal family and the monarchical state as framework for an authentically Christian life and for personal appropriation of the message. A Christian charity that could not find enough to do there would in Luther's view be of little use under whatever other conditions could be imagined.

At all events, Luther's way of treating traditional ideas and ecclesiastical authority was amply sufficient to saddle him with a sentence of heresy; furthermore, his preaching and writing acquired an unprecedented response in a situation where explosive matter had accumulated, and where the art of printing had provided writers and thinkers with new possibilities for rapid and massive dissemination of ideas. From 1520 onward Luther gave voice to the "complaints of the German nation" against the papacy. He acquainted princes and municipalities with the religious meaning of their resistance to papal interference — or provided them involuntarily with a pretext to resist on other grounds. He showed how individual piety could be meaningfully united to churchly solidarity and consciousness of the objectively given, the divine word coming from outside the world of men. And he gave humanist reformers grounds for hoping they had found a powerful ally in their struggle against obscurantism and irrationality.

In consequence, a wave of reform went over Germany. In the course of one generation a large part of the empire abolished catholic forms of worship and founded "evangelical," "Protestant" churches with creeds on more or less Lutheran lines; with German-language ritual, preaching, hymn singing, and schooling; with two, and only two, sacraments: baptism and the Lord's Supper; with a married ministry; and in close alliance with city councils and princely governments. The form assumed by old European Christianity during this process, and its degree of accordance with Luther's intentions, are issues to which we shall have to return. In the meantime we shall look at the most important among the immediately post-Lutheran reform movements.

Here, as in Lutheranism, the founder's personal role was decisive. The Frenchman John Calvin (1509-64) was Luther's disciple in that his version of Christianity in important respects presupposes Luther's faith and action. But he was another sort of person and a different kind of thinker. Whereas Luther expressed his most important ideas in occasional writings or biblical commentaries, Calvin's main contribution to theology consisted in a big, systematically organized doctrinal treatise, a work in

59. John Calvin, an epochal figure in the Protestant Reformation, and its foremost theological system builder. (Courtesy of The Royal Library, Copenhagen, Department of Maps, Prints, and Photographs.)

which nothing is left undiscussed, where everything is in its proper place and the style — clear, stringent, elegant — stands in a curiously instructive relation to the ideas it serves to express: ideas about an anything-but-rationally fathomable God and his sovereign actions toward his creatures.

195

Also, Calvin was far more interested than Luther in providing the new church with a definite form. While Luther's priority was the "negative" one that nothing be allowed to *prevent* the free preaching of the message and the free administration of the sacraments, Calvin aimed at a positive definition of the framework of church life. By prescribing that early Christian offices be reintroduced in the congregations, he took the revolutionary step of letting laypeople take a formalized part in church government. Together with the "pastors," lay "elders" were to supervise the public and private life of all church members and take disciplinary action in cases of failure to conform. Calvin's preoccupation with discipline — he called it the church's "musculature," doctrine being its "soul" — was a consequence of his somewhat un-Lutheran use of the Bible. According to him, church and state were in duty bound to safeguard the moral prescriptions contained in both Testaments of the Bible. True believers were to observe them in their capacity as a holy people and as a sign of their undeserved salvation, whereas infidels and hypocrites must do it for the sake of God's honor. Calvin's church was a hard school. Against a great misery, brought about by age-old popish falsifications, a great and pure severity of doctrine and life must be set in action in order to make the church become what it had been in the beginning. Luther's tolerant attitude to "Romanist" remains in ceremonies and church art, and his fear that "evangelical purity" might develop into a new form of coercion of souls, found no adherent in Calvin, and Calvinistic church life has testified to the fact ever since.

The state in which Calvin operated and whose help he required and expected was of quite another kind than that of Luther. That was a difference that became important for their churches. True, the two Reformers had largely similar ideas about the duty of the state to enjoin one and only one form of worship in its dominions and to take measures against that quintessential blasphemy, the Mass as traditionally understood. They were also at one concerning the state's role in God's government of the world: it must be free of ecclesiastical interference in secular matters just as surely as it was forbidden to interfere with the freedom of the church in preaching and teaching. But in a long perspective as well as a short one, it became important that the original politico-social context of Lutheranism was a monarchical state, whereas that of Calvinism was the republican city-state of Geneva. That was not only due to the possibilities of influence and maneuver offered to Calvin by the Genevan system of elected assemblies, or to the fact that experiments with moral supervision and control of an entire population were practicable in Geneva, but not in Saxony, but because the ideas held in common by the Reformers about the "priesthood of all believers" were considerably easier to carry into some sort of reality in a city-state than in a princely monarchy. That came to be of benefit to Calvinism during its dissemination to France, Scotland, England, and Germany, a process that began as early as Calvin's own lifetime and was destined to turn his church into a denomination on a par with the Lutheran and Roman Catholic communities.

Luther's and Calvin's interpretations of Christianity, and their consequences during the middle decades of the sixteenth century, constitute the most radical new departures in the history of old European Christianity. It was a matter of new thinking — in Luther's case indeed, so new that it opened perspectives far beyond his own old European context of thought and life. But his own it was, his and his disciples'! They endowed the old European dynamic with a form and direction that it would not have got without them, but that does not disavow the fact that the questions they grappled with were those of the old Europe, and that their answers had a common horizon of understanding with those of their contemporary adversaries. To put it another way, the new things they said were accessible and meaningful on the background of a tradition that had never been without its tensions, be they partially or entirely perceived.

That is something that will become clear when we consider modern European Christianity later in this book. In other words, it will become clear when we look at a manner of thinking among whose premises we shall *not* find such assertions as that the Bible delivers a full and correct description and explanation of history, geology, and astronomy; that Moses wrote the Pentateuch; that Israel's prophets predicted future things correctly; that the workings of the devil in human affairs can be clearly pointed out and that witches enter into covenants with him; that civil rights and Christian confession presuppose and condition each other; that heresy is something for the police to investigate; that the end of the world, with judgment, heaven, and hell, is close at hand because such and such signs and portents appear. And above all, it will become clear when we consider the difference between whether the central religious problem is the existence of God or whether it is his state of mind toward — in Luther's words — "me, lost and doomed creature that I am."

But something else has to be added to that; namely, that the new initiatives were far from fully realized in subsequent centuries. Luther did not, so to speak, bind the company. Other considerations than his, other interests, became dominant, not only in places where his movement was rejected but also where his doctrines and his example were officially in force.

b. Warring Creeds

From the outset, the new movements made the same claims as the old church: that they were the true church, *the* authentic expression of the common and general — catholic — faith; and for a long time people in all camps were convinced that church unity could and would be preserved or restored by everybody adopting the ideas of one of the camps, their own. When that proved impossible, and when the religious question became increasingly mixed up with controversial issues of politics, war, and economics, then a characteristically old European process was set in motion: that by which the movements — Protestant and Roman Catholic — became crystallized as the religio-political phenomena known as confessions or denominations.

Such was the main trend, but when viewed in a shorter perspective of time, the situation was somewhat more opaque. Furthermore, one new phenomenon portended future things. That was the movements that criticized Luther and Calvin for being timid or self-serving halfway Reformers. Many different ideas and strivings met and collided in those movements: apocalyptic expectations of a coming realm of justice and purity; social protest, as in the German peasant uprising of 1525; preaching of an inner enlightenment, granted by the Holy Spirit without intermediaries such as Bible and church; actions for total extirpation of popish remains; demands for adult baptism as the sign of conscious adherence to the community of the saved. Many of those tendencies were released by the general upsurge, occasioned by Luther's protest, but not a few were continuations of earlier movements such as the ones we have already met. And not least, they were portents of developments that would not be permanently realized until much later. In the Reformation period itself, the radical movements were rarely able to stay alive for long, at least openly, and they were savagely persecuted by the mainstream confessions.

The religious aspect of confession building took the form of normative catechisms and orders of worship, and above all, more or less extensive creedal statements such as the Lutheran one from Augsburg in 1530. Those were documents setting forth and explaining the doctrinal and organizational assertions by which each of the churches, or rather, their trendsetting theologians and lawyers, defined the Christian truth, gave reasons why they were in possession of it, and explained — not without acrimony — why others were not.

As for law and organization, the confessions expressed themselves in a variety of organizational forms, which were more or less clearly adapted

60. Luther, as conceived by a Roman Catholic polemicist. A devil has taken possession of him and inspires him. Wood-cut by Erhard Schön, ca. 1535.

to or incorporated in structures of state and city government, and more often than not acted as participants in the national or international power
game.

Such was the case even where, as in parts of the Calvinist movement,
a certain amount of independence could be preserved in relation to state

power. And it became increasingly the case with the steady strengthening of centralized states and their more or less naked interests in expansion in all available directions. That could lead to confessionally absurd situations, as in Cardinal Richelieu's France (1624-42), where the government fought the Protestants inside the country, because that served domestic interests, while simultaneously financing Protestants externally because that furthered the designs of foreign policy.

The combination of an absolute aversion to theological compromise and a wide-reaching dependence on secular powers resulted predictably in coercive mission as well as wars of religion. Only after a succession of bloody and protracted struggles, merciless persecutions, forced emigrations, and large-scale material destruction did the confessions gain their final identities and the religious map of Europe its finished form, with a Roman Catholic monopoly or preponderance in southern Europe, in France, Belgium, Austria, Hungary, Bohemia, and parts of Germany, and the rest of the continent as well as England and Scotland being Protestant.

Stability and peace were bought at other costs than war and persecution. One was the thought control and structural rigidity that were distinctive marks of the "finished" confessions — not least as a consequence of the increasing power of central governments. That contributed to a faint but growing disillusionment concerning the traditional old European relation between religion and society. Such an attitude could lead in several directions; at all events, it is an important factor in the rise of modern European Christianity.

c. The New Churches

All the confessional churches — the Roman one included — were more or less new as compared to the old unitary church. As we shall see later, all were stamped with the mark of modernization and striving for efficiency — as expressed, for example, in the stress on pedagogical communication of the message, systematic consciousness shaping, and inculcation of moral discipline.

They were also different one from another. The Protestant confessions had abolished the papacy, five of the seven sacraments, the cult of saints, purgatory, monasticism, priestly celibacy, and the Latin language in worship. And they disagreed among themselves about the Holy Book from which they had taken their reasons for abolishing all those institutions and usages. As religious wars and processes for heresy showed, such differences could and did cost lives.

3. Old European Christianity: The Time of the Churches

Nevertheless, churches they all were, blood relations, as it were, of what had gone by the name of church in earlier centuries. They were not associations of like-minded individuals with individual experiences behind them. They were, in principle, all-encompassing institutions that, each in its own way, claimed to be the sole place where experiences were made because God had instituted them for that purpose. He had willed to let salvation happen by means of the gifts with which he had entrusted them: words and acts that were "objective," that is, independent of human powers and faculties.

Salvation, the focal point of old European Christianity, the act of rescue from confusion and despair to order and hope, comes to men by means of the church. Such was the common conviction of thinkers and practitioners in all the churches. No Roman Catholic could express that conviction more clearly than did Calvin by using the word "mother" about the church, and continuing: "There is no other entrance to life than the one she vouchsafes us by conceiving us, bearing us, nourishing us at her breasts, and

SIX-TVS.V.
PONT. MAX.

61. Sixtus V (1585-90), a Franciscan of modest origins, became one of the Catholic Reformation's most vigorously active popes. His reorganization of the papal apparatus of government and his performance as a large-scale urban planner are mutually related expressions of the efficiency and rationality aimed at by the revived Roman church. (Courtesy of The Royal Library, Copenhagen, Department of Maps, Prints, and Photographs.)

62. *(Following pages)* The movements of Protestant reform till ca. 1580.

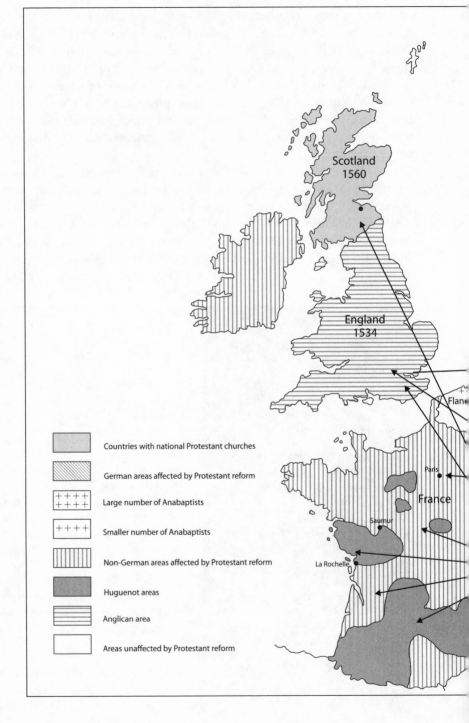

Countries with national Protestant churches

German areas affected by Protestant reform

Large number of Anabaptists

Smaller number of Anabaptists

Non-German areas affected by Protestant reform

Huguenot areas

Anglican area

Areas unaffected by Protestant reform

Scotland
1560

England
1534

Flan

Paris

France

Saumur

La Rochelle

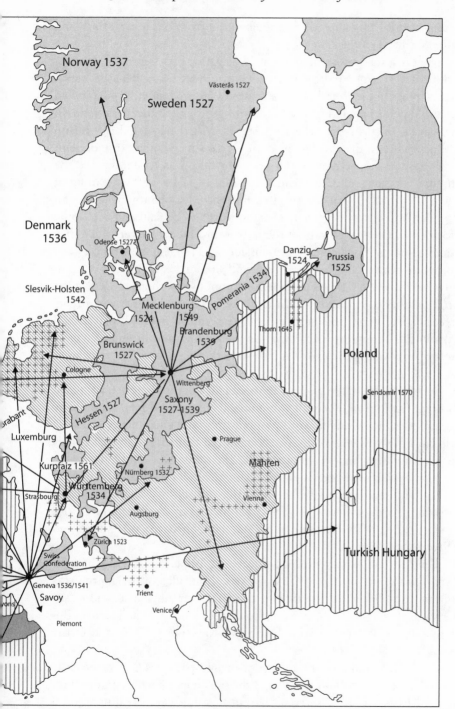

Norway 1537

Sweden 1527

Västerås 1527

Denmark
1536

Odense 1527

Danzig
1524

Prussia
1525

Slesvik-Holsten
1542

Mecklenburg
1524

Pomerania 1534

Brandenburg
1539

Thorn 1645

Poland

Brunswick
1527

Cologne

Wittenberg

Saxony
1527–1539

Prague

Sendomir 1570

Brabant

Hessen 1527

Luxemburg

Mähren

Kurpfalz 1561

Nürnberg 1532

Vienna

Strasbourg

Württemberg
1534

Augsburg

Turkish Hungary

Zürich 1523

Swiss
Confederation

Geneva 1536/1541

Trient

Savoy

Venice

Lyons

Piemont

guarding and leading us until we are liberated from our mortal flesh and become similar to angels."

The Protestant movements protested against the church on behalf of the church. The target of their protest was not the Roman claim that salvation took place in the church, but the church's failure to uphold what it had been appointed to do and its pursuit of things it had no business to do. In other words, according to the Protestants, it had neglected the raison d'être of a church: the proclamation of God's sovereign act of judgment and liberation. Consequently the pressing task was to emphasize the "churchly" character of Christianity by pointing out that the meaning of the word "church" lies in the fact that God has deigned to take care of a guilt-laden and errant people by causing words to be said and acts to be performed that the fallen cannot themselves produce and over which they have no disposal. They come from outside, and the church is where they become audible and visible. There men and women hear what they cannot say to themselves, and they see what they cannot show themselves. But the church's ability to say and do just that presupposes that it never forgets where the gifts come from, that it does not set itself in God's place. God speaks in the church in its capacity as the community of empty hands; therefore, everything that turns it into something else must be done away with.

Such is, in short, the original Lutheran idea of the church. It is an idea *both* of an institution where the annulment of guilt and fear happens by means of the independent word in preaching and sacraments *and* of a Christian liberty that owes its freedom to the fact that the word comes from God and that he will allow nothing and no one to stand in its way.

That explains the breach of church unity, but it is also enlightening as to a fundamental continuity between the old unitary church and the Protestant churches as well as a basic community of essence and purpose between the heir of the old church, the Roman Church in a new shape, and the Protestant churches.

This became, however, especially evident because much of what had constituted the originality of the early Protestant idea of the church was lost in the established Protestant churches. That circumstance, and its social as well as religious causes, is something to which we shall return. Before that, we will glance at what became of the Roman Church after the breach.

After the initial uncertainty, or downright paralysis, it became clear that the Lutheran rebellion stimulated the old church's will to internal reform and external self-assertion. The protesting ways of thinking and speaking about reform on biblical lines and about man's direct encounter with God impacted many Roman Catholics, who busily studied Paul and Augustine. But above all, the will to reform originated in a rethinking and a sharper formulation of what was distinctively Catholic. In a longer perspective of time, that became decisive for the lines along which the "confessionalization" of the Roman Church was worked out.

The theoretical aspect of reform was expressed in the theological work of the great church assembly in the north Italian town of Trento during the middle years of the sixteenth century: the Tridentine Council. Here an attempt was made to clarify the position developed by Augustine, namely, that salvation is initiated by God alone, but that man participates in the ensuing process by his love, his obedience, and his striving for perfection by constant use of the church's sacramental and pedagogical means of support.

But even more important were the practical reforms initiated by the council, which fall under three main headings. One was a reorganization of the central government — the Curia — aiming at increased bureaucratic efficiency on the basis of a better exploitation of the age-old papal dominion in central Italy. Those lands now acquired a decisive importance for the papacy's survival as a European power. Another was a complex of prescriptions concerning the duty of bishops to reside in their dioceses and about Roman supervision of how they discharged their duties. And the third consisted in a calculated action in favor of raising the level of education of the parochial clergy and of safeguarding their spiritual authority. The cure of souls on the grassroots level — the parish priest's work of governing, teaching, comforting, and protecting the people — was the essential target at which the entire reform work aimed. That was what the whole apparatus was there to serve.

That can also be clearly discerned in that section of the reformed Roman Church which did not directly belong to the normal clerical system of services and demands, namely, the new orders. All were designed with a view to the cure of souls as largely defined, along lines such as popular preaching, school teaching, poor relief, or care of the sick. It is eminently characteristic of the new spirit that the Society of Jesus, the most important of the new orders, not only observed stricter rules of training, command, and supervision than any earlier order, but also to an unprecedented degree freed itself from activities close to the hearts of earlier monks: the practice of common prayer and worship, the regulated life together in one place. Mobility, efficiency, dynamic engagement with the world in order to win it and shape it — that was the principal aim of the Jesuits.

The large-scale, albeit only partially successful, attack on abuses and inertia for the sake of winning and keeping souls, in combination with Catholic rulers' military actions against heretics, was decisive for the church's survival in its struggle against the new movements. And the reform was equally vital for the church in its self-defense against those same Catholic princes whose power interests grew to be an ever more serious internal menace to its institutional identity the more their help was required externally, and the more the centralizing tendencies in national life gained force.

Among the other new communities, a special position was taken by the Anglican Church, insofar as it gave the common claim to being the catholic church a character of its own. In its normative creed it had accepted the fundamental Calvinist assertions concerning relations between God and man, the Bible as norm for preaching and life, and the number and meaning of the sacraments. But at the same time it flatly refused to take over Calvinist notions of church organization. On the contrary, it retained the episcopal office in its traditional form, accepting the bishops' character of being "successors of the apostles" as that character had been defined by the ancient church. In Anglican eyes the existence of that old dignity was the principal sign of the unbroken life of that old church in Queen Elizabeth's dominions. That was exactly what the Roman Church had abandoned by introducing a papal monarchy. It is not by accident that Cyprian of Carthage, the early antagonist of that monarchy, could appear as something like an Anglican ancestor.

Clearly, the combination of that idea with main ideas of the Continental Reformation was anything but easy. It contained possibilities of conflict which later erupted into actuality during the English civil war. The Anglican Church nevertheless proved to be a resilient institution, under an episcopal leadership that was generally supple as well as firm; with a vivid national consciousness and a will to self-defense that — for a time at least — made the strong influence of the state acceptable to many; and with a theology that, perhaps more than any other Protestant thinking, maintained one of the central concerns of the past: the attempt at a plausible and

63. The Spanish Carmelite nun Teresa of Avila (d. 1582) was a strong and active leader and reformer in her order. But she was also a mystic. In her autobiography she described her experience of divine love in the shape of an angel who pierced her heart with a flaming arrow. This passage inspired Gianlorenzo Bernini to sculpt one of the most famous works of reformed Catholicism, located in the church of Saint Maria della Vittoria in Rome (ca. 1650). (Courtesy of the Danish National Art Library, Copenhagen.)

meaningful union between, on the one hand, the doctrine of the fall and restitution of man, and on the other, that of the God-given order of the universe and the laws of nature and national community. Richard Hooker (d. 1600), the prototypical Anglican thinker, reasoned along such lines. Significantly enough, he was also an artist of language, as were the men behind the King James Version of the Bible (1611) and preachers such as Lancelot Andrewes and John Donne, whose richness of expression and power of imagery has perhaps only been equaled by the Dane Grundtvig — a late-born nineteenth-century old European.

The self-professed "genuine" Reformation churches: the Lutheran ones in Germany and Scandinavia and the Calvinist, or Reformed, ones in Switzerland, France, the Netherlands, Germany, and Scotland present a good many organizational differences. The Calvinists' office of elder and their tradition of regular regional meetings between clerics and lay representatives endowed their churches with a stronger internal coherence than was possible for the Lutherans, whose parish minister was largely left to himself, in a vulnerable position between a controlling state and an encroaching squire.

But irrespective of such differences, all those churches were clerically dominated, as were the Romans and the Anglicans, in the sense that the gifts of salvation were everywhere administered by professionals of preaching and teaching, over against whom the laity stood in a receiving position. That the Calvinists — especially where in a minority — had conceded an influence to the laity in disciplinary matters was important in the long run, but it does not affect the fact that the Calvinist churches as well as the Lutherans stood and fell with their ordained administrators of "word and sacraments."

Of course, the process of salvation was defined in quite another way by Protestants than by Roman Catholics. That was important in other regards, but less so in the practical understanding of the nature and function of a church. Something similar can be said about the original Lutheran idea of the church and of the priesthood of the baptized. Naturally, that idea was never disavowed in theory. But in practice it was unimportant. Some of the reasons for this lay in the Lutheran churches' strong dependence on state power and in other social or cultural circumstances. But there were also theological reasons, one of which perhaps stands above all others. The "Word of God," the formula used by Luther to characterize God's judging and saving action and understood by him as the critical counterforce against each and every attempt at forcing the conscience, came to be understood as being identical with the Bible, the Holy Book that was fully accessible only to experts. As expressed by an orthodox Protestant: "To us, the Bible is what the pope is to the Catholics." If that is your way of thinking — and it was in Lutheran lands until the breakthrough of biblical criticism and until Grundtvig's attack on the "paper pope" — then there is, quite irrespective of social and political circumstances, no theological way of avoiding an authoritarian office of mediation.

Our rapid survey of the "new" churches — Roman and Protestant — has shown that they agreed not only on certain fundamental ideas of the church as an institute of salvation, but also on the clericalist character with which they endowed their administration of word and sacraments. We keep that in mind as we consider the churches' relationship with the secular structures that constituted their social contexts and contributed to shaping their ideas about the meaning of Christianity.

d. Churches, Societies, and People

The social role of the churches from the sixteenth to the eighteenth century was played on old European premises, above all the conviction that society and church were two aspects of one and the same thing: the same people as seen from two angles. That manner of thinking was active on all levels of society, right down to the family. Or rather: up from the family, considering that the patriarchally governed "house" — a nuclear family with servants — now as before was the basic unity, setting its stamp on the other formations. Pope and king were viewed in the image of the providing, defending, teaching, punishing father of the house, the intercessor and the model for conduct. Indeed, God himself could be imagined in that light, surrounded by his closer or more distant "holy family." Church and state were families, and the family was state and church in a nutshell. That was a viewpoint on which all churches were agreed; it was nourished by Bible and antiquity; and in a good many respects it made the reality denoted by the words "state" and "church" into something distinctly different from what is meant by the same words in the modern world.

One of the forms in which this viewpoint became important in our period was given it by the Christian humanism of Erasmus of Rotterdam and his fellows. Their interpretation of Christianity on the lines laid out by ancient moralists contributed to shaping one of the model images of the increasingly centralized European state: the prince as a father of his people, who provides for the spiritual as well as the material needs of his "children." The men who administered that kind of state power were indeed often Erasmians, irrespective of their formal creed. In such an atmosphere, the age-old joining together of secular and religious society underwent a characteristic deepening while at the same time specifically Lutheran insights were lost. Luther was as keen as any on the idea that everything began with the family and that the governing and punishing father was a minister of religion for his children. And he was willing — as an emergency measure — to let the Christian ruler take responsibility for the external order of the church as its "foster father." But that did not make him abandon the distinction between the "kingdom" of power and that of grace. The gospel of forgiveness of sins and restitution of joy is God's undeserved gift and has nothing whatsoever to do with external discipline or moral schooling. Therefore the task of the pastor is, in principle, utterly different from that of the ruler, even though the father, or the mother, of the family performs both tasks in relation to minors in their charge.

The "Erasmian" model contributed to the common understanding of the two closely related entities, state and church. But the decisive factor in the development of their mutual relations was the growth of state power toward absolutism in most European countries. That process was politically, socially, and culturally conditioned, but it was hastened by the weakening — by confiscations of lands, etc. — of the economic and political power once wielded by the church.

The growth of state power became part of all the churches' destiny, insofar as they all had to consent to extensive control by the Christian princes. For a state more and more firmly intent on dominating, it was a logical necessity to secure control over an institution that claimed to "cover" the nation spiritually.

More or less, that became the general state of affairs. It is true that the Roman Church tightened the papal grip on those parts of church life with which the Catholic state powers did not normally see an interest in meddling. But over against those powers' will to control the nominations to higher offices in the church and supervise its legislation, jurisdiction, and finances, the pope was helpless, so much the more as he was thrown upon their military and financial assistance in his struggle for survival and reconquest against the Protestants. As for Spain, the king there was a rather more important figure than the pope, and something similar was the case with the independent-minded French church, where the saying ran: "We do not go for Tiber water when there is a fire on in Paris." So much the more was it the case with the Protestant churches, which, unlike the Roman one, had abandoned the idea of being a kind of "state." They had to submit to far-reaching supervision and in many cases formal direction by the state.

WITEBERGA,
GLORIOSA DEI CIVITAS,
SEDES ET ARX VERÆ DOCTRINÆ CATHOLICÆ, SE-
PTEMVIRATVS SAXONICI METROPOLIS, ACADEMIARVM IN EVROPA
CLARISSIMA, ET POSTREMI MILLENARII LOCVS
LONGE SANCTISS:

64. Prospect of Wittenberg, Luther's home town, from the Cranach workshop. The Latin text goes like this in translation: "Wittenberg, the glorious city of God, seat and stronghold of true catholic doctrine, capital of the electorate of Saxony, most famous among the universities of Europe, and by far the holiest place of the last thousand years."

Most glaringly did that appear in the Lutheran churches of Germany and Scandinavia. Broadly speaking they lost their character of separate institutions and, practically speaking, became organs of the state. In those lands the coherence of the church on all levels above that of the parish stood and fell with the prince and his government. No independent book of church law was in existence, and none of the church's own supervisory organs was able to take independent action. In short, the church was the extended arm of the state. No wonder that the Russian czar Peter "the Great" drew inspiration for church order in Lutheranism such as he knew it.

This development went directly, and tragically, against Luther's original intentions. It can with reason be called tragic because Luther's decision to refrain from establishing an order of self-government for the church was intimately grounded in his passionate wish to see the church as the place where the message of judgment and liberation could be proclaimed freely, without coercion of any kind. "God," he said, "will let no one govern the souls but himself alone." But such words were apt to lose their impact when the carriers of the message were left without any institutional support for the power critique exercised fearlessly by Luther himself, although

— as may be added — Lutheran pastors had no qualms with chastising the sins of the common people.

There is, however, another side to the dependence on the state suffered by all the new churches, and it reveals something important about the distinctively old European character of the situation as compared to the church policies of, for instance, twentieth-century totalitarian movements. The states in question were *Christian* states in whose theoretical self-legitimization the Christian images of the world and of history were vital ingredients, and whose practice — legislative, administrative, and educational — in a thousand ways drew its inspiration from those images as communicated and interpreted by preachers and theologians. As Hans Wandal, the Danish bishop, expressed it in his anointing sermon to King Christian V (1671): The Bible must be in the king's hands wherever he goes; it is his "church-book, house-book, war-book, law-book; it is God's own coronation charter for the king, a rule and a guide that must determine all the king's business and actions." Such words could have been uttered everywhere in European Christendom, because everybody was agreed on the ideal formulated by Wandal's contemporary, the French bishop Bossuet: a "rule of politics extracted from Holy Scripture."

The obligation thus described could be neglected, and often was, but seldom without excuses being deemed necessary. In other words, never was it neglected without the tribute that vice pays to virtue, thus making clear to posterity what virtues have been taken seriously. Not a few rulers have let their course of action in cases of doubt be determined by the advice given them by their theologians, in accordance with what the respective confession defined as "pure doctrine." And neither is it an accident that theologians of all confessions became systematicians with the duty not to leave anything unexplained.

From this state of affairs sprang two sets of specific obligations, one for the government, one for the clergy. The government acknowledged a duty to defend the one and only salvific creed and exclude all others. It did this by provisions for compulsory church attendance and religious schooling; by censorship; by laws about holy days, interest, and matrimony; and not least by police action against heresy. The denial that this implied of God's "sole government over souls" did not disturb mainstream church people — it was age-old catholic tradition; as for the Protestants, even Luther himself accepted punitive measures against certain categories of heretics, and indeed not only because of their being potential rebels but in their capacity as heretics in religion. So much the more willingly did Luther's successors approve the practice, for instance, during the great persecutions of witches that swept over Europe in the decades around 1600 and which in fact were religious ones insofar as the witches were accused of worshiping the devil. Behind all this lay the shared conviction that the survival of an ordered and peaceful human community depended on the correct form of faith and worship; and in those centuries, when religious correctness was a more hotly disputed quantity than ever before, and when state power was in the ascendant, it is no wonder that state action against false religion became sharper and more uncompromising than ever before.

The government was also obliged to endow the clergy with the means needed to inculcate correctness of faith and conduct among the common people. In Protestant as well as Roman Catholic areas, the clergy became a privileged class, and in countries where church land had been confiscated, the bishops were given a livelihood. It could be modest enough — with the positive effect that the earlier gap between high clergy and low was somewhat narrowed. Negatively, the loss of landed property meant that the clergy's chances of presenting a corporate counterweight against the powers of state and aristocracy became even further weakened. The clergymen — at any rate the Lutheran ones — became functionaries, and it was unclear where exactly they belonged, because the influence of the nobility on the local level made itself strongly felt. The pastor might be formally appointed by king or bishop, and he was ordained by his bishop, but in a great many cases he was in actual fact an appointee of the local squire and was seldom allowed to forget it.

On the part of the church, the obligations were partly theoretical, partly practical. The theoretical ones were fulfilled by theological arguments for the legitimacy of royal power and by the efforts made by preachers and catechism writers to promote civil obedience. Hans Wandal, mentioned above, was one of the theoreticians of royalty. In a voluminous Latin treatise entitled *On Royal Rights,* he drew his arguments for absolutism not only from the Bible and from Luther's doctrine of the God-given task of secular authority, but from the ideas of Hellenistic political philosophers about the ruler as universal reason incarnate. Here the power-critical tradition of Christianity had ceded the ground in favor of an almost totally unembarrassed identification of the absolute monarch's will and actions with those of the Creator and Savior.

The practical obligations continued, in Roman Catholic lands, to include some of the directly political tasks incumbent on the higher clergy in preceding centuries. Here "princes of the church" were still in evidence, but it is significant that they commanded much less elbow room than they had when royal power had been weaker. In Lutheranism, such concerns were eliminated after the nationalization of the landed property of the bishops; and the room for action left to "superintendents" or bishops was modest, in some cases ludicrously so. But the practical support of the clergy was important for the state, most of all in the lower levels of society where the parish minister not only acted as preacher, teacher, and administrator of sacraments, but as communicator of government notices, as registration officer, as the sole educated person, in short, as a vitally important connecting link between the state and the common people.

When asking about the social role of churches on the grassroots level, it is important to be clear about the range of meaning covered by the question. When considering the relations to central state authority, we found that the social role could not be exhaustively described by referring to the inculcation of obedience or to the community of material interests between high clergy and royal government. It was at least equally important that the state and its rulers accepted the message of the church as the

65. Lutheran worship, as shown by an altar painting in a Danish country church, 1561. Just as in van der Weyden's altarpiece (above, pp. 139-41), Christ's sacrifice on the cross occupies the center; but here only two sacraments are depicted: baptism and the Lord's supper. At the same time, the proclamation of the Word by preaching has become strongly emphasized, as well as the listening and receiving people. (Courtesy of the National Museum of Denmark.)

truth about life in this world and the next: as "consolation in life and death." But that consideration is even more valid on the level where personal encounter counts for more than that of institutions, that is, on the level of the parish. Here it becomes clearer than elsewhere how much it meant socially that the church preached the message for the Sunday congregation, distributed the sacraments, blessed the marriages, taught the children, and brought solace to the dying. Here the condition is to be found for every other part of the social role to be played. That is a point forgotten at our peril. But so is the historically and theologically relevant fact that preaching, distribution of sacraments, teaching, and consolation cannot be understood apart from their social context. Therefore the question about the social role is also one about how, in those centuries, the local context and its social constraints influenced what went on in church. It is worth our while to look into that, despite such things as the paucity of sources and the insufficient research of available sources hampering our effort, to say nothing of differences of place and time.

The country priest or pastor and his flock were parts of a social system that included the lord of the manor and, to an increasing extent, the king and his officers. The social theory of the church, Protestant as well as Catholic, accepted the notion of society as a "pyramid," a hierarchical organism, with peasants and laborers at the bottom, the squire higher up, and the king or the pope on top. And it was understood that a Christian must conduct his life where God had placed him, enjoying the rights and fulfilling the duties of that particular condition. An Italian manual for preachers recommends that that doctrine be incorporated in the sermon and illustrated by pointing at a tablet graphically depicting the social ladder.

There is much indication that this element of old European–style thinking often overpowered the Christian assertion of the equality of all the baptized before God, thus neglecting or blurring the idea of the church as the place where social differences were canceled. That happened, for instance, when the minister acceded to upper-class demands for private baptism — or at least private water — and special forms of address when bread and wine were distributed. The introduction of reserved pews for "the quality" and of pompous memorial tablets for noble or bourgeois families on the walls of the church is further indication. Not a little water had flowed under the bridges since the church was able to insist that the great acts to be celebrated on the walls must be those of God and his saints — irrespective of who paid for the pictures.

An ironical relation existed between the key position enjoyed by the minister in accordance with current clericalist thinking and his lack of certainty as to where he belonged. In the eyes of the squire, the priest or pastor was neither an equal nor a person he could treat as dirt; and he did not belong among the peasants either. His much improved education could prove a two-edged sword. In one sense it made him better fit to serve in a church that placed a higher value on preaching and teaching than had been the case before. But it contributed little to his understanding of the conditions and needs of parish people. He, and perhaps most of all if he were an unmarried Roman Catholic priest, could be a lonely man in an exposed situation, vulnerable in the face of threats from several sides.

His relations "downward" presented many similarities to earlier situations, but also much that was different, be it due to the emergence of new varieties of church organization or to tendencies of development inherent in European Christianity.

The Protestant pastors arrived in their parishes carrying the knowledge acquired at the university — and from their fathers: many of them were sons of pastors — about "the clear daylight of the gospel," the Christianity of the Bible, purged of "superstition" and "idolatry" as well as of "justification by works." But in the congregations they came to serve, the "superstitions" were deeply rooted. In the eyes of the peasants, those practices were anything but devilish delusion: they were vitally important vehicles of the support for well-ordered community, peace, and fertility that they felt themselves entitled to expect from their religion. A prime instance is the cult of the saints, God's friends and men's helpers in adversity. They were close while God was distant. As is clear from visitation reports, Luther's discovery — that God himself was close to men in Christ — had far from enough impact with the preachers of his church to make it clear to the people. A void was at any rate left when the closeness of heavenly things was no longer incarnate in holy men and women, associated, each of them, with his or her parish church, fraternity, and holy day, with that day's words, images, and gestures.

It was no less important that many of the old church's acts of consecration and safeguarding, its feasts and processions, etc., were done away with by the Protestant churches. Practices that the reformers — many Catholics included — condemned as magic, incompatible with the pure message of the gospel, might perhaps be dispensed with by city dwellers, but they were age-old necessities in agrarian society. The struggle of modernized churches against magic in favor of a piety nourished by preaching based on the Bible did not meet with the hoped-for response. Visitation reports from Lutheran Germany show that even the most diligent catechization had exasperatingly meager effects, and that — far from disappearing — traditional fertility-protective usages lived on under irregular forms. What could not be got from the priest or pastor was sought from "wise people." A similar impression is conveyed by recent research into English popular religion of the sixteenth and seventeenth centuries.

The struggle against magic was a common concern of all churches, even though it was, in the nature of the case, not conducted as radically by Catholics as by Protestants. But reformed Catholicism did initiate action against other ancient forms of popular Christianity in the interest of sharpening priestly control over the entire range of religious expression. A case in point is the fraternities, which in some places had assumed the character of irregular churches, where the clergy had considerably less authority than officially required. Another is the socially strengthening uses connected with baptismal feasts. And yet a third victim of reform was the expressions of the people's inclination to amuse themselves independently. The carnivals, initiation feasts, etc. of earlier centuries were thorns in the side of the new, often morosely principled clergy of all confessions, not only because they gave rise to moral disorders — not least, sexual ones, an increasingly important concern of the churches — but also because they threatened clerical leadership.

Behind all this can be discerned a growing need, felt by all elite groups, for drawing an ever sharper distinction between the holy and the profane. Ideas and practices that had earlier been considered a legitimate use of the holy in everyday life were now condemned as a desecration of the holy. This is an omen of developments in modern European Christianity, but it is also a reminder of one of the permanent tensions in the old European variety.

Summing up, the role of all churches on the grassroots level expresses a gigantic renewal of an old effort at Christianizing and "rationalizing" European life, and is, at the same time, a sign of a beginning withdrawal, or forcing back, of ecclesiastically organized Christianity from some of the central concerns of popular life. The first-named effort was crowned with considerable success, inasmuch as the "internal mission" led thousands to a deepened consciousness of what was involved in being a Christian. But the tendency of withdrawal was under way. That both things can be stated simultaneously is partly due to the fact that those who called popular Christianity magic were both "right" and "wrong," but also to the fact that conscious Christianity was on its way to becoming a more individual and private matter than had earlier been the case.

e. Personal Christianity

The attempt at understanding the churches as institutions — their official ways of arguing for their legitimacy, their organizational structures, their practical activities, and their social roles — is one way of getting to know the Christianity of those centuries. But it must be looked at in another perspective also: that of the Christian individual.

It was one of the central tenets of the new churches, as of their predecessor, that their ultimate raison d'être was the salvation of the individual soul. That purpose was now formulated more decisively than ever before and was followed up more energetically in practice. In part, that happened because the reforming initiatives — Catholic as well as Protestant — had sprung from intensely personal experiences. Another factor was the interconfessional strife that inevitably implied a motivation to personal reflection and decision. But in addition to that, it had to do with general trends of cultural life: the individualizing and rationalizing tendencies considered earlier in this book — and the technical revolution brought about by the invention of the printing press.

At any rate, the new churches' appeal to realize the confession of Christianity in personal life took a broader aim and reached further than had been the case in earlier centuries. The question now becomes: How did the individual cope with the message and the appeal of his or her church?

We can learn something about that from the books the individual used in his or her religious self-education. Apart from the Bible — which was far from a direct source of inspiration everywhere — that literature consisted of the immensely increased multitude of printed devotional works and hymnbooks. But religious autobiographies — a new genre in lay circles — and funeral sermons eulogizing the exemplary Christian life are also illuminating.

In a sense everything centers on coming to terms with guilt and the anguish flowing from guilt. This anguish of the individual soul — fear of death and of hell, of God's demands, his wrath and his judgment — which was a central concern in monasteries, can now be seen as the point of departure for personal pious practice in much wider circles. Not only were anguish and the ways of overcoming it important motifs in what was said to people from the pulpits, but they were consciously accepted by buying and devouring devotional books. Being a Christian is thus understood as acknowledging one's existential anguish and doing something about it, or allowing something to be done about it.

That was not everywhere understood in the same way. The most profound characterization of the anguish of guilt and the most radical understanding of what it means to "allow" something to be done about it is Martin Luther's. Luther summarized his experience and reflection in the words: "Where there is forgiveness of sins, there is life and bliss." What he meant by that was: The only salvation out of the anguish of guilt comes from the "foreign justice," lovingly granted by virtue of the Crucified One having taken human anguish on himself and undergone human suffering. That justice "from outside" is tantamount to God's acceptance of the anguished human being in the place where he or she is to be found; God is present with the lost ones. Nothing more is required. Liberation has taken place, without conditions, without presupposing a future movement toward being found worthy in the sight of God. Such a train of thought has two consequences. One, that freedom and joy can never be capitalized as a possession, an acquired quality. It must be sought and granted to empty hands every morning. And the other, that the Christian freedom is a freedom *from* concern and worry about oneself and freedom *to* outward action: concern for the needs of one's neighbor.

Such is the complex of ideas that, according to Luther, constitutes the quintessential core of the daily "practice of Christianity." That practice runs along two interconnected tracks. One is the daily family worship, based on the *Lesser Catechism* and centered on the commandments, the creed, and the Lord's Prayer. And the other is, quite simply, the life in accordance with one's calling and station, the working and communal life, out into which the liberated are sent and which, by the way, will often prove to be fraught with the adversity and suffering for which Luther used the expression "the cross in the calling," the sharing of Christ's fate that the monks and friars sought elsewhere than where Christ himself wanted to be found. For Luther it is an important point that the *lived* everyday Christianity is worship and work in one, and that the church — consequently — is in fact rather a profane quantity, a bundle of activities in everyday life rather than a separate institution.

Such ways of thinking are hardly found in this radical form outside of Luther and the Lutheran tradition. But that does not mean they remained inviolate in Lutheran circles, nor that more or less related ways of thinking were absent in Catholicism and elsewhere. To understand those centuries, it is important to remember that, as far as individual piety was concerned, their dominant trait was a set of largely common presuppositions and lines of thought, formed, more often than not, by means of mutual borrowings and influences.

The key concepts in those interrelated forms of "practice of piety" are: anguish, repentance, conversion, imitation of Christ, and methodical asceticism. And one of their historically most influential expressions is found in the *Spiritual Exercises* of Ignatius of Loyola (1491-1556), the founder of the Society of Jesus. This short book was a manual of planned training in self-control, renunciation of irrelevant impulses, and purposeful turning of the mind to divine things. In other words, it was a manual of conversion, imitation, and ascetic training. The method of inculcation to be used by the reader under supervision by a spiritual adviser was meditation on the objects of fear — death and perdition — and on the goal to be reached: life with Christ in his church. It was carried through by repeated calling to mind of great images: scenes, appealing to all five senses, from hell, from Satan's warfare against God and humanity, from heavenly bliss, and above all from the earthly life of Christ, the life the convert was to imitate and gradually make his own so that henceforth no fear could affect

66. Ignatius of Loyola composed his *Spiritual Exercises* in the 1520s. This is the title page of an edition printed in Antwerp in 1689. (Courtesy of The Royal Library, Copenhagen, Department of Main Collections.)

him. By means of this planned and supervised process of image forming, appropriation, and decision, the trainee was to establish himself as an unshakably firm Christian person, prepared to place himself at the disposal of the church in whatever capacity, wherever and whenever his superiors might decide to use him. Evidently the exercises were primarily intended for the professional elite, the members of the order themselves, as a preparation for the tasks they were to perform as internal and external missionaries, as teachers, confessors, relief workers, heresy fighters, and intelligence agents. But it is highly characteristic of the period that the exercises were put to use by laypeople, and that they were imitated and modified by literate Christians in other confessions, such as German Lutherans and English and American Calvinists. By such means they contributed to a broad current of interconfessional piety and proved able to set their mark on European ideas about what a Christian must shun, what he must seek, and how he ought to shape and make sense of his life.

The "standard piety" of the age had, of course, a broader content than that designed by the Jesuits. A number of other motifs were in play. But its ideas about the meaning and practice of repentance, conversion, and imitation were nevertheless remarkably similar from place to place. And it is worth noting that they — irrespective of what might prove possible in actual practice — were more or less sharply incompatible with what Luther had meant by those words. That becomes clear by considering two basic features. One is that the standard piety is concentrated on just that "religious self" — its qualities, its experiences, its growth — that in Luther's eyes constituted the very source of anguish, and indeed of every other form of human misery. The second (and it is really the first, regarded from another angle) is that what this piety struggles against — the sins of "the flesh" and "the world," everything that threatens to disturb and dismantle the rounded personality of a Christian — is entirely different from the evil from which Christ (according to Luther) brings liberation, namely, the selfish will, be it "religious" or not, that seeks its own and strives to make everything else serve it.

We are thus once again confronted with the fact that Luther's church was busy with many other things than listening to its father in the faith. But it is no less important to note the historical fact of a broad community of ideas and practices across the confessional divides. This testifies to tendencies that had long been active as part of the inherent tensions of old European civilization. One is the tendency toward concentration on the needs of the individual and toward loosening of the individual from his surroundings — it is no accident that the closed Catholic confessional stems from this period — and another is the tendency toward an ever more widely disseminated and ever more strictly performed planning and disciplining of life. But the "standard" piety is also worth keeping in mind when, at a later stage, we shall look at what happened at the transition from old to modern European Christianity. It is highly significant that, in Protestant circles, the tendencies became strengthened and deepened during our period.

There is, however, another factor to be considered, namely, that of mounting crisis and repeated reform efforts in the life of the churches. To those things we shall now turn.

f. The Crisis of the Churches: Causes and Expressions

The crisis of the confessional churches, that is, the process by which the dissolution of old European forms was set in motion, is a many-sided phenomenon. The question about its nature and causes must be attacked from several angles.

One of the first things that spring to mind when surveying the last old European centuries is the much debated complex of events that goes by the name "the crisis of the seventeenth century." That crisis shook Europe as a whole, with wars, epidemics, decline of population, and economic distress as the most conspicuous manifestations. One of the phenomena of crisis is particularly glaring: the decline of population. Not until the mid–eighteenth century did the population reach the level of the year 1600. That means that the crisis bears comparison with the most calamitous of all earlier crises: that of the fourteenth century, the time of the Black Death; and it had similarly far-reaching effects on the domains that interest us here. No ecclesiastical organization could remain unaffected by war and poverty, and no personal view of Christianity could avoid the impression made by omnipresent death and decay. Fear of Judgment Day — or longing for that day — filled many minds, and the note of repentance and turning away from an evil world, which, as we have seen, was a salient feature of the individual piety of the age, became particularly insistent.

Our theme is not sufficiently clarified, however, by studying those phenomena alone. We must first track the variegated forces and tendencies that contributed to putting the churches under pressure, and in a following section consider the consequences of those tendencies, and the responses from the churches and individual Christians to which they gave occasion.

The new churches — Roman and Protestant — represented in many respects a fulfillment of what earlier old European centuries had meant by

the word "church," insofar as they were better organized and more efficiently comprehensive than ever before.

On the other hand, this was a "victory" in which the seeds of "defeat"
lay hidden. Because the "victory" could only be won on the background of
a conscious religious choice, it was inevitable that conscious questioning
and doubt must occur alongside conscious acceptance. And not only that.
Such a situation might give rise to conscious and articulate denial, based
on the same premises of an ever advancing demand for personal choice.

When this is considered in connection with the advancing differentiation in European social life, it is no wonder that the pressure against the
churches became harder and deeper-reaching than it had been when
churchly Christianity itself had been less articulate.

One of the things working for crisis was nothing less than the "personal Christianity" considered at greater length above. It is certainly an important point in that form of piety that it stands for much else than a potential protest. When the churches insisted, as they did, on a conscious
appropriation of the faith and a planned "practice of piety," they did so
within their own context and on their own premises, in the sense that the
appropriation was regarded as something that must be grounded in the
church's "objective" means of grace, and be accompanied by diligent use of
those means — sacraments and preaching. It is significant that two of the
most important characteristics of the methodical individual piety insisted
on by the Roman Church were frequent use of the confessional and of the
Eucharist. The traditional cult of saints could also without difficulty be incorporated in the framework of the new piety. But, as in Origen's and Augustine's time, the combination was fraught with disruptive possibilities,
and as a result the objective, "mysterious" factor could either be retained in
a manner revealing that it had become nothing more than a stimulant for
individual efforts, or it could be consciously and openly done away with.

Such attitudes had been present in several variations for centuries,
but they became particularly conspicuous in the Reformation period, and
increasingly, in the seventeenth and eighteenth centuries. The last-named
attitude could take shape as a radical "spiritualism," as for instance in the
ideas propagated by Sebastian Franck (d. 1542/43) about God's unmedi-
ated illumination of man, or in those of some English civil war thinkers, as
well as in the radical forms of German Pietism in the eighteenth century.
But it is perhaps even more significant that related attitudes can be found
with more "normal" theologians, as when Johann Agricola (d. 1566), Luther's enemy and former collaborator, found the meaning of the word
"church" to be "a heart in which God's spirit rests and makes himself

known." The first-named phenomenon, the tendency toward hollowing out the "objective" factor while retaining, more or less strictly, its exterior forms, was the most important, however. That is one of the things to be learned from the Pietist movement. Here it is clear that personal conversion by direct encounter with the Bible; methodical cultivation of the soul through prayer, meditation, and ascetic practice; and exchange of experiences with like-minded fellow believers are felt to be much more important than what is objectively played out in the all-encompassing institution of the church — "the ark with clean and unclean animals." As for the Catholics, it is worth noting that not only the somewhat aristocratically minded Jansenist revival movement in seventeenth-century France, but also the Society of Jesus, its great enemy, each in its own fashion reveals a similar way of thinking. The case of the Jesuits is particularly important because they were influential members of the official ecclesiastical establishment.

Such tendencies cannot but have been partially inspired by the engagement of the state churches in the world of power and earthly purposes: the more or less dubious alliances and combinations that were bound to hurt pious sensibilities. In particular, the critical trend was stimulated by the pressure exerted by the established churches against new forms of personal interpretation of the message and individual ways of arranging one's religious life. Nothing much was needed to make the absolutist state feel menaced. People were to keep awake in the pews — helped, if necessary, by the verger's stick — but they must beware of getting other ideas into their heads than those the preacher found suitable to put there. In an increasingly differentiated society with ever more efficient governmental systems, the typically old European combination of Christian state authority and a church that understood itself as "the nation at prayer" could not fail to be felt as a straitjacket by many. In some places it took the form of something worse: a blatant perversion of its own nature. That was the case when the absolute monarchy presented itself as a manifestation of divine world order, with the monarch as a kind of earthly god at its center. During chapel services in Louis XIV's Versailles, the entire court personnel sat with their backs to the consecrated host on the altar — Christ present in person — and their faces turned toward the king.

Another threat against the established churches came from the sociopolitical crises accompanying the development toward absolutism. Social groups whose interests were hurt by that development found natural allies in the movements of protest against the church establishments. An object lesson is provided by England, where the anti-absolutist resistance of burghers and gentry in the House of Commons merged with the

Puritans' opposition to a church that refused them the right to free biblical preaching and organizational experiments. This alliance — which implied something more than Realpolitik, because many links existed beforehand — led to a breakdown of the Anglican establishment, with consequences to be considered in a moment.

"Secularization" is the name usually given to the freeing of political and cultural life from ecclesiastical tutelage. It is a meaningful word for a trend that was discernible from the later eighteenth century onward. When speaking of the preceding period, a certain reserve is called for. "De-Christianization" of institutions, customs, and styles of thought was as slow a process as had been their "Christianization." Furthermore, several forms of secularization are just as old as European Christianity itself — they have indeed drawn nourishment from that religion. Nevertheless, the weakening of the influence of the churches on political and cultural life was a reality in the seventeenth century and was felt as such by many. "The reason of state is a strange animal," a participant in the peace negotiations of Westphalia, 1648, said; "it devours all other reasons." And the Anglican John Donne expressed a more general unease in his words about the "new philosophy" that arouses universal doubt, to the extent that not only has the nature of the earth and of the heavenly bodies become problematical, but the order of society and the individual's identity has become out of joint: " 'Tis all in pieces, all coherence gone." When Galileo Galilei (1564-1642), one of the pioneers of the "new philosophy," let fall the remark that, after all, Christianity was not a matter of how the heavens moved but of how to move to heaven, he gave voice to a sense that certain old European positions were being abandoned. The new sciences of nature and society took a long time prevailing in wider circles, but they spread uncertainty and thus began to prepare the dismantling of a form of Christianity more than a thousand years old, a form whose idea of human and religious order was intimately connected with a concept of a knowable cosmic order.

Also contributing were the frequent and necessary practical compromises. One example is the reordering of church arrangements carried out by the elector of Brandenburg after his conversion from the Lutheranism of his country to the Calvinist faith (1613). That situation made it necessary to begin treating the two confessions equitably; and in the long run it contributed to turning the ruler in the direction of becoming an impartial regulator of church affairs.

A partial analogy to this softening of traditional monopolistic systems can be found in ecumenical initiatives, as for instance that of the German Lutheran Georg Calixtus (1586-1656), who enraged his fellow theologians by calling for reunion on the basis of the creeds of the ancient church. Neither he nor like-minded individuals had any success with the enterprise; practical experiments like the Brandenburg-Prussian one carried more weight — to say nothing of the trends in personal piety which made Jesuit writings welcome in Protestant circles and also gained expression in a common use of the fifteenth-century devotional treatise *On the Imitation of Christ* — one of a tiny number of widely and massively read works in the whole of premodern literature.

To that must be added that the confessions could find a meeting point in what constituted their common and permanent phenomenon of crisis: their problematical relationship with the common people. It may be that most influential clerics were busy with other things, but some saw the problem as a pressing one, and they tried to cope with it by reform and "internal mission."

g. The Crisis of the Churches: Consequences and Responses

As pointed out above, "internal mission" is one of the great "constants" of old European Christianity, and it is worth remarking that in this period, after centuries of the church's presence, it still requires doing — and is now being done in a way that reminds us of the other characteristic features of the age.

Religious and moral confusion, lack of knowledge about the most elementary doctrines and precepts — that was what anxious and worried church leaders found with people in the countryside, the overwhelming majority of Europeans; and they found it in a great many national and denominational contexts. Some areas of southern Italy went by the name of *Indie di qua:* "our own America," inhabited by our own "Indians."

It is probable that some of the complaints — like similar ones in our own age — were caused by the fact that those who ask questions about religion express themselves differently from those who answer them — quite apart from the circumstance considered earlier: the difference between clergy and people concerning what one was allowed to expect from one's religion. But the problem was real enough, and some of those who had acknowledged it tried to do something about it. Their solutions were still very much solutions from above — that could indeed be called one of the reasons why the problem was a permanent one! In other words, they were clerical solutions, worked out on premises cherished by priests and pastors. But, as mentioned above, they were also remarkably consonant with the period's general tendencies and style of thinking.

That is convincingly apparent in the great missionary enterprises carried out in seventeenth-century France. They aimed at a massive attack on the areas commonly regarded as the retarded ones, the villages of the countryside, which had remained more or less untouched by the urban reforms. The missions were organized as something resembling military campaigns, fought by special troops, and each of them concentrated on a narrowly defined area where a number of villages could be periodically visited through a number of years. In each village the missionaries stayed on long enough to be reasonably sure that the teachings would stick. As expressed by Jean Eudes, one of the great missionary leaders, staying less than six weeks in one place would produce more noise than profit — "du bruit mais peu de fruit." The key words were objectivity, planning, and limitation to essentials. In other words, missionaries engaged in catechization, not elegant sermons; daily inculcation of the creed, the Lord's Prayer, and the Hail Mary; systematical and confidential confession of sins by each and every villager at the close of the instruction period; and finally a great Communion service as a manifestation of the liberation now accomplished by means of teaching. The endowments that financed the campaign ensured that the village would be revisited according to needs.

Clearly this is methodical action, in accordance with important tendencies in the individual piety of the religious elite. The rational planning of life and the religious activism that had in earlier centuries been cultivated in the monastic houses and then disseminated to the reading population of the cities was now sought to be transferred, in a simplified form, to the people at large, irrespective of qualifications. Here, in other words, was an attempt to practice the appeal to the rationality of common people, which had always, in principle, been part of the church's purpose without always having become more than that. And it could be added that one of the points of departure can be found for the popular cultural advance that was to take place, on other premises, in the nineteenth century.

"Internal mission" was a more or less permanent response to a permanent old European problem, notwithstanding the characteristic form it took in this period. The response to be considered next is, on the contrary, one that could hardly have been given until now.

It was given by the Pietist-Puritan "core congregation," "gathered church," or as it has sometimes been called, the *ecclesiola in ecclesia* (the little church in the greater one). Puritanism and Pietism differ from each other in many respects. The Puritan movement in England had as one of its points of origin the problematical compromise between Calvinist and Catholic Christianity in the established Anglican Church — a compromise that suited a good many people by its comprehensiveness but was deeply unsatisfactory to more radical spirits wanting to carry out to the full a biblical Christianity as understood by Calvinists. The Pietist movement in Germany, on the other hand, never forgot its Lutheran roots when claiming to realize the fervor of the pious soul, which they regarded as the distinctive trait of the young Luther. The note of Old Testament piety, the demand for a shaping of life in accordance with the Law, was considerably less in evidence in Pietist than in Puritan circles. Here the religious atmosphere was rather a New Testament one, implying a hope that pious souls in the Roman Church would agree. Such Catholics were regarded as *gute Gemüther* who were longing to escape "Babylon" but who, seeing that the Lutheran church did not practice as it preached, must necessarily feel tempted to regard *all* churches as a "Babylonian jumble."

But in a manner typical of the times, the two movements were in complete agreement concerning the need for "biblical" reform, concordance between teaching and practice, and clear criteria of the personal holiness demonstrating that conversion had taken place. And they pursued mutually similar ways of organizing the "true believers" within the framework of the institution of the church, as a base for mission among its members, for a gathering of genuine Christians before it should become too late. Those organizations took the form of voluntary associations where the members strengthened their common commitment by Bible reading, prayer, preaching, and pious converse. Significantly enough, all those activities were aimed at realizing something like the "priesthood of all believers," Luther's great, and largely neglected, idea. But it is equally significant that Philipp Jakob Spener (1635-1705), the pioneer of Lutheran Pietism, found clerical supervision of the activities to be necessary. Not by accident did he, in his programmatical work *Pious Wishes,* demand that preparation for the ministry should include common and regular pious exercises by professors and students as well as a thoroughgoing control of the personal conduct of the future shepherds of souls.

After initial difficulties and controversies, Lutheran Pietism in its "Spenerian" form became an established link in normal, institutional church life, and lost much of its first glow of enthusiasm in the process. But the idea of a core congregation within the great church of the "merely" baptized was destined for a great future. It became a characteristic expression of modern European Christianity's often somewhat flickering conceptions about the nature of a church.

The case of the Puritans was somewhat different, not least by reason of their much more clear-cut ideas about organizational reform on a biblical and Calvinist model. Their conflict with state church and royal power, which

The Orthodox true Minifter,   the Seducer and falfe Prophet.

67. A polemical woodcut from seventeenth-century England. To the left, the Anglican priest speaks, as is meet and proper, from his pulpit in church; while to the right, the Puritan minister leads souls astray from the open window of a tavern.

contributed strongly to the English civil war of the 1640s, was so deep-reaching that it proved impossible to incorporate the movement in the established institution. After a brief flowering under Cromwell, who allowed a multihued variety of Puritan sects to dominate the religious picture, the movement was forced away from the centers of power by the restoration of the episcopal state church. Those Puritans who retained their nonconformism became to some extent victims of civil discrimination, but they could avail themselves of the freedom of organization introduced by the Act of Toleration of 1689. It is, anyhow, a proven fact that the methodical, ascetic, Old Testament–oriented Puritan piety projected a deep and lasting influence on English cultural and social life, and on that of North America as well.

In the periphery of both movements, however, persons and groups emerged whose responses to crisis were much more radical than reform from within. They demanded a total showdown and doing away with the entire idea of an all-encompassing institution of salvation. In such circles the church was conceived as the association of the tiny number of true believers. Its holiness could be ascertained on the basis of the holy conduct of its members, and indeed, the church became identified with that personal quality. Here the thing that was later called the "sect type" in Christian organizational history assumed a number of individual forms. Some sects regarded themselves as a "new Israel," bound together by a pact with God and each other; others demanded and proclaimed a social revolution on presumed biblical models. Yet others were Baptists, demanding adult baptism as practiced in the primitive church. That movement had already played a part in the Reformation period and had been savagely persecuted almost everywhere it appeared. In some groups prophecy and visions were cultivated as God's new ways of addressing the world; and the Society of Friends, or Quakers, abandoned formal worship and let everything depend on the direct illumination granted by the Spirit in the gathering of the faithful. Common to all was the idea of the church as an association of persons, and a profound hostility against traditional forms. As written by intrepid sectarians on church doors in Stockholm: "Babel, Whore, Sodoma; here is nothing but lies."

Such phenomena are foreign to the typically old European ways of thinking, although they testify to its inherent potential for conflict. They belong in the seedbed of modern European Christianity.

Something similar can be said about the forms assumed by Puritan Christianity in England's North American colonies, while those forms also realize some typically old European intentions. Here, in the special situation of settlement, where everything could be organized from scratch, the "association church" was the natural form of religious community, but its religious and moral principles proved able to deliver the norms for secular society too. The agreement concluded in 1620 by the "Pilgrim Fathers" to stick together in the "community of the Gospel" and the pact entered into by other immigrants with God and each other were church-constituting acts, implying popular election of ministers and "democratic" government of church affairs. But inasmuch as the congregation was more or less identical with the people in its capacity as a political quantity, those churches came to play a much larger role in society than could be played by comparable groups in the old world. What happened here was not a more or less voluntary isolation from the rest of society, but acts that *created* a new society. What was strived for was carrying the "kingdom of God" into social reality by means of legislation. Admittedly, that could not succeed in the long run, if not for other reasons, then because of the steady influx of new immigrants; but the attempt has had effects on American life ever since, in remnants of Puritan moral discipline, but above all in the intimate links connecting a worldview and a conduct of life with the democratic form of government. After the virtual disappearance of the totalitarian tendencies inherent in congregational "democracy," other possibilities in popular government came to be realized. Forces were released that were theoretically implied in the ideas of Protestant Christianity about the saved human creature's relationship with God, but which did not till much later come to be realized in Europe. That is one of the ways the Americans became pioneers of important elements of modern European Christianity.

We are led in a somewhat different direction for the last in our series of "consequences and responses," namely, the apocalyptical upsurge of the age. Certainly the expectation of a rapidly approaching end was a frequently occurring trait of peripheral-sect religiosity, and certainly, such ideas had likewise been rather eccentrically in evidence earlier. But the hope and the expectation of the breakthrough of the "last times" and the second coming of Christ was, as a matter of fact, also a central element in old European "standard" Christianity. It appeared in many quite unsectarian guises and, naturally enough, was particularly strong in situations of distress, when the concerns of the earliest Christians gained renewed importance: the idea about this world being a world under judgment, about the salvific acts implying a radical questioning of every human purpose, about the future world as a new heaven and a new earth, not just a new version of the old one. That men lived in the "evening of time" was something of which they were constantly reminded when the evening sun touched the west portals of churches, with their relief sculptures displaying the last judgment. No priest or pastor allowed his congregation to forget the doctrine of everlasting suffering in hell. The guilty fear that played so extensive a part in personal piety, and against which the confessional, the sermons of consolation, and the literature of devotion served as instruments of combat, is above all a fear of the "last things," those things men and women were painfully aware of being confronted with at life's end. In the time of the Black Death, during the Reformation uproar, and now in the Europe of the seventeenth century, with wars and plagues in abundance, those things were especially present to European minds, as objects of fear, as instruments of polemics and of manipulation, but also as bearers of hope: the hope of liberation, of the final breakthrough of the kingdom of love on Judgment Day, "the dear last day," as Luther had called it. Many ingenious spirits, and some simpler ones, kept a steady lookout for the signs of the last times, the presages from all over the world that the art of printing, and especially the emerging daily newspapers, brought close to people: the Turkish advance in eastern and central Europe, the victories of the

Catholic Counter-Reformation, portents like comets and deformed creatures, moral depravity and declining church attendance.

When such expectations and fears begin gradually to lose their grip on European minds, in the eighteenth century, then that is one of the signs of an emerging modern European Christianity.

4. Old European Christianity in the Mirror of the Poets

Old Europe was also the home — in all senses of the word — of two universal poets of Christian conviction: the Florentine Dante Alighieri (1265-1321) and the Londoner John Milton (1608-74). Their poetical interpretations of the world they lived in open an entrance to that world that is not opened by other approaches. In their works, central themes of old European life and thought are played out in a way that makes certain connections and certain lines of development clearer than is the case elsewhere.

The two main works, *La Commedia* — later called *Divina Commedia* — and *Paradise Lost,* are universal poems insofar as they aim at keeping everything in their grasp: the entire world order and history as a whole, and demonstrating the inner coherence of everything. Dante does that by letting his narrator traverse the beyond — hell, purgatory, and paradise — and making him, in the course of the journey, experience history through the histories of the dead, in such a way that history is made to comment on the shape of cosmic order and become commented upon by that order. And Milton does it by telling the story of the "first things" — the rebellion and fall of angels, the creation of the world and of man, the fall of Adam and Eve — in such a way that the whole of later history shines forth from it, closely intertwined with the world order in which it takes place.

The great common theme in and behind the mutual shaping of history and cosmos is divine order, its establishment, the attack on it by the powers of evil and nothingness, its restoration by divine intervention, and the divinely ordained struggle of rational creatures for meaning and coherence. All of that is demonstrated by poetical elaboration — in metaphor, narrative, and drama — of the great common images of European humanity: life without fear and guilt in the garden on top of the mountain; the devil, the fallen angel of light who has chosen his own nothingness instead of God-given fullness of life and has given himself over to the hatred that narrows instead of the love that is enlarged by many sharing it; and the self-sacrificing Savior meeting his fallen creatures in the depths.

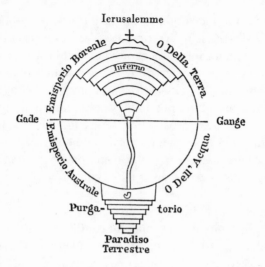

68. Schematic representation of the earth as described by Dante in his *Divine Comedy*. The "land part" of the earth is situated on the northern hemisphere, with Jerusalem at the top. Beneath its surface lies hell, divided into a system of circular terraces. From its bottom, where Satan sits caught in ice, a narrow passage leads to the surface of the southern hemisphere. That part is covered by water except for the Mountain of Purgatory in the middle of the ocean, formed from the earth masses thrown up by Satan, the rebellious angel, when falling from heaven, while all other land "fled" northwards. The mountain, which is divided into terraces where the purification of the saved souls takes place, carries on its summit the earthly paradise, once inhabited by Adam and Eve, where Dante's extraterrestrial journey begins: the ascent through the nine spheres circling the earth, into God's heaven.

In both poems, this tale of cosmos and history is organized in such a way that not only do those individual components speak for themselves and to each other, but they also speak by means of the experiences of *one* person. They become gathered up in him, and incorporated in the world he himself is. The order and love with which everything begins; the hatred and disorder that accompanies them and clings to them as their parasite in the course of human history — all go into Dante's narrating pilgrim and Milton's Adam, and each undergoes change through his experiences. Above all, each becomes the person God reaches out for and sends out onto the way of order and love.

When it is furthermore considered that each of the poems is built on the claim that its voice is a prophetic one, in continuation of the inspired and universal interpretation of existence contained in the church's Bible, then it becomes abundantly clear to what extent a European tradition of a thousand years is summed up in them. Each theme mentioned here — order in time and space; the interaction of orders; God's action as action in and by history; human choice as a choice between true love and false inclination; the gathering up of everything in the microcosm of the individual person; and above all, the self-sacrifice of the God-man as the event that alone makes meaningful life possible — is fundamental in the version of Christianity we have been considering here; and under the freely organizing hands of the poets these themes are developed more clearly and coherently than elsewhere. It is a remarkable testimony to the stability of old European tradition that it expresses itself so concordantly across an interval of 350 years.

But there is more to be learned from the poems. They teach us something about the tensions and the inherent conflicts of old European Christianity. Each does that by reflecting the problematical relation between God's sovereign action toward the powerless creature and man's "natural" striving for self-fulfillment. This, as will be remembered, is a tension that occupied Luther as well as Augustine.

But our understanding of the conflicts is furthered by the poets in yet another way. Something happens from one poem to the other. Dante's formulation of the common attitudes is governed by the idea that everything that is not God, or does not long for God, is, in the last resort, a nothing. God's ultimate opposite, the frozen devil at the earth's center, is therefore regarded as existence on the extreme border toward nonexistence. In Milton that is not so. There God's enemy is an active force. Certainly Milton's readers knew this enemy's enterprise, the rebellious struggle against the source of being and goodness, was absurd, but he is nevertheless experienced as an actively menacing, persuading, coercive power. He is also a mobile and incalculable power, coming from outside this world, a counterworld. Far beyond the world structure that in Dante serves as the devil's prison lies the point of departure of Milton's Satan: his basis for the attack against order in the world of humankind. Milton's universe is an asymmetrical conglomerate of worlds, between which a struggle is going on until the end of time. Behind this "development" from one poem to the other we can glimpse a sharpened consciousness of the internal uncertainties of old European Christianity. The world has become more dangerous and less calculable. Another characteristic difference comes to light in the poverty of social perspectives that characterizes the goal of Milton's history, as compared with that of Dante. The restored human creature is not, as in Dante, incorporated in a society; on the contrary, the goal is the "Paradise within," enjoyed by the lonely follower of Christ.

part four

Christianity as a
World Religion

1. "Modernity"

From the viewpoint of Christian history, the period we are turning to now, from the late eighteenth century to the present, is dominated by two themes: the development of the modern European and North American form of Christianity, and its dissemination to other parts of the world. We will better understand this form of Christianity by looking at the greater context in which it belongs and to which it stands in a reciprocal relationship: the civilization of modern Europe and America, or — as it is also called — modernity.

Discussing the distinctive traits of that civilization implies special difficulties, both because it is a living civilization with an open future and because it is our own. But even though we — as historians must — confine ourselves to "prophesying backward" by looking at its past, we ought to be able to identify some features that — considered separately and in their interplay — are characteristically different from what we met in old Europe.

Agriculture has been replaced by capitalistically organized industry as the dominant trait in the picture. In consequence, a global economy has been established, with much stronger mutual dependence than hitherto seen. And yet another consequence is the application of industrial methods to agriculture.

Socially and politically the keywords are: population growth, urbanization, legal homogenization, mass democracy, nationalism, and concentration of power in the hands of the state — as well as, lately, in those of supranational bodies. A steeply increasing population has to an unheard-of extent been concentrated in urban communities where people have adapted themselves, voluntarily or not, to the disciplined and calculated lifestyle required by industrial production and which the new social elite, the bourgeoisie, made into a central element in the formation of ideals. A presupposition as well as a consequence of the migration to the cities was the elimination of differences of legal status between social groups: a breakdown of privileges and a removal of compulsory links to special interests.

Something similar can be said of the diffusion of political rights to ever wider circles and the emergence of interest parties and mass movements. Nor is it possible to explain the growing influence of nationalism without reference to the dissolution of traditional rural structures. Last but not least, the ever expanding regulation of ever more numerous areas of life by the national state and by statelike bodies has been a direct consequence of the economic changes while at the same time representing an exploitation of the vacuum created by those changes. To that must be added that the abolition of ancient differences of status and the breakdown of traditional institutions have resulted in a situation where the state and the citizen confront each other without, or with far fewer, intermediaries.

Finally, if looked at from the perspective of culture, the new civilization is characterized by the diffusion of elementary formal culture to entire populations and an accompanying tendency toward isolation of creative individuals from the everyday concerns of the ruling elite and the rest of the people. Correspondingly the humanities as well as the sciences have been split up in ever more specialized disciplines, and the humanities have attempted to apply the methods of the successful natural sciences and the principles of partition of work known from industrial production. Science, or the thing commonly understood by that word, gained unprecedented prestige as provider of exclusive explanation of the world and of human existence, on a par with quasi-scientific and quasi-religious ideologies such as nationalism and socialism. It is significant that those two ideologies, and their compounds, figure side by side with Christianity, the old monopolistic religion, on a world market of worldviews. This can, however, only be stated with the proviso that a new monopoly, that of a new paganism, has been periodically established in several places — reducing Christianity to the new, although also old, role of a religion of the oppressed.

All those tendencies — economic, political, and cultural — are parts of an interplay where the tendencies presuppose each other. Modern European industry and science are mutually dependent, and so are the legal equalization and the bureaucratically governed national state. The same is the case with universal culture, urbanization, and suffrage, and with political democracy, ideological pluralism, and mobility of the workforce. And all those individual tendencies as well as their interplay are markedly different from what we have found to be typically old European — while at the same time much of the new can be seen to be embryonically present in past ideas and practices.

It is no concern of ours — in a context of the history of Christianity — to go into more detail concerning how the peoples of Europe moved from the old situation to the new. But it is useful to reflect on the role played by Christianity in that process.

The modern European industrial economy has many other roots than the Christian ones. But it could hardly have come into being without the Christian tradition of renouncing the impulses of the "flesh" by an ascetic discipline and a rational planning of life with a defined purpose, carried through on the basis of time schemes and universally valid sets of rules. In other words, it is unthinkable without monasticism. It is not thinkable, either, without Christian insistence on a critique of tradition based on a concept of past and future perfection. And it would not exist at all without the natural sciences, which can only be understood in the light of the Jewish and Christian assertion about God, in relation to whom everything else, all individual phenomena, is both "accidental" and "regular" — governed by laws.

Modern European politics and government must likewise be understood against the background of Christian tradition in its old European shape. That becomes clear, for instance, by reflecting on one of the underlying assertions of European political life — one considerably less trivial than appears at first glance — namely, that human society, and in the last resort humanity, is a coherent entity, reaching out beyond the small local communities; and that this universal whole has a historical dimension, documented and handed down in written texts. The concepts of church, people of God, and sacred history belong among the basic presuppositions of the modern state, and the same goes for the ideas about a divinely sanctioned, universally valid system of laws and about a hierarchy of similarly sanctioned officials, bound by rules, entrusted with the task of communicating knowledge and welfare, and endowed with authority from above to judge and to command without respect of persons. And yet another example is the connection between the popular and democratic movements of the nineteenth century and the Christian "appeal to the rationality of the common person." That connection is, of course, particularly clear where that appeal is bound up with the idea of a Christian's relationship to God being independent of clerical intervention. It is, at any rate, a proven fact that democratic movements could begin as Christian lay uprisings against a clerical tutelage that was at one and the same time a religious, a social, and a cultural one.

Finally, behind vital elements in modern European intellectual and spiritual culture lies, among other things, the Christian idea of the individual person's salvation as the absolute and supreme purpose of earthly life, one that must not be sacrificed for any other. But it is evident that Christian critique of traditions and the educational systems of the churches are among the presuppositions too. To that must be added the concept, cultivated by the churches, of a separate intellectual profession. The old European university clerk who disputed and taught independently of social origin and priestly functions is one of the direct ancestors of the modern European intellectual. Last, not least, each and every modern European ideology of progress — or of revolution — is stamped with the mark of the religion and the church against which they have raised their protest.

Obviously, such Christian contributions to characteristic features of modernity testify to one kind of shaping presence of Christianity in modern Europe and North America. But it is a characteristic of the new situation that Christianity has no longer been present in the same way and to the same extent as before. During the last couple of centuries it has lost its function as common and sole "basic myth" of society and culture. And the church has lost its function as bearer, communicator, and social expression of such a "myth."

That state of affairs is one of the two poles toward which our consideration of modern European and North American Christianity has to be orientated. None of the changes in the character of Christian faith and practice, as compared to earlier times, can be understood without keeping the phenomenon of secularization in mind: the loosening of social and cultural life from Christian purposes and ecclesiastical regulation. That is true of Christianity as a matter of individual piety and of theology, and also when it is considered as a collective and institutional quantity.

The other pole consists in the fundamental fact that traditions, institutions, and styles of thought inherited from old European Christianity are present as living ingredients of the modern incarnation, both in its individual and its collective aspects. The Christian religion in nineteenth- and twentieth-century Europe and North America poses and answers many of the old questions in a new way because of the shifting of accents occasioned by the new cultural context. And because of changes in the way the world runs, it poses questions that have not been posed before. But at the same time, it is a salient fact that the old questions are being posed and answered in ways which would be recognized as their own by sixteenth-, thirteenth-, and fourth-century Christians respectively. In a religion that is historical in all senses of that word, nothing really dies, and everything new has to come to terms with the old that never dies.

That has never come about without conflicts and internal contradictions, and least of all in the age of industrialization, revolutions, and global wars — an age in which the framework of civilization has been more profoundly shaken and changed than in any earlier period.

69. The church in Temple Square in Helsinki, Finland, built into the rock by the architects Timo and Tuomo Suomalainen, 1969.

70. Interior view of the Temple church, where raw rock walls, concrete structures, and glass roof make for a remarkable unity.

2. The Ways of Secularization

Perhaps the most important contribution of Christianity to the birth of the modern world is secularization itself, in that one of its presuppositions is to be found in Christian assertions about creation and incarnation and in the various ways in which those tenets have been interpreted. Using a pointed expression, one could say that secularization came about *both* because Christianity talked about man as a free creature whose shape was assumed by God himself, *and* because the church did not dare take its own statements about that free creature seriously, for fear of what would become of "the holy," "the things of the spirit," if they were in earnest allowed to "become flesh."

That is, however, only one very general point about the causes lying behind the emancipation of social and cultural life from ecclesiastical tutelage. More directly important was the steadily growing differentiation and professionalization of European life, which, as we have seen, often enough happened on distinctly Christian premises. Bureaucrats, merchants, teachers, scholars, and artists might be — and perhaps mostly were — believers, but they were also professionals with an insight into the rules governing their specialties; with professional pride; and, not least, with a material interest in the independence of their various fields of endeavor. Another highly important factor is the general tendency toward rationalization, which, as we know, had one of its points of origin in the claim made by the Christian religion itself: it was entrusted with a rationally accessible explanation of the world and of history as well as a set of rationally coherent rules of conduct. Under the name of the "Enlightenment," this tendency made itself more broadly felt in the course of the eighteenth century than in any previous era.

In its capacity as a conscious and articulate movement, the process of secularization ran along two lines: a political and institutional one, and a cultural one. For the first line, the decisive breakthrough occurred in the period of the American and French Revolutions late in the eighteenth century when, almost simultaneously, the demand for full separation of church and state was raised and met. In America this meant that the state declared itself confessionally — though not religiously — neutral. It proclaimed liberty of worship as one of the "rights of man," and defined its own purpose as upholding and protecting humankind's natural striving for life, freedom, and happiness. The Americans, in other words, went considerably further than the elector of Brandenburg (p. 225). The Parisian revolutionaries, however, went further yet. There the movement for casting off ecclesiastical shackles became a movement for total and ruthless extermination of Christianity and its churches in the name of revolutionary humanism, as well as for replacing Catholic church services with the state's cultic celebration of itself under various guises. State-organized rites for weddings and funerals, as well as exclusively secular and state-controlled forms of education, were established; recalcitrant Catholic clergy were mercilessly persecuted; church lands and buildings were confiscated and desecrated; and the consecrated oil for royal unction was thrown into the gutter. In short, a thousand years of Christian nationhood were thrown overboard in the name of a rational human nature that stood in no need of a history, and in the name of an ideal image of the pre-Christian Roman republic — commonly regarded as the quintessential bearer of pure and severe civil virtues.

Even though this campaign of de-Christianization — set in motion by a fanatical minority — was quickly allowed to peter out, it was nevertheless an event of great import. More than any other single event did it contribute to the waning of the aura of awe-inspiring inviolability that had hitherto surrounded the Catholic Church. And more than that. Like the persecutions of pagan antiquity, it served as a reminder that Christianity was a matter of personal conviction and, under given circumstances, personal risk. It contributed also to a setting up of deep and long-lasting divisions in the French nation, and not least, it made clear to cooler-headed statesmen everywhere that even a religiously indifferent state, which in principle regarded religion as an exclusively private concern, would in the long run be unable to avoid coming to terms with Christianity and churches. Without such an arrangement — including, be it noted, an amount of government control over church affairs — there was an imminent risk of encouraging forces that were essentially incalculable and potentially dangerous to the state. That, clearly, was the rationale behind the church policy of Napoléon Bonaparte, the French military dictator (1799-1815); but the reasoning of liberal and social democratic leaders of later periods was not much different from his. A totally different situation did not outline itself until the twentieth-century totalitarian regimes once again put the extermination of Christianity on the order of the day — naturally enough, considering that those regimes did not acknowledge the concept of private life at all. There nothing was allowed to remain outside the reach of state ideology.

Within the main current of the secularizing process, it was, on the contrary, emphatically asserted that the competence of the state does *not* reach beyond common and public affairs into the sphere where the individual makes up, or declines to make up, his mind about God and eternity.

71. The totalitarian powers of the twentieth century appropriated elements of the Christian tradition in their attempt to shape their subjects' attitudes. One instance is the Soviet cult of Lenin, which was carried out under the catchword "Lenin lives" and expressed itself in — among other things — pilgrimages to the Founder's embalmed corpse in the mausoleum in Red Square in Moscow. The photo shows a queue of waiting pilgrims. The mausoleum lies in front of the Kremlin wall to the right.

Dearly bought experiences from religious wars, heresy trials, and coercion of ideas had inspired a number of sixteenth- to eighteenth-century thinkers to raise the demand for self-limitation of the state. Now that demand came close to becoming realized, but not, however, without another problem emerging and demanding to be solved. It arose out of the practical experience that the matter of "eternity," the question about ultimate meaning and purpose, has proved impossible to banish from political life. The solution presented by the doctrines and practices of Lenin and of Hitler had no power of attraction where people were allowed to choose. It is, by the way, certainly the case that the early critics of old European religious coercion would have stared incredulously at the sight of the possibilities of terror, technical and otherwise, at the disposal of a modern to-

2. The Ways of Secularization

talitarian ideology that has cut itself free from the inherent self-questioning of Christianity, its power-critical tradition, and its notions of human dignity. Anyhow, as is evident from recent discussions of the meaning of social life, universally convincing solutions have been — to put it mildly — scarce on the ground.

Be that as it may. At any rate, politico-institutional secularization went from one triumph to another, although at different speeds and with many local and regional variations, during the later nineteenth and the twentieth centuries. Among its forms of expression were the introduction of "civil" rites of passage such as weddings, partial removal of legislative control of public and private morality, abolition of blasphemy trials and compulsory holidays, and above all, de-confessionalization of public education. In the last-named area the stage was set for the most dramatic collisions between the old and the new — and for more than a few compromise solutions.

None of those social and political processes are, however, fully understandable without insight into the cultural and spiritual aspects of secularization, a process that was initiated by the pan-European "Enlightenment" movement of the eighteenth century. What philosophers, scholars, and artists of that period did and thought in the way of a critical reckoning with old European ways of thought and feeling came to stand in a lively mutual relationship with the initiatives taken by liberal and social democratic statesmen and administrators in their confrontation with old European institutions.

One of the most important expressions of the cultural secularization movement is presented by the natural sciences, not only because of their practical and technical implications and consequences, but also because many Europeans found that science could provide an alternative explanation of the world and of human existence, or, at any rate, rich material for criticism of the Christian explanation. Once when Laplace, the French physicist and astronomer, was asked by Napoléon what became of God in his science, he answered, "Your Majesty, I had no need of that hypothesis." Such was his way of lending words to a situation that had become common to all practitioners of the sciences of nature, be they Christian believers or not. When all was said and done, it was a basic rule of the scientific game that one had to make do without "that hypothesis." That meant, also, that the literally understood Bible lost its position as arbiter of scientific research and theorizing, irrespective of the unease felt by personally believing scientists. The geological discoveries concerning the age of the earth were among the earliest to make the problem clear to wider circles of people, but a much stronger impression was made by Darwin's theories about the descent of man from the animal world and about "natural selection" and "survival of the fittest."

Those discoveries and theories acquired additional weight because, at the same time, the traditional Christian view of history as an intelligibly coherent process, visibly governed by the Creator and reliably documented in the Bible, was subjected to more or less destructive criticism by the disciplines of political and religious history as well as archaeology. Not only did those disciplines widen the perspective as to time and space. They made relative what had till then been absolute: the sacred history of Israel and of the church, the process whose coherence and intelligibility rested on divinely sanctioned prophecy about coming things and interpretation of past things.

Most important of all was the closer application of critical methods to the Bible itself, the demonstration of its very human genesis and of the links connecting the Holy Book to its profane surroundings.

It can be said that the threat such tendencies presented was one against traditional ways of thinking about Christianity, more than against

72. "God with Us": German military belt buckles from the Second Reich, the Weimar Republic, and the Nazi state respectively.

that religion itself. As a consequence, the sciences of nature, and especially of history and religion, became discussion partners of Christian thought, with consequences to be considered later on.

The land lies somewhat differently as far as one further phenomenon

73. This drawing was made by a German priest who was sent to prison for having taken part in the resistance against the church policy of the Nazi regime. Through the bars he visualizes his Bavarian parish, and underneath he has quoted the biblical passage: "The word of God is not bound."

of secularization is concerned: the all-out war waged on Christianity by some nineteenth-century intellectuals. There were of course precedents for such an attitude. But its main interest derives from its radicalism — a telling testimony to changes of atmosphere — and its inner relatedness to Christianity itself. The great atheists of the nineteenth century, Feuerbach, Marx, and Nietzsche, and their somewhat lesser twentieth-century successors, Freud, Sartre, et al., were uncompromising in their rejection of Christianity. But they were also deeply influenced by what they rejected, and resembled the heretics of earlier times in a good many ways. That is perhaps most conspicuous with Marx, whose ideas of alienation, of the liberation of the oppressed and their acquisition of full humanity, and of the march of history toward a final revolution and revelation of all things are not without a kind of subterranean connection with Christian thinking about original purity, fall into sin, and restoration of the fallen. That is a matter for the historian of Christianity to ponder, as is the influence exerted by simplified editions of those thinkers' ideas on political movements and on parts of public opinion.

But by saying that, we have touched upon an aspect of secularization that was articulated neither as an institutional nor as an intellectual concern. In other words, it was a gradual mass de-Christianization, which, while being partially conditioned by what has been considered above, was primarily due to industrialization, to the population explosion, and to the mass migration into the cities and across the Atlantic. One result of those processes was the isolation of multitudes of people from Christian influence in the traditional sense of that word. There were no churches and no ministers available to them, and the new form of working life they were constrained to lead isolated them quite effectively from most of the contact that the churches had previously managed to establish.

To that must be added something that naturally had much to do with industry and technology, and with a gradually rising standard of living, namely, the growing conviction among Europeans and North Americans that the world was material for increasingly successful human elaboration and shaping, and that the forces of nature could be domesticated; in short, that the natural surroundings were delivered to the discretion of mankind, and not the other way round. The forms assumed by Christianity in old Europe had to a large extent been conditioned by the experience of being at the pleasure of the "powers." It could not fail to have religious consequences that the powers were now — for a time — regarded as passively subject to man.

3. Modern European and American Christianity

a. Churches, Congregations, and People

Nothing testifies better to the survival of old Europe in the new era than the part played in theory and practice by the idea of an all-encompassing church of men and women who have been baptized as infants. That idea, and its institutional expressions, was more severely criticized than ever before. To a large extent the churches went in other directions from the "spirit of the times," and their powerlessness before some of the most burning problems of the age was painfully evident in the eyes of friend and foe. Nevertheless, the idea and reality of such a church refused to die, and did not die. Why was that?

Part of an explanation can be found in the terror struck into many Europeans by the French Revolution, in the fear of desperate action by the industrial proletariat, as well as in a general unease at the rapid social changes that swept away many time-honored institutions and customs.

But there were other causes too. Quite apart from the fact that nothing ever disappears completely in a historic religion, it was natural for the traditional concept of a church to survive as long as men and women in Europe understood the restoration of the "courage to be" as something that had to come from outside, independently of human powers. Only when this motivation is taken into account are the waves of church-orientated religiosity of the period anything like fully understandable.

But those movements were highly different from each other, and they tended also to be somewhat different from what had been known before. That can be demonstrated by two examples. One is Grundtvigian church piety in Denmark. That movement is akin to quite a few reform movements in other parts of Europe, but it has its own distinctive character and is more instructive than similar tendencies by its way of uniting something old and something new. In full accordance with tradition, it rests on the assertion that Christian faith and life stand and fall with God's sovereign action in his people, manifesting itself most clearly in baptism and the Lord's Supper. The creed, which is recited in the context of worship, is, as N. F. S. Grundtvig (1783-1872) put it, "a word that creates what it says"; one of the things created by that word is a community that is independent of human will and power. In such ideas, old European basic premises are in evidence. But the ideas are also new ones, in that they are churchly without being in the least clericalist. Grundtvig regarded government by priests and experts (the "paper pope") as a betrayal of the very

74. Danish nineteenth-century comment on lay preaching: "Sophie tries to convert some ministers to Christianity." Drawing by Fritz Jürgensen.

idea of a church wanting to proclaim God's deeds among the people. He was closer to Luther in that respect than Lutherans had been for three hundred years. At the same time, the strain of ideas inherited by old European Christianity from the first centuries of the church finds, with Grundtvig, a much clearer expression than the political and legalistic features in European tradition had allowed. This way of thinking about the church is also open to cultural life in another sense than before, owing to Grundtvig's experiences with history, poetry, and folklife, and to the conclusion he had drawn from those experiences: "First a human being, then a Christian!" Here, too, an originally Lutheran insight is being renewed, even though combined with a kind of liberal democratic optimism of progress that was utterly foreign to Luther.

The other example is the Roman Catholic Church. About that church, too, it can be said that, in spite of its strong links with the past, its modern incarnation differs in two significant respects from the old form of churchly Christianity. One difference is the sensational growth of papal ideology and of central Roman control during the nineteenth century, culminating in the dogma, adopted at the First Vatican Council (1869-70), of papal infallibility. When the pope, thus goes the dogma, pronounces officially on behalf of the whole church in matters of faith and morals, then he is endowed with the infallibility promised to the church by Christ himself, and he is thus endowed independently of the church's assent. This decree, which can never be abolished or modified and which has presented a severe test for the interpretative skills of Catholic scholars, is theologically significant, both on account of the links connecting the dogma with the past and because of its points of difference from earlier thinking.

But the dogma is even more important as a symptom of deep-reaching changes in the situation of the Roman Church after the French Revolution. In a general sense the experiences of Catholics in the wake of that upheaval sharpened the need for an indisputable authority. But above all, the Revolution and the Napoleonic Wars had destroyed most of the established institutions that had for centuries prevented the theoretically asserted papal monarchy from being fully implemented. The "Most Christian" French kings had disappeared, and with them the institutes and customs of a truly national church. The old French episcopate — recruited from the ranks of a proud and self-confident aristocratic caste, and disinclined to "fetch water from the Tiber when there is a fire on in Paris" — was gone too; something similar can be observed wherever the troubled years had led to a weakening of age-old safeguards of local and national independence. In this situation the "Roman idea" grew immeasurably more attractive in ever wider circles, not least because the lower clergy considered it in their interest to seek a direct connection with the Roman see and began agitating for the Roman cause in their congregations. Such tendencies were ably exploited by the Curia and, not least, by a revived and extremely active Jesuit Order; and they were deepened by intensive cultivation of old and new pious practices close to the hearts of the laity, such as a rich variety of Marian devotions and the cult of the Sacred Heart of Jesus. New technical means of communication were used with considerable success: devotional pictures were mass produced; multitudes of people were rapidly transported to the places of pilgrimage; and well-planned newspaper campaigns were conducted against recalcitrants. Under such conditions, bishops and theologians of dissenting views were powerless. Deprived as they were of a foothold in traditional arrangements, dependent on financial support after the loss of church lands, and increasingly ex-

posed to pressure from below as well as from above, they had no chance of stemming the tide, let alone turning it. To a previously unheard-of extent, the Roman Curia realized its pretension to total control of faith and life, defiantly resisting the claims of "modernity" but — ironically enough — deftly exploiting the conditions and methods created by it. The centralizing process would have been unthinkable without distinctive traits of the age, such as the popular upsurge of piety, the cutting of ancient roots, and the industrial standardization of the forms of life.

But the cost at which unity and efficiency were bought was high enough to trouble many Catholics. The "new" church that provided a meaning and a spiritual home to millions of perplexed women and men did it at the price of isolating itself from the longing for liberty and the critical questioning that were *also* among the signs of the times. Catholics who dared to engage with such aspects of the modern world were suppressed without mercy and with scant discrimination as to means. As a natural result of all this, the Roman Church's reputation in the eyes of progressive opinion, that of being a quintessentially reactionary and obscurantist body, became consolidated.

This is the background against which the other event that gave modern Catholicism a distinct appearance must be seen. That was the reform movement that culminated in the decrees of the Second Vatican Council. This meeting, held from 1962 to 1965 on the initiative of Pope John XXIII (1958-63), not only carried out such far-reaching changes as the introduction of vernacular languages in the liturgy and acknowledgment of the partial validity of other Christian communities, but tried to modify the centralized and authoritarian structures of the church by establishing a consultative synod of bishops. Most importantly, the view the council formulated of the nature and tasks of the church was much more "religious" and much less "juridical" than it had been for several centuries. Ideas inspired by the Bible and the ancient church about the church as a dynamic and outreaching community to whose life all members contribute actively, and not as a "state," found so forceful an official expression that it sur-

75. Pope Pius IX's proclamation in 1854 of Mary's "immaculate conception" — that is, her freedom from original sin — was one of the epochal events in nineteenth-century Roman Catholicism. It is celebrated on this mosaic in Pius's chapel in St. Peter's, Rome. To the left is the author of Revelation, whose "woman clothed with the sun, and the moon under her feet" (shown standing in the center) was identified as Mary. To the right, the pope is shown kneeling with the dogma document in his hands.

prised the entire Christian world. It was certainly a situation with a good many ironical overtones, apt to resound in the ears of theologians who had propagated such ideas long before the leadership began adopting them and who had paid for their outspokenness with career stoppage, banishment to distant places, and ban on publication. Another kind of historical irony can perhaps be found by pondering the difficulties run into by the reforms after the council, but they are far from ready for closer historical analysis.

The same is true of the reform council itself and of its prehistory. Much must have happened beneath the surface that cannot yet be ascertained. But what is in fact known suffices to tell us something important about the scope and range of modern Catholic Christianity, as well as about its distinct character in comparison with its old European predecessor.

We have acquainted ourselves with the continuing vitality of the "church type" of Christian association under the conditions of modernity. But it is nevertheless a fact that the other collective forms — the "gathered church," the "core congregation," the specialized society, the sect — have taken up considerably more space in the modern European and American landscape than they did in old Europe, and that the Protestant church, in much of what it has done in this period, has presented itself less as a church in the inherited sense of the word than as an association of like-minded people.

Such forms were, now as before, results of and vehicles for one or the other variety of "internal mission." They began as the conversion of baptized Christians to what they regarded as a "new" life, renouncing the "world." That did not necessarily lead to a breaking of relations with the church that had adopted them as infants — that church did indeed itself aim at performing "internal mission" and serving a "new" life by its preaching and sacraments. But breaking with the church — or, what amounted to the same thing, denying its fully Christian character — was nevertheless bound to appear as the obvious thing to do whenever a man or a woman drew a line between "Christianity" and "true Christianity."

Such features did not constitute the distinctive character of these forms of modern European Christianity as compared to similar phenomena in the old world. The new is to be sought elsewhere.

76. One of the things emphasized by the popular Pope John XXIII in his work of reform was the pope's position as bishop of Rome, responsible for the care of its inhabitants' souls. The photo shows him on a visit to the inmates of the "Queen of Heaven" prison in Rome.

It drew its origin from the situation to which the movement for "internal mission" now had to react. The dissolution of rural society and the migration to the cities and across the ocean resulted, in a few generations, in a wide-reaching transformation of the traditional relationship between the Christian religion and the people — a relationship that it had hitherto been the task of the churches to maintain. A chasm of "alienation" was opened, more gapingly obvious than ever before. That was bound to have consequences for every conceivable attempt at coping with the missionary task, whether one wanted to reintegrate the alienated into the old churchly forms or create congregations of "real" Christians.

One of those consequences is implied in the famous saying of John Wesley (1703-91), the founder of Methodism: "My parish is the whole world." A Christian ministry among those who had been torn loose from old contexts and frameworks could not allow itself to be bound by those frameworks, so much the less as one had to reckon with sluggish or hostile reactions from the normal clergy. Itinerant preachers who were able to cover great distances and gather large numbers of people at open-air meetings became the bearers of the "awakening" message, not only in Methodism but in many other confessions.

Other consequences of the new situation were inter-Protestant cooperation in the diffusion of Bibles and disregard of specific denominational traditions in the interest of practical efficiency. What the confused masses were to hear was one thing only, the "thing that is needful": that Christ had died and risen for each one of them and would let him or her share his life. That was to be said loud and clear and must lead to a clear decision — Wesley was able to date his own conversion accurately to the minute — and to a form of conducting one's life that could make clear to everyone that the world, the flesh, and the devil had been renounced and the law of God made manifest. The "law" was equivalent with the specific directions of the Bible about which activities to pursue and which to shun. The "holy people" were to be known by their keeping away from games, drink, and dance, and their observation of the "Sabbath" by public worship and private prayer and devotional reading.

This basic substance of revival piety and conversion practice could express itself in many ways in different European and American movements: stricter or looser definition of the law; more or less passionate dwelling on eternal punishment; more or less interest in calculating the time of Christ's second coming; variations of preaching and meeting techniques; practice or nonpractice of ecstatic and spectacular manifestations such as speaking in tongues, healings, etc. No less variegated a picture could be drawn of the organizational structures resulting from the spread of the message: centrally governed mass movements; small independent groups, connected or not to a church; the pioneer family, assembled around its house Bible in the wilderness; and so forth. What was important was the elementary fact that new human communities came into being in a situation where historical or natural-grown bands had been cut and replaced by the impersonal discipline of the industrial workplace. Proletarianized laborers who were followed into the cities by the Methodist movement were given a foothold that — in spite of, or by reason of, cultural narrowness, robust moral discipline, and rigorous mutual supervision — could make all the difference between a human and an inhuman life. In such firmly knit groups of awakened people lies one of the points of

77. Salvationists on the march. The Salvation Army took its final form as a militarily organized battle unit against spiritual and material misery and want "in darkest England" in 1878. Its dauntless drive and resolute use of modern propaganda techniques made it into a sort of Protestant counterpart to the Jesuit order.

origin of the industrial workers' movement for social and political self-help.

The case is not unique. The powers of independent organizational initiative, the Bible-based critique of authorities, and the purposeful planning of conduct characteristic of revivalism could not fail to have effects outside the field of religion. The worldview and lifestyle of awakened factory owners — the awakening was more than an underclass phenomenon — as well as of awakened workers, artisans, and country folk gave rise to economic and political consequences, similar to those of the Cistercian movement 700 years earlier. Christian asceticism and industrial efficiency could form interesting combinations, and the same goes for hostility against established churches and resistance to public authorities and social superiors. Such lines of connection belong to the most disputed themes in recent research into nineteenth-century popular movements — where, by the way, much remains to be clarified, beyond the basic fact that the awakenings can be called neither "purely religious" nor "disguised social protest."

Another established fact concerning the relations to the new civilizational context is that neither "traditional" nor "modern" forms of mission succeeded in turning the current and overcoming the impact of "de-Christianization." The movements gained access to parts of the people; and the ambulance services rendered by churches and Christian societies toward those who had suffered most severely from industrialization — the sick, the hungry, and the abandoned — were enormous, and much greater than those of any other organs of assistance. But the hoped-for "re-Christianization" of the masses did not materialize. In the new working class as well as in other social groups, Christianity was and remained one possibility among many. The traditional role as the communal "myth" and frame of reference was gone.

The needs and aspirations, the ideas and emotions that are ingredients in the tense relationship between "church type" and "sect type" or "gathered church," belong to the "perpetual companions" of Christian history. And the result of Christian association building in each respective period has always reflected both types of ideas and practices as well as the constraints of the wider social context. A sect is never without similarities to a church, and vice versa; and both types have to come to terms with their surroundings.

Examples of such complex and more or less opaque combinations could be taken from almost everywhere. An illuminating one is the Danish national church. It is a church of men and women baptized as infants. It is built on the premise that salvation comes "from outside," known and experienced through Scripture, sacraments, and hymns. And it operates, furthermore, on the more or less conscious assumption that being Danish — imbued with Danish history and language — and being a church member according to Lutheran confession of the "common faith" are largely overlapping things. One of the expressions of that is the democratic organization of the church. But at the same time, the national church serves as framework for the "Christianity of awakening"; it is a "civil arrangement," an umbrella organization providing room for a number of special interests and for widely differing notions of "true Christianity." It is an opaque, if not downright turbid, situation, in accordance with the inherent tensions of a two-thousand-year-long history. It is admirably reflected in the church's hymnbook of 1953, a medley or — unkindly spoken — a jumble of all the things that can neither die nor agree on anything except the need to relate to Jesus of Nazareth and to the question of the meaning of his person and work.

That question also occupies the pastor or priest in his sermon. And it has — in a special way, conditioned by the times — been a central one for nineteenth- and twentieth-century theology.

b. Christian Thought Confronted by Modernity

The modern European and North American way of thinking, feeling, and acting presented a challenge not only to the churches as institutions but to Christian thought. That perhaps becomes clear in a specially palpable manner when the words "thinking, feeling, and acting" are taken in their wider and looser sense, remembering that modernity is not only a matter of profoundly meditated and highly articulate attitudes, arguments, and actions, but is also an atmosphere and a bundle of views that, while being anything but deeply pondered, determine what may or must pass for reflection. An example: when the problem of God is broached, the question that comes first to mind is no longer that of his disposition toward his creatures, but that of his existence and plausibility. Trivial though that fact is, it is historically important. Something similar can be said about another automatically accepted presupposition: that the validity of a worldview depends on its power of moral impact and its contribution to material well-being and happiness, individual or collective. If something else is asserted, then the burden of proof rests on the person who asserts it. A third example: not uncommonly the point of departure for any discussion of ideas other than one's own is the claim that such ideas are determined by finan-

78. Bertel Thorvaldsen's statue of Christ (1839) in the cathedral of Copenhagen, Denmark, represents Christ risen from the dead. It has often been interpreted to depict the Gospel words, "Come unto me, all ye that labor and are heavily laden, and I will give you rest." Reproductions of it were put up in many Danish homes, and it may be perceived as communicating one of the typical nineteenth-century understandings of Christianity. In the following century, this statue gave Karl Barth occasion to remark that the Antichrist might well be imagined to look like this when he came trying to lead humankind to perdition. (Courtesy of the Danish National Art Library, Copenhagen.)

cial or political interests, or by forgotten childhood experiences. He who says they are not must prove it. A difficult task — no less difficult than the old European one of having to prove that one was not directly inspired by the devil. Fourthly, the nonhuman environment exists for being ever more intensively exploited. And finally, death is an unsuitable topic for civilized conversation; and the good death is a sudden one.

A description like the above is, of course, as insufficient as it is irreverent. Its purpose is to point out that the civilization of modernity resembles its predecessors by containing elements of the more or less indisputably agreed. Such modern "matters of course" play a part that can be compared to that played by similar ones in the old Mediterranean world (pp. 91-92). Now, as then, they help draw up the horizons of thought, Christian as well as non-Christian. And just like then, the attempts at reflecting on those presuppositions lead to many different kinds of reorientations of Christian thought, spanning a scale from outright surrender to the "spirit of the times" to a refusal to have anything at all to do with it.

Another lesson to be drawn from the analogy with the Mediterranean past is that the Christian religion now as well as then provides its environment with fewer "matters of course" than it receives from it. In old Europe, as we know, the case was quite the reverse.

Keeping those considerations in mind is useful when turning, as we do now, to the ways Christian thought, and more specifically theology, reacted to the more articulate attitudes of modernity concerning nature, society, and history. In the beginning the problem raised by the new sciences of nature provided a popular occasion of scandal whenever a heavy-handed use of the Bible as scientific textbook ran into confrontation with discoveries that were obviously incompatible with the biblical information. But then the conflict was comparatively quickly defused, for two reasons. One was the self-limitation of the natural sciences. Scientists did not as a rule consider their task to be explaining everything and proving or disproving the "hypothesis" of God, but gathering and ordering data concerning a given subject, formulating theories on that basis, and testing the theories on fresh data. "Solution of the world riddles" was no purpose of theirs. The German biologist who wrote a book with that title was clearly outstepping his brief. The other reason was the deepened acknowledgment by theologians of the fact that the validity of the Bible as an interpretation of human existence was independent of its being scientifically accurate. It was certainly regarded as a problem when it was not, but the problem was, after all, an old one, which experience had proved it possible to live with.

But it is worth noting that there was another problem lurking behind the encounter with natural science, one that was important for both sides. It sprang from the loss of the ancient and old European concept of an animated order of the universe, as expressed in the idea of the hierarchy of things — the "great chain of being" — and that of the concordance between macrocosm and microcosm. In theology that meant that the problem of the relations between the Creator and the world of nature became more difficult than before, and that many theologians became reluctant to handle it and preferred to entrench themselves inside the "religious" confines, the place of "God and the soul." That development in theology may have been one of the conditions producing the modern European view of nature as an object of exploitation, without soul and without rights.

The social thinking of modern Christianity is one that relates to the challenges of industrialization, secularization, and totalitarianism. Its most salient feature is perhaps represented by the spokesmen for more or less modified old European ideas. One variant of this attitude was expressed in the claim of some French postrevolutionary writers, that "church" and "state" were words for two aspects of one Christendom. Another was the combination by German Lutherans of two traditional concepts: that of the "Christian state" and that of the two "kingdoms" of law and gospel, respectively. That meant, on the one hand, that the problems of society were regarded as the prerogative of the patriarchally ruling, God-fearing prince and his ministers, while, on the other hand, the task of the church was considered to be the salvation of souls exclusively, so that it must refrain from meddling with the exercise of political and economic power.

Such ideas were not only traditional, they were prisoners of tradition. That becomes clear by the fact that the democratic way of understanding the origin and exercise of political power remained without influence on the German Lutherans' notions of secular government. They had taken over and retained Luther's fruitful distinction between the domain of grace and that of power, his passionate refusal to let the message of grace be falsified by being mixed up with political and moral coercion, but they had used it in such a way that it became largely irrelevant in the modern world. In other words, a Christian wanting to act politically would find the

79. Worship in the Women's Penitentiary in Copenhagen, as shown in a popular periodical in 1893. The paper comments: "Whatever one may think of the cell-system — with the purpose of churchgoing does it agree so perfectly that it most certainly ought to be introduced into the free life. Then, churchgoers would be undistracted by comings and goings, they would have no occasion to study each other's attire or similar profane objects, no possibility of controlling each other's devotion — one could be alone with oneself." It is worth noticing that the altar table is not prepared for the sacrament.

theory useless. This combination of "correct" theology and "reactionary" politics proved to be a serious obstacle to the formation of a productive relationship between official Lutheranism and democratic ways of conducting public life. And it proved less than helpful when German Protestantism found itself confronted with Nazism.

In the Roman Church things developed somewhat differently. Pope Leo XIII (1878-1903) tried, in his encyclical *Rerum Novarum* of 1891, to sketch out a way of grappling with some of the most pressing problems of industrial life. He was no radical — the framework of his propositions was traditional paternalism — but the document was nonetheless important by its explicit acknowledgment of the right of industrial workers to organize, and by its protest against the way unrestrained capitalism abused the workforce. Its main importance, however, derived from its indirect encouragement of efforts like those of progressive Catholics in France and elsewhere to reconcile church and workers.

When all is said and done, such private attempts at practical reform were what counted most in the long run. "Christian Socialism," "Social Gospel," "Christian Democracy," and similar movements certainly did not succeed in presenting a viable alternative to the workers' own movements for social reform, but they contributed — together with the much more influential relief work of Christian associations — to mitigate the tensions and prepare the ground for the European welfare state. The ideas behind that twentieth-century phenomenon can be identified neither with Christianity, nor with old European paternalism, nor with socialism or liberalism; but it owes something to all those traditions. It is, by the way, possible to discern an interesting consequence of a modern trend in the fact that the ideas of Paul, of Augustine, and of Luther have now been given a larger breathing space than before. That is so because the thing all those thinkers had rejected: political action "in God's name," has grown to be a less obvious temptation than it was in old Europe.

Finally, the challenge of history. This challenge gave Christian thought the most to be concerned about and influenced its modern form and direction most profoundly. Christianity was based on the claim that one single event in time and space was of uniquely decisive importance for the relation of the individual and of humanity to the ultimate meaning of everything. And as traditionally understood, it was based on the further claim that that event was linked to other unique events in a demonstrably coherent history of a special kind: the history of creation and fall, of conservation and restoration.

Those claims could be contested philosophically, with arguments that were given a classic formulation in the words of Lessing, the German thinker of the eighteenth century: "Eternal truths of reason cannot be proved by accidental truths of history." It is, by the way, worth noting that the problem had occupied theologians as early as Origen and Augustine.

But the attack could come from another direction also: from the historical sciences, which were now constructing a picture of the past on quite different premises — a picture that incorporated the basic writings of Christianity as well as its subsequent history. That attempt was not without precedent either. Humanists and reformers in the fifteenth and sixteenth centuries had used source criticism as an instrument of church criticism; and by a subtle turning around of traditional perspectives a German Pietist, Gottfried Arnold (d. 1714), had made the history of heterodox and heretics appear as the real and authentic history of Christianity. But contrary to such initiatives, which had, as a rule, aimed at replacing one orthodoxy with another, the modern research into historical sources resulted in making *all* orthodoxies relative. That state of affairs was expressed with admirable clarity by the Protestant theologian and philosopher of culture Ernst Troeltsch (1865-1923) when he pointed out that the axioms governing historical research made absolute claims about past things impossible.

What he meant was, first, that the process of testing and verifying historical sources must, in the nature of the case, be an endless one, because new sources might be found and old ones might be interpreted in new ways. Secondly, each and every historical phenomenon must of necessity be understood by the experiences of the researcher. And thirdly, any such phenomenon can only be understood as a link in a chain of causality

80. Ernst Troeltsch, asker of uncomfortable questions.

from which nothing can be excepted. Every link in such a chain is itself conditioned and has therefore been relativized. Consequently, if you want to deal with the past in a meaningful way, you will have to limit yourself to strictly preliminary, relative statements and claims, and can entertain no hope of anything more than that.

Such views were fundamental for the new sciences of nature also, but they did not give rise to serious unease until they were applied to history, for the simple reason that the most basic tenets of Christianity concerned the course and meaning of history, not the order of nature.

The historical work that caused the unease was done mainly by Protestant theologians from the time of the "Enlightenment" onward, and quite specifically in the decades up to and after 1900. The practical challenge was, in other words, put forward by the Christians themselves. Their efforts ran along two principal lines, the most important of which was biblical scholarship.

That was a highly variegated activity. Some researchers concentrated on questions of philology, widely defined: comparison of manuscripts with a view to determining the most reliable form of the biblical text; dating of texts and identification of the older material put together in them; attempts at clarification of the relations between oral and written tradition and between primary testimonies and "redactions." Others were chiefly interested in the history of religion. They compared biblical texts with other Near Eastern and Hellenistic texts in order to discover possible lines of influence. And they tried to identify governing motifs in the biblical traditions and the differences and similarities between them. Such researches could not fail to produce deep-reaching consequences. It became clear that the very basis of Christianity as a scriptural religion, and not only its interpretation, was at stake. That must have caused many to acknowledge the truth of the words uttered by Troeltsch in one of his addresses: "Gentlemen, everything is being rocked!" It became clear that the history of Jesus was open for discussion in every detail, so that the question to be asked was no longer "What does this act and this saying of Jesus mean in the biblical context?" but now was "Has Jesus said or done this at all, or is the text a piece of theology, a result of experiences and reflections by the early Christians after the death of Jesus? Can, then, anything at all be said with certainty about the person whom the church confesses as the Savior?"

The question was not laid aside or suppressed. It became *the* question of theology and was answered in many ways, some of them rather eccentric. Such solutions disappeared gradually from the discussion, as a consequence of an increasing conviction that the person of Jesus was, after all, a less indeterminate quantity than the hypercritics believed. But the change in the situation was nevertheless a radical one, because every single attempt at portraying and interpreting had become wide open for discussion and revision. That could not fail to have effects on the ideas formed by church people about what the church can afford to think when it confesses the Christ who has been Jesus.

The other line pursued by students was church history and the history of dogma. Here, too, the creeds were put under the lamp of criticism, and a traditional idea broke down: that the dogmatic formulations of the ancient church were immune from history and change. If, as claimed by Adolf von Harnack (1851-1930), these dogmas were "products of the Greek spirit on the basis of the Gospel"; if, in other words, they were dependent on philosophical and political concerns in their pagan context, then that must have consequences for the way in which God was today confessed as the triune one — supposing that one indeed wanted to confess him as such. If not, where was the line to be drawn between what was Christianity and what was not? And how could it be possible for a church to get along without a common creed, agreed on by everybody?

Such were the questions that arose from the biblical and historical work and stimulated further work. But they were not all answered by the men who asked them. It was a sign of the times that so many refrained from hazarding an answer and confined themselves to their "purely historical" domain. Specialization — not unlike the industrial version — and unease with the difficulties of the task contributed to a splitting up of theology in independent disciplines. Not least, it created difficulties for the relations of theological scholarship with the church and the believers at large.

The answers that *were* in fact given in the Protestant world in a discussion that is still going on and is unlikely ever to be concluded covered a broad scale from which only a few samples can be sketched out here. One way to go — especially in the earlier part of the period — was the rationalist one. Here the Christian message was, as far as possible, stripped of its "supernatural" elements and its dependence on unique events in time. What was left was then shown to be consonant with reason and morality, thereby implying a guarantee that its claims held good beyond earthly life. "God," "virtue," "immortality" were the keywords. This manner of thinking surfaced again from time to time, in a modernized form, such as the "political theology" of recent times. But other approaches have been much more important. The one that was most influential until the 1920s was a Kantian trend represented by men like Friedrich Schleiermacher (1768-

1834) and Albrecht Ritschl (1822-89). Here an attempt was made to demonstrate that the religious approach to reality was valid independent of other approaches, and that the core of Jesus' message — the proclamation of God's mercy toward the prisoners of meaninglessness — contained the uniquely valid answer to the religious person's quest for meaning and fullness of life. In spite of its dependence on the conditions of its time, this biblical message could be believed as a message from the divine origin of meaning and life, and its adequate human context was the church, where truth and meaning could find expression in the shape of image and metaphor, and in the common engagement in devotional practice.

Another preponderant tendency in modern theology was in many respects diametrically opposed to the one just mentioned. The counterclaim put forth by the so-called dialectical theology, and in particular by the Swiss Calvinist Karl Barth (1886-1968), was that the message of Christ implied a judgment on all religious aspirations, and not a fulfillment of them. God is the one who comes from outside; he is the one who as Creator and Savior is the presupposition and condition of everything else. Over against him, man, with his desire for confirmation of self, is and remains in the wrong. The liberation, brought about by Christ in his life, death, and resurrection, is equivalent to a judgment on self-centered illusions of fulfillment and happiness; and faith in the deliverer assents to that judgment.

In this theology — developed in *Church Dogmatics,* Barth's many-

81. Karl Barth, photographed in March 1933 during a visit to Denmark. The Nazi rise to power in the same year resulted two years later in Barth's expulsion from Germany. He was one of the authors of the declaration by which the "Confessing Church" rejected the regime's attempt at turning Christianity into an instrument of its propaganda. (Courtesy of The Royal Library, Copenhagen, Department of Maps, Prints, and Photographs.)

volumed, unfinished treatise — a rich store of ideas from Christian tradition was brought into play, and formulated afresh. The whole Bible is there; and Augustine, Aquinas, Luther, and Calvin are put to use in a spirit of critical solidarity. More than anywhere else in twentieth-century theology was it made clear that the tradition is something more than a lumber room for worn-out goods or a device for harmless entertainment. It was shown to be a living presence, a challenge to all the challenges of the age.

Barth's theology was also rooted in its own time and engaged itself in it. It is to be understood on the background of the collapse of idealistic illusions in World War One, and it came to play an important role in inspiring a group of German Protestants in their resistance to National Socialism and its attempt at turning the church into a tool of its propaganda. But it also had to pay a price for its sharply hewn decisiveness. It did so by more or less evading the "challenge of history." When all is said and done, it disregarded Troeltsch's problem.

That problem remains in force, and it has not been solved either by another influential modern trend, the Kierkegaard-inspired, existentialist one.

This development of two centuries did, however, make at least one thing clear: theology finally had to acknowledge that it must share the fate of the other "textual" disciplines and stand in the same exposed and vulnerable position they do. In its dealings with its texts from the past, it has no other recourse than those other disciplines have when dealing with theirs; namely, to engage in that never ending, disciplined, but risky adventure: the attempt at understanding on the conditions posed by the ambiguous text, the ever disputed tradition, and the prejudiced reader. It cannot pull an ace out of its sleeve by referring to a divine guarantee of the one and only meaning. And when the theology of the church (that of the university works on other lines) ventures the judgment that here, in this text, God is speaking and acting through Jesus of Nazareth, then the venture is one of *faith*. Basically, there is nothing entirely new in that. Theology has never been satisfied with the "inspired" text alone. It has always acknowledged that the text can be rightly understood only when God himself opens it up for the reader by awakening his faith within the context of public worship and private prayer. But in the modern situation, that has come to be more clearly and sharply acknowledged than ever before.

There are good reasons for other observers than Danish ones to conclude this discussion by yet another glance at a Danish thinker who is too little known internationally, and who cannot be placed in any single category: Grundtvig (cf. pp. 249-50). Granted, he has not "solved" any of the problems left unsolved by other thinkers, nor has he foreseen specifically

82. N. F. S. Grundtvig, photographed in August 1872. He died on September 2 of the same year, at the age of 88, after having preached his last sermon on the previous day. (Courtesy of The Royal Library, Copenhagen, Department of Maps, Prints, and Photographs.)

twenty-first-century problems, but in his mind the old Europe and the new, tradition and present, cohabited in a unique and fruitful way. This is connected with the fact that his instrument of communication was poetry — irrespective of whether he wrote verse or prose. When Grundtvig spoke of the church in a way that was Catholic, Protestant, and democratic, and when he reflected on man and on human possibilities in a vein that was humanist as well as Lutheran, then one of the causes must be sought in his distinctively poetical power of envisaging many things at once and letting their interplay, their tensions, and their contradictions come to meaningful expression. That is something he shares with old European theological poets such as Dante and Milton, but the possibilities contained in that mode of doing theology have by no means been exhausted yet.

4. The World Religion

a. "A House for the Sufferings of Christ"

Christianity aims at reaching all of humanity; it is meant as a universal message. That claim is expressed by the words, recited at baptism, from the Gospel of Matthew by which the risen Christ commands his disciples to go forth into the world and make disciples of all humankind. And it is also expressed — in a manner typical of old Europe — by Thomas Aquinas when he writes

269

that Christ was crucified outside the walls of Jerusalem, under the heavens, so as to make it clear that salvation was no prerogative of the Jews, but that "the entire world was to become a house for the sufferings of Christ."

In practice, however, what has first and foremost become clear is that viable Christianity has always been a religion that entered into an existent cultural context and united itself with that culture in such a way that it set its stamp on it while at the same time being influenced and shaped by it. Or it has been, as the case might be, a religion that became the principal builder of a culture and was in turn influenced by it. Christian faith, worship, and conduct does not exist in a "pure" form. The form it assumes has always been more or less conditioned by its context, and its pretension of being "for everyone" can only be realized on the premises provided by a cultural situation.

That is one lesson to be drawn from our consideration of Christian history in Mediterranean lands, in the Near East and Russia, and in old and new Europe and North America — those areas where it proved viable in the first place. In each of those civilizations Christian beliefs and communal life assumed an individual shape and put a special stamp on their surroundings. In each of those contexts and phases, except the latest, Christianity became the religion of "everyone," at the cost of having difficulties with being accepted outside the respective ambient of culture.

The first great example of this in earlier times is the relationship with the Islamic world. It was encumbered from the beginning by the Arab conquest of wide areas of Christian culture. And Islam was, from the first, resistant to Christian influence, regarding itself as the fulfillment of all previous divine revelations, Judaism and Christianity included. But the relations were made yet more difficult by a Christian intransigence that was to a large extent culturally conditioned. The form of Christianity responsible for the final breach of understanding was that of the early phase of old Europe, a religion that, because of special conditions of life, had been turned into a socio-politico-military power — one without which human society could not exist and which looked to feudal society for its material sustenance and for much of the inspiration for its way of looking at the world. In the Crusades and their consequences — massacres of Muslims and colonization of the Holy Land — a complex of religion, politics, and culture became manifest and made further Christian expansion well-nigh impossible when confronted with a religion whose adherents did not forget easily and who worshiped a zealous God. The definitive failure of the crusading and colonizing movements at the end of the thirteenth century decided Christianity's fate for centuries, as far as Islam was concerned. Ever since then, the resistance of this "daughter religion" toward Christian mission has proved all but absolute. The case is an instructive one as to the vital relations between religion and culture.

The next satisfactorily documented phase of expansion is the Roman Catholic mission in Central and South America and in Asia in the sixteenth and seventeenth centuries. As could be expected, it was launched in connection with a more general movement of European expansion: the Spanish and Portuguese voyages of commerce and exploration. Those enterprises enabled missionaries to go out, and to survive. But the commercial expansion preconditioned the missionary undertaking in a deeper sense also. The religion the missionaries carried with them was European Catholic Christianity, imbued with European history, culture, and customs; and the Indian, Chinese, and Latin American peoples who accepted the message about Jesus of Nazareth — he who "walked about doing good" and gave his life for the sins of humankind "outside the city" and rose from the dead to give life to men — had to accept several other things in the bargain.

But that is only one, very general characteristic of the missionary process. The course of the mission, and its results, were different according to place and time.

The areas later called Latin America became a "house for the sufferings of Christ" in another sense than the one intended by Aquinas. The new religion arrived in those parts hand in hand with a conquering military power for whom the "Indians" were inferior creatures one could treat at one's pleasure. That must have influenced native ideas about the religion Spanish plantation owners indoctrinated them with, as the price they promised Madrid for being allowed to make unrestrained use of the natives' labor.

It is true that the Indians were shown the other face of Christian Europe too. Bartolomé de Las Casas (d. 1564) and other fearless Christians pleaded the natives' cause and obtained some elementary alleviations of their fate. And with the "reductions" — that is, closed collectives of Indians — in Paraguay, the Jesuit fathers made it possible for some to live a human life. But everywhere the guidelines were European ones, not least in the reductions, where the type of organization of work and division of time reveal their origin in European rationality and the monastic lifestyle, and where everything was done under the paternal leadership and control of the missionaries. By that attitude was the seed sown for a pressing problem of contemporary Latin American Catholicism: an age-old unwillingness to leave any initiative to the natives has resulted in a serious shortage of native-born priests.

The Society of Jesus was also one of the principal bearers of the mis-

83. Illustrations from a tract used by the Christian mission to China. The Chinese texts are quotations from Psalm 69, 1 Peter 1, and Psalm 40.

sion to the East. With Portuguese support, Francisco Xavier (d. 1552) covered immense distances through short-time campaigns to chosen places; and in India and China his brethren used methods that are enlightening for their understanding of problems arising from the combination of Christian preaching and European culture. In India a Jesuit donned the yellow gown of the "holy men," studied Indian philosophy, and discussed with the learned in their own language. In China the Jesuits accepted the use of Chinese names of gods for the God of the Christians and interpreted ancestor worship as harmless acts of familial piety. But such attempts at bridge building were not without their problems. A missionary who wished to be accepted among Indian high-caste people was obliged to cut himself off from low-caste Christians — to serve them the eucharistic bread on the tip of a stick — and acceptance of pagan sacrifices such as those to ancestors was highly contestable when viewed against the background of traditional European Christianity. Understandably enough, a controversy broke out among Catholics, and the pope decided the question in 1742 by putting an end to the Jesuit experiments. That decision had far-reaching consequences for Christianity in the East.

An important ingredient in the situation was the rivalry between

Catholic missionary orders. Together with the beginning Dutch commercial activity, that rivalry proved fateful for the mission in Japan in spite of initial successes by the Jesuits. Religious and commercial competition aroused Japanese suspicions and was among the causes of a series of persecutions, with crucifixion of Japanese Christians and burning of missionaries. In effect, that put an end to the Japanese mission for nearly 250 years; but small groups of Christians kept the faith and came to light again when the country was reopened to European influence in the later half of the nineteenth century.

b. World Mission and Its Problems

Without forgetting the geographical reach of the old European missions and the perspectives opened by them, it must be acknowledged that world mission in the proper sense of the word was a work of modern European and American Christianity. Not until the later half of the nineteenth century did Christianity acquire a large following of people outside traditionally Christian lands.

That development cannot be understood in isolation from the drastically increased general relations between Europe and North America and the rest of the world. Colonial expansion, inclusion of the colonies into the global market, and the shaping influence exercised by industrial methods of production — all helped pave the way for Christian mission.

In speaking of those connections, some reservations are in order. Often the missionaries were in place before a permanent European presence had been established — some died in the attempt — and the missionaries' religion was often the governing factor in making the overseas peoples acquainted with European modes of thinking and living. Also, the history of missions is full of frictions between missionaries and imperialists. It is significant that the East India Company, which represented British interests before an official colonial government was set up, tried to place obstacles in the way of the mission because it threatened commercial and political interests. A Christian campaign of propaganda and lobbying in Britain itself had to be launched before those obstacles were removed.

But none of that contradicts the fact that a lasting Christian presence overseas presupposed that of traders, colonizers, and soldiers. Mission could be a consequence of military action, as was the case in China, where a firm foothold could only be acquired in the wake of the Opium War, ending in 1842. But it was more important that the colonizers appreciated the pacifying influence of the missionaries on the subject peoples, and — not

273

least — that devoted Christians among officials and soldiers took a personal interest in the mission and gave it active assistance. Even more important, however, was the elementary protection made possible by colonization, and most important of all were the attractions of European power, wealth, and technical skill — they could, when all was said and done, hardly be isolated from the attraction of the Christian message as such.

The form of Christianity for which possibilities of dissemination were thus provided was the modern European and American one. That can be seen on both sides of the most important confessional divide. Least, of course, on the Catholic side, where the continuity with the past was stronger than in Protestantism; and the Catholic Church could, furthermore, build on a tradition from the missionary activities in former centuries, and on the personnel that could now as then be recruited from the religious orders. But there are many signs that the immense Catholic work of mission in the nineteenth and twentieth centuries in Africa and Asia is at least partially dependent on specifically modern tendencies in Catholicism. That is apparent in the use of popular information campaigns and appeals for financial support. And it can be seen in the increased influence of central authorities on the organization of the undertakings. To be sure, the Catholic colonial powers, France and Belgium, were indispensable partners in their domains, but the relationship was by no means one of total dependence, such as those with Spain and Portugal in earlier times.

Nonetheless, the modern character is far more conspicuous in Protestant missions. We can catch a preliminary glimpse in one of the earliest enterprises, in the Danish colony of Tranquebar in South India, from 1706. It drew its origin from the piety of awakening; its bearers were German Pietists; and the aim was personal conversion and formation of an independent Indian congregation. All of that points in the direction of important features of subsequent Protestant mission.

In its origin and initial development, that mission was profoundly imbued with the eminently modern European form of Christianity, that of the awakening. There the Christian life was regarded as an obviously holy, strictly regulated life, the result of a conversion, following biblical preaching. And the Christian community was seen as an association of the converted, in which traditional distinctions between clergy and laity had been at least partially dismantled. This form had dominated a number of modern European attempts at "internal mission," and it became equally prevalent in the external variety.

In accordance with the awakenings view of Christian community, the most important organizational form on the "home front" was the missionary society: a free association that, while not necessarily without links to traditional church institutions, operated independently and was financed by voluntary contributions. This view of mission as being a specialized activity implies an enlightening lesson about the state of the traditional Christianity of the churches. As for the missionary work itself, it was of great importance that it could be deployed in some independence from established forms of action — bound up, as those forms were, with political, social, and clerical obligations and interests.

That freedom finds expression in the early missionaries' very modest social origins. William Carey (1761-1834), the pioneer figure, was a highly intelligent but totally self-educated cobbler, and his two closest companions in India were a teacher in a paupers' school and a typographer. No less characteristic of the freedom from traditional bonds were the possibilities the mission opened for female initiative from the mid–nineteenth century onward. Women as equal partners in preaching and missionary work were almost unheard of in Europe, at least in the established churches where, for centuries, women had been reduced to subordinate functions or dispatched to the nunneries. The new female missionaries took up the heritage from very distant predecessors, the women preachers of very early times, whose existence is barely visible in the sources. And they became pathbreakers for twentieth-century acceptance of the ordination of women.

The guiding impulse for the great missionary enterprise in the nineteenth century was, then, the desire, inspired by the piety of the awakening, to make the "one thing that is needful" known to the heathen. But therein lay the seed of additional activity. If the proclamation of the "one thing needful" was to be biblically based, and if the "new life" of the converts was to be a biblically regulated life, then the Bible had to be translated. But that presupposed that languages other than that of the Bible had to be studied, as well as the cultures expressing themselves in those languages. It was, furthermore, inevitable for the missionaries to seek to clarify the ways of thinking — in other words, European rationality — with which the "one thing" was inextricably entwined, to the people they wished to convert. Those people were to understand as well as believe. As a natural consequence, Protestant mission understood itself as a schooling activity as well as a preaching one — just as had more or less always been the case with Protestantism as a whole. "School," *coetus scholasticus,* was one of the names used about the church by early Protestants.

The teaching activity could assume more or less wide-reaching forms, and it could become more or less closely linked to the missionary concern proper. From one of the school mission's great pioneers, Alexander Duff (1806-78), a detailed report has been preserved about his method of informing young Indians about European ways of thinking and experience. After having, courteously and attentively, made them repeat what their *guru* had taught them about rain coming from the trunk of Indra's heavenly elephant, he gave his account of what he had learned from his Scottish "gurus." The method is Socratic. Step-by-step, beginning with the lesson to be drawn from seeing steam from boiling rice hit the lid of the pot, the disciples are led to discover for themselves how the causal chain of physical processes behind a weather phenomenon can be empirically demonstrated. Duff's ideas and methods were perhaps not typical, but the story demonstrates something that is: the connection between salvation and reason, which has been more or less evidently active in the whole course of Christian history.

By that we have touched on one of the many aspects of the problem that occurred when European Christianity met non-European peoples. In the missionary movements of the nineteenth and twentieth centuries, a message about God, the world, history, and conduct is brought to people with entirely different ideas and lifestyles. And it happens in close connection with an economic, political, and military expansion. How does that encounter turn out? In what manner is it experienced?

One answer must be that a liberation takes place, just as it always has at a transition to faith in Christ. In the modern mission fields, as elsewhere, the central theme of Christianity, Christ's conquest of "the powers" (death, demons, and despair), has been experienced as a living reality, even though there is no way of knowing which particular powers have plagued the individual and how he or she has experienced the liberation. As the book of Proverbs has it: "The heart knoweth his own bitterness; and a stranger doth not intermeddle with his joy." But both the misery and the salvation from misery take different forms according to the cultural context, depending on whether it was a Hindu or a Bantu or a Maori who believed what he heard. It has also been important whether the approach to religion has been a predominantly individual or a collective one. An example of a collective approach can be found in a report of how some Papua tribes in the interior of New Guinea decided on their conversion. According to that report — which is apt to remind us of what had happened on north European mission fields nine hundred years earlier — the process began by the chiefs making known to their people, with symbolic gestures, the choice they had to make between the evils that plagued them before they "knew God" — tribal wars, sorcery, infanticide — and a life of freedom from such evils. Thereafter, everybody confessed the God of the Christians, symbolized by a pole

276

rammed into the ground in the middle of the meeting space: "Nobody can draw it up, nobody can upturn it, it stands firm."

Liberation was a wide concept. Often it led into new servitude under "powers" — compulsory European dress and sexual practice; loss of old customs and festivals that had secured daily life; surly moral supervision by missionaries. The "religious" aspect of conversion was always connected to the social changes caused by the European presence in a wider sense. The offer of schooling and medical help was important. So was increased trade. And so was, in Africa, the common struggle of missionaries and colonizers against the traffic in slaves. David Livingstone (1813-73), missionary and explorer in central Africa, expressed an important truth by appealing to help the Africans by giving them "commerce and Christianity." Christian faith was one of the things by which human dignity could be served and upheld; honest trade with goods other than slaves was another.

By leaving the old and adopting the new as a group, such as took place in New Guinea, some new Christians avoided a problem that caused much difficulty to others, those who broke with the old religion and thereby cut themselves off from the community of the tribe, or who had been outcasts in the first place. As in earliest Europe, religion was only one aspect of the right conduct of life in a wider sense — that which the Norsemen called *sidr*. One solution of the problem consisted in gathering the converts in special villages where they could avoid being forced to take part in activities that were incompatible with their new faith. Such a ghetto could never become a definitive solution, but it could serve as a midway house from which native evangelists could be sent into the normal villages in order to work for a general conversion.

In connection with the general process of political and cultural expansion, the massive missionary effort, made possible by the generosity of countless European Christians, led to a spreading of Christianity without precedent in history. From the mid–nineteenth century until the First World War, Christians came to be counted in millions on almost all mission fields, with the Islamic world as the great exception. This is true even though there were differences of depth and breadth from one cultural context to another. In India the results were relatively modest, and especially wherever another religion was present in an articulate and sophisticated form. In Africa there were many places where Christianity became the religion of an entire society. Both in colonial times and afterward, Africa was the great Christian area of expansion. It is estimated that there were 40 million Christians south of the Sahara at the end of the colonial age, and the increase has continued since then.

The conversion was followed up by the forming of congregations, with the accompanying problems of organization. The new congregations were offshoots of the European and American societies that carried the responsibility for personnel and finances. The society was the supreme authority, and the missionary, its local representative, was the undisputed daily leader. His authority could sometimes — as when new Christians were gathered in special villages — become all but total: he was pastor and chieftain in one person. But it was in any case considerably more extensive than originally intended.

In principle the desired aim was to make the new communities stand on their own as soon as possible. They were to govern and finance themselves, so that the missionary could be free to go on to new places. The outcome in practice was different, as long as the colonial situation lasted at any rate. Training and ordination of native ministers did not keep step with the needs, and no serious attempt was made to make the congregations independent of the missionary society. This state of affairs was clearly due to the colonial situation and the more or less well-meant attitudes of superiority caused by that situation. As long as native initiative was suppressed or limited in secular affairs, the chances of its being developed in matters ecclesiastical were limited. Paternalism, the attitude of a protector and guide, became in practice the natural one, irrespective of principles.

It is no wonder, then, that ecclesiastical independence did not come until the Asiatic and African colonies became independent states, in the mid–twentieth century. Not until then was the decisive condition created for the missionary congregations to acquire the status of "young churches" and for their European members to find it natural to serve under native leaders.

This organizational liberation from missionary tutelage was apt to be felt as the logical continuation of the personal and religious liberation preached by the missionaries. But there is more than one side to both liberations. Both the message of liberation and the life as a free organization assumed their basic forms in a context that was foreign to Asians and Africans. That has not prevented Asians and Africans from accepting the message of Christ as the truth about themselves and about their life as men and women in society. But it has at all times caused the question to arise about the relation between the message and its organizational expression on the one hand and, on the other, the human and social contexts that are alien to the European and American ones, which have contributed to shaping the message as well as the organization in the first place.

The raising of that question meant that the new Christians were set out on the road toward making Christianity their own religion — the road that had been entered by people in Mediterranean and old European times: artisans and slaves and philosophers, peasants, warriors, merchants, pioneers, ascetics, and artists: each group in its own fashion and with results that were often regarded as eccentric, weird, or downright perverse by fellow Christians.

It can with reason be said that the question arose at the very moment when the keywords of Bible and worship were translated and put to use as vehicles of Christian preaching and teaching. As in the Mediterranean and old European civilizations, but in a much more deep-reaching sense, did it prove difficult not only to find passably equivalent words, but to come to terms with what the chosen words implied by way of associations of ideas that were more or less foreign to what had to be communicated. "Conscience," "sin," "grace," "faith" — suchlike fundamental concepts whose meaning has taken a long time to become to some extent agreed on among Europeans cannot without more or less painful compromises become meaningful to Asians and Africans. And there are, quite apart from the individual words and concepts, some trains of thought that are as foreign to them as they are familiar to Europeans. One example is the difficulty felt by many Indian Christians in coming to terms with the dogma of Jesus of Nazareth as a human being of flesh and blood at a definite point in time and space. The notion of Christ as the heavenly Savior was somewhat more accessible — contrary to what has often been the case in Europe.

There can, thus, be no doubt that the way to an African or Asiatic Christianity, embedded in African and Asiatic life, has already been entered by the conscious or unconscious choices that translators, listeners, and readers made between the various possibilities of understanding provided by their respective cultural milieux.

But the new Christians, just as the "old" ones, have been selective in their dealings with message and doctrines, in accordance with their several indigenous traditions. They have stressed some elements and neglected others, as had the Europeans before them. Interestingly enough, the way that has happened is apt to remind us of far earlier European situations. African Christians who take the farmer's and warrior's world of ancient Israel to heart make us think of similar tendencies in very early Europe. And when the Bataks on Sumatra tell us that Christianity is a new and better version of what they had until then called *adat,* the sacred order of things, governing the life of society and the individual, then it strikes us as similar to what the newly converted Norsemen meant when they spoke of Christianity as the new *sidr.* Something similar can be said of the cases when church organization has merged easily with the tribal one; again just as in early Europe. The missionaries were aware of such things. The great Catholic organizer of missions and archbishop of Algiers, Cardinal Lavigerie (1825-92), put his knowledge of church history to direct use when planning his "strategy" south of the Sahara.

Along such lines, the new Christians connected their new religion with their life as men and women in society; they made its meaning concrete in relation to what that society fears, hopes, and lives by. Christian sense has been made of the traditional African relationship with the ancestral "spirits" by strongly emphasizing the idea of the church as the "Christ tribe" of the living and the dead, with the Savior as the great tribal father; as well as by taking a special interest in the feast of All Souls. The Gospel stories of how Jesus cured demonic possession are heard with ears that are intimately acquainted with traditional tales about evil spirits, the powers of chaos that threaten prosperity and peace. Ritual traditions have also been worked into the web of Christian worship, by missionaries as well as by the Africans themselves. An example is the initiation rite introduced in southern Tanzania by an English missionary bishop, under inspiration from Pope Gregory I's directions for mission among the Anglo-Saxons in the year 601. Everything possible was preserved of the traditional ceremonies surrounding the initiation of boys into adult life — circumcision, the chieftain's instructions on the tribal concepts of honor, dance, and music — and was then combined with Christian preparation for confirmation, confession of sins, and divine worship.

Just as in old Christendom, the possibilities of such combinations of traditional and Christian ideas and practices have their limits, simply because the powers of absorption of the Christian message are not unlimited. It is true of that religion, as of Judaism and Islam, that there are many things that it is *not* and cannot become. That could be "negatively" demonstrated by looking at some of the pseudo-Christian sects and syncretistic religions that were so strongly in evidence in southern Africa in the twentieth century. To that must be added that the development toward Africanization or Asianization of Christianity was impeded by the colonial status of the missionary areas, and above all that the rapid social transformations taking place in the developing countries — the processes of urbanization and industrialization that threaten to destroy all traditional patterns — must presumably result in turning the religious development in new directions. Be that as it may, it is an incontestable fact that the enormous spread of Christianity in the non-European world has given the old problem of relations between culture and religion a new appearance, with incalculable future possibilities.

5. Challenges and Tendencies
at the Turn of the Millennium

As pointed out above, nothing ever really dies in a historical religion, and everything new must come to terms with the old that refuses to die. "Institutional" church and "enthusiastic" sect; scripturally based social protest and equally authentic affirmation of the powers of order; the "people of God" engaged in common worship and the solitary person meditating on the Savior's sharing his lot and calling him to discipleship; delight in the revelations of divine love in earthly life and fierce rejection of "the world, the flesh, and the devil"; liberal and conservative theological thinking — to a greater or lesser extent, all those things have been there together from the beginning, in conflict, but also in constant interaction, on the terms offered by changing cultural situations and exposed to the challenges their own inbuilt contradictions have always presented to Christian individuals and communities. Thus also in A.D. 2003.

The situation at the beginning of the third millennium is characterized by the acute strengthening of the main tendencies of "modernity," such as they have been sketched out in earlier sections of this book, and by the fact that some of those currents have assumed new shapes, presenting new challenges for Christian faith as well as for Christian churches and congregations.

a. Social Trends

The movement toward establishing a "global village" has accelerated in a downright breathtaking way. It has been favored by technological developments, not least the digital forms of communication, as well as by the end of superpower conflict in its traditional "cold war" version, and by the consolidation of supranational bodies such as the European Union. Among its most recent expressions are the steadily intensified economic interaction, the worldwide network of speedily transmissible money and commodities, the recurrent global currency unrest and oil crises. Yet another of its manifestations is a massive demographic pressure against the rich parts of the world. Mass immigration into those lands has been set in motion by poverty, social upheavals, and wars, and has been facilitated by modern means of communication. Among its effects are social tensions in the receiving countries and, not least, a confrontation of religions, laden with much sharper challenges and problems than hitherto. In the rich countries, earlier tendencies toward a leveling of spiritual as well as material internal differences, and toward demolition of traditional attachments, familial and otherwise, have been considerably strengthened. Connected with such currents, but also in some tension toward them, the same can be said about the way Western societies have cultivated moral and religious pluralism and relativism, and asserted the sovereignty of the individual as to decisions about the conduct of life and the meaning of existence. In more or less paradoxical combinations, a flattening out of differences and a cult of individualism are, ever more clearly, among the distinguishing marks of those societies. The situation of the poor countries is notably different. Although they have become subject to some of the effects of globalization, traditional patterns of life are much more in evidence there than in the West.

On that background of modernity, and not without undergoing strong influences from its challenges, old and new tendencies in Christian religious attitudes and forms of organization are active.

b. A New Balance

Perhaps the most conspicuous recent tendency is the transfer of Christianity's numerical center of gravity to countries outside Europe and North America. Considered under the perspective of future possibilities, that trend is perhaps also the most important one. But because of the continued material superiority of the older parts of Christendom, because "young churches" have not yet worked out decisive differences from Euro-American Christianity, and because of the beginning social transformation whose effects in those parts of the world are more or less unpredictable, an attempt at assessing the future consequences of the "transfer" cannot amount to more than guesswork. But there is no denying that far-reaching perspectives for Christendom as a whole can be expected to be opened by events and conditions in the so-called third world, especially when it is remembered how widespread are the loosening and decline of Christian faith and behavior in the "first" one.

c. Organization of Community

In all the "worlds" a time-honored interaction — variously hinted at above — is at work; namely, that between, on one side, a conception of the church emphasizing objectivity, tradition, sacramental and institutional order, and consequently aiming at becoming an all-encompassing organization of men and women who have been baptized as infants, and on the other side, that of the church as a "gathered" community of like-minded people, with an emphasis on personal decision, on renunciation of "the world," and on holiness of life in accordance with Scripture, and sometimes also on extraordinary spiritual experiences and "charismatic" practices. It is worth repeating that interaction, or interweaving, is the proper word for the relationship, insofar as the two main types of understanding what can be meant by "the people of God" not only present an authentically Christian challenge to each other, but also — the Christian message being what it is — present that challenge *inside* one and the same organization, be it traditionally "churchly" or not. They are present with and in each other. Nevertheless, clarity may be served by, to some limited extent, considering them separately.

The first-named type has continued to evince a tenacity of life that is especially remarkable considering the many and ever growing countercurrents of the age: its pluralism, its individualism and antitraditionalism, its outbursts of social protest. As before, that has to do with perennial features of Christian faith and with corresponding needs felt by Christian men and women. But neither is it without some connection with the countercurrents just mentioned. Both sides of the matter are, as before, but in new ways, evident from the vicissitudes of the Roman Catholic Church. Rome's hardening of attitude in the years following the upsurge of reforms in the 1960s — its stubborn rejection of demands from below for ordination of women, clerical marriage, permission of artificial birth control, as well as its refusal to countenance liberal tendencies in theology — is only understandable when *both* churchly tradition *and* modern currents are kept in mind. Correspondingly, the articulate or discreetly silent resistance put up by wide circles of laity and lower clergy against Roman commands and guidelines is both a typical sign of the age and a prime example of inbuilt tensions in churchly tradition. It is, by the way, worth noticing as yet another combination of age-old tradition and modern needs and aspirations that Latin American bishops have lent their support to movements of social protest, and in so doing have been backed up by Rome.

The churchly, "objective," and institutional type of Christian organization has shown itself to be a living reality. That is true in the religious sense, but also in a political and cultural one, as can be seen not only in more or less all-encompassing national or "folk" churches where a number of direct or subterranean influences on society as a whole can be discerned, but also in things like the Roman Catholic influence on structures and guidelines of the European Union. One instance among several is that the Union's so-called principle of subsidiarity, presented — or, unkindly put, masquerading — as a democratic safeguard of national, regional, and local government, is directly descended from the Roman principle of allowing certain decisions to be taken on lower levels of the secular command structure.

The disintegrating and transforming forces of modernity are also factors behind the contemporary expressions of the *other* main type of organization and communal activity among Christians. Such expressions can be found in a wide and varied spate of communities all over the world, inside the traditional churches, such as the striking phenomenon of the charismatic movement in the Roman Church, or outside, as in evangelical groups in Africa and — under particularly difficult conditions — China. A specially impressive case of evangelical awakening is the massive growth of Pentecostalism in Latin America. That part of the world is also conspicuous as the original homeland of the "base communities." That phenomenon must be seen on the background of the shortage of priests in Latin American Catholicism and of the encouragement given by the hierarchy to social activity by and for the poor. The communities — small groups of laity, gathered for Bible reading and charitable and political action — are thus affiliated to the church, but their manner of working is recognizably related to that of scripturally orientated groups outside the Catholic context, and as a matter of fact some of them are not universally popular with the clerical establishment. It is no accident that similar informal groups of laypeople with devotional or practical purposes have struck roots in quite different surroundings elsewhere. Yet another sign of the times is the "television church" in the United States, an extreme example of how a fundamentalist form of biblical preaching with a stridently moralistic bent can be combined with state-of-the-art technology. But addressing itself, as it does, to a solitary viewer, it is above all a powerful reminder of a salient feature of modernity: the tendency to privatize religion.

d. Ways of Thinking

We already met one of the currents of recent Christian thought while considering the base communities, one of whose aims and purposes was the political liberation of the poor and oppressed. "Liberation theology" has been a powerful ferment in Latin American Catholicism, but its affinity to, or agreement with, a Marxist turn of mind and some theologians' advocacy of armed rebellion have given the Roman Curia occasion to denounce the movement. It is, however, a telling sign of troubled times that a wide range of politically radical theological thinking has been in evidence in many other places all over the Western world, while at the same time churches and individual Christians have been actively engaged in resistance against and overthrow of totalitarian governments, notably in central Europe.

Another feature of contemporary social thinking and action is found in the more or less concerted efforts of churches and theologians to look at the message of creation and redemption in the light of pressing ecological needs. Not only poverty and oppression among humans, but human misuse of the nonhuman environment, has moved toward the center of many Christians' concerns.

Yet another example of a theological response to contemporary social and cultural change can be drawn from the wave of feminist theology in recent decades. As part of the wider movement for social, political, and cultural emancipation of women, feminist theology has cast a critical eye on Christian history in general and the masculine bias of biblical images of God in particular. In doing that, such feminists as have not given up the struggle and despaired of Christianity altogether have provided a fruitful impetus to the work of rethinking Christian origins, discovering forgotten women in history, unmasking latent misogyny past and present, and helping the cause of a female priesthood.

In the churches of Africa and Asia, such tendencies are much less in evidence. To a large extent, thinking and practice in those parts of the world are concerned with hammering out a viable relationship between pre-Christian traditions and "foreign-born" Christianity. African theologians and church people have reflected on and experimented with ways of interpreting and formulating the message in indigenous terms, and Indian Christian thinkers have attempted the same from their quite different points of departure (cf. pp. 279-80). It is an ongoing process, beset with dilemmas, as witnessed, for instance, by the problem of polygamy. But when it is remembered how long it took early European thinkers to turn theology into something other than it was in its original context, there can be no cause for wonder in the difficulties experienced by their African and Indian counterparts at the turn of the third millennium.

The question of the outcome of such endeavors is still an open one. But there is no question as to the importance of third-world Christianity for the phenomenon to which we shall finally turn.

e. The Ecumenical Movement

Since the missionary and church-building work in that world was carried out in quite another cultural context than that of Europe and North America, and especially since it implied daily encounters with religious beliefs and practices that were utterly different from the Christian ones, it is a matter of no surprise that the interdenominational turn of mind that many missionaries took with them from home became strengthened "in the field," and that the experiences gained there led to the old world becoming increasingly conscious of the relative character of all differences of confession among Christians. Another, and presumably yet more powerful, factor behind that consciousness has of course been the growth of secularism and neopaganism in the older parts of Christendom. The movement to which those various tendencies gave rise assumed many shapes. Regionally, the Church of South India (1947) unites a number of Protestant denominations; in Europe and the U.S.A. denominational mergers and interdenominational talks and consultations have taken place, significantly enough with some Roman Catholic participation; and since 1948 the World Council of Churches, comprising almost all communions except the Roman one, has held meetings and formulated common attitudes to contemporary religious, moral, and social problems, such as those presented by apartheid, world poverty, and ecological crises. For some participants in the ecumenical endeavor, the goal is formal and institutional union, while others — not without a background in theological conviction as to what "oneness" means, but also taught by practical experience — are satisfied with the churches gaining a deeper knowledge and understanding of others' ways of teaching and living the common faith.

Meeting of minds among Christians is one thing, and one beset with a number of problems. Quite another is the encounter of religion with religion. Globalization and migration have made that encounter much more lively in recent decades. That means reawakening old grudges and indeed hatreds, not least as the result of the massive influx of Muslim and other newcomers into Western urban life. In such environments the notions of mutual understanding and practical compromise do not — to put it mildly — meet with universal approval, although feeble attempts in that direction have been made.

In that as well as in each and every other respect, the question of Christianity's future in the third millennium is an open one. Open in the radical sense of its message.

conclusion

One Thing — Many Things

Even a rapid glance at the history of Christianity makes clear that that word covers a good many things.

That is true of Christian theories of the world, of history and society, and of the human condition. It is also true of Christian conduct of life or Christian ways of organizing human life in common.

The differences come to light as differences from one culture to another, in the sense that the widely different cultural contexts in which Christianity has lived its life have used it to satisfy their needs and give vent to their prejudices. Christian piety is not the same in a collectively minded culture of peasants with "magical" traditions as in an individualistic urban culture with "rational" traditions. But palpable differences can also be found within one and the same civilizational framework. Old European crusaders, monks, university clerks, merchants, and laborers did not by any means have identical ideas about salvation or the good life and its duties. In more recent times, one Spanish valley is described by a British anthropologist as the home of three versions of Catholicism simultaneously: early European peasant Christianity with more than a tinge of magic, sixteenth-century reform Catholicism with its rigid moral discipline, and the Second Vatican Council message preached by the young generation of parish priests. Last and by no means least, no Christian needs to seek far and wide to find religious ideas and sentiments of widely different origin gathered together — in a more or perhaps less coherent manner — in the head of one individual believer. This is indeed one of the things that can be meant by saying that Christianity is a historical religion, and that "all history is contemporary history."

287

It is the task of the historian of Christianity to try to come to terms with those differences and to gain insight into the network of shaping influences between each single version of Christianity and its "place in life." But it is also his task to determine what those versions are versions *of*. It may be useful to conclude with a few remarks about that — in continuation of what has been said earlier in the book about the uniting features of Christianity.

Such remarks may, for instance, be of use regarding the problem of the relations between Christianity and the other world religions — a problem that has become especially topical in an age where the Christian world is beginning to become a mission field for outside religions, instead of — as was earlier the case — being *the* place from which missions set out. That problem — which would require a separate book — is intimately connected with the question of what unites the different versions of Christianity, and must therefore be touched on in a context like ours.

Christianity belongs to the group of world religions that also includes Judaism and Islam. With those two it shares features that make it, and them, notably and characteristically different from religions such as Hinduism and Buddhism. One such feature is the role history plays in them. Between God and his people, they say, there is a historical relationship. God causes his will to be known through the course of a history, and the people live by what he speaks to them and what he lets them experience in time. Truth is God's eternal truth, but it becomes known on the terms of changeable and ever changing time.

This duality is important. It is in his capacity as the Eternal, the Almighty, the Lord of time and space that he reveals himself in time and history. In other words, he lets himself be known as the Creator, as the will without which nothing exists, as the potter who has power over the clay, who fashions and destroys.

On these premises the common expressions of the three religions manifest themselves. All three speak of God's law: commands and prohibitions that are no part of the "nature of things," but originate in divine acts of will. They speak of the institutions of the people: the forms of government and law by which the creation is upheld and continued. They speak of departure, passage, and peregrination: that of Israel from Egypt across the Red Sea and Jordan to the Promised Land; those of the Prophet from Mecca and of his followers to Mecca; that of the church toward the "New Jerusalem." They speak of remembered and expected things, gathered up in that present moment into which God speaks. Their sacred acts, such as the paschal rites of Jews and Christians, actualize history by incorporating the past and anticipating the future. They think materially: flesh and blood are the bearers of holiness and of divine will; man lives by bread.

With all those common features, it is not surprising that the things that divide the three religions have given them occasion for embittered mutual rejection. It is no accident that Jews and Muslims have always been the most passionate and articulate of resisters to Christian mission.

The thing that distinguishes Christianity from those two religions and constitutes its internal unity expresses itself in many ways, but all of them derive from one single claim, that of God the Creator's disclosure of his own nature in the man Jesus. Not his making use of that man as a prophetic or priestly or kingly instrument of his will and his message, but his own appearance as that man.

The claim is an exceptional one. It is, as Paul the apostle says, "unto the Jews a stumbling block, and unto the Greeks foolishness." It has been so for Christians as well, and still is. The fact that they have, again and again, interpreted it in such a way as to soften or falsify its radicalism shows the difficulty they have dealing with it. But it has been retained in the creeds of the Christian churches, and it has made everything said by the Christians about death, about evil and suffering, about human relationships, society, politics, and religion into something else than what has been said by other religions.

If the Creator and Lord of the universe has appeared in the world as a man who has given his life for mankind; if, that is, God himself has assumed the human lot and is present where it is hardest, then — say the Christians — another light is cast on suffering, evil, and death than if that claim were not valid. That is so because God's giving himself up to suffering and death is a judgment and a liberation in one. It is judgment because the fact that nothing less sufficed shows what humankind has come to. And it is liberation because the fact that the source and origin of life shares suffering and death with his human creatures means that not death and suffering but life and joy are the ultimate realities.

The central claim of the Christians has also affected their thinking about man in society by being the ultimate cause of the assertion of human equality. If, namely, God's self-abasement constitutes a total judgment and an unqualified liberation, then there is, in the absolute sense, nothing to choose between men. In other words, irrespective of the reasons that may otherwise be given for superiority and subordination among men, those reasons can never include differences of rank in the eyes of God.

And finally, the fact that the central claim of Christianity is what it is and not something else causes Christian thinking about religion to be a thinking about a relation of faith. That means it is not about an achievement but about a receiving: acceptance of the judgment and the liberation implied in the presence of God in the man Jesus. Out of that receiving and accepting comes — according to the entire Christian tradition — everything that can be called by the name of religion. In that, and in that only, lies the root and cause and condition of everything else: worship, prayer, love of neighbor, moral instruction and personal self-discipline, everyday habits and high exploits of courage and sacrifice.

From that claim spring the coherence and the distinctiveness of Christianity. According to the Christians, their religion's character of being "many things" must be seen in the light of that claim. That is so because Christianity, by proclaiming the incarnation — God's becoming man in a definite cultural context, his acceptance of that context, and his "obedience unto death" within its framework — is a message of countless open possibilities. Acceptance of the "humble God," him who is present where men and women live, is therefore necessarily something that takes place in many different ways according to situation and context; and it results in widely different forms of Christian behavior, theoretically and practically.

In other words, the Christians maintain that the authenticity of Christianity as Christianity depends, not on whether life in the faith assumes this form or that, or whether it emphasizes this or that, but on whether it is a life in that faith.

According to the Christians, that is a faith which has always been accompanied by the unbelief of the believers. They find confirmation of that in the attempts by Christians of all times at making the tremendous claim into something other than it is: their efforts to turn the creed into an instrument of religious self-assertion, moral tyranny, and political coercion. Christians have exploited the fear and anguish of fellow men, and ruined their joy. The Christian is well aware of that. But it does not keep him or her from maintaining that unbelief and its consequences have been accompanied by faith and the consequences of faith — and that the immeasurable claim is put forth as before, and gets itself heard as what it is.

index

Index

Kierkegaard, Søren, 268

Laplace, Pierre-Simon de, 245
Las Casas, Bartolomé de, 271
Laurentius (Lawrence), 89
Lavigerie, Charles, 280
Lenin, V. I., 244
Leo XIII, 263
Lessing, Gotthold Ephraim, 264
Livingstone, David, 277
Louis XIV, 224
Loyola, Ignatius of, 220
Luther, Martin, 57, 186, 189-94, 196,
    197, 210, 211, 212, 219, 221, 228, 231,
    234, 250, 263, 268

Marcion, 44
Marriage, 55-56, 60, 142, 144, 279, 285
Martyrdom, 70, 71, 79, 273
Marx, Karl, 248
Mary, 10, 52-53, 104, 105, 174, 176, 251
Melchizedek, 18, 43
Mendicants, 164-68. *See also* Monasti-
    cism
Methodism, 256-57. *See also* Church;
    Confessions
Methodius, 102
Milton, John, 92, 231-34, 269
Ministry, 29, 191, 196. *See also* Church;
    Episcopacy
Mission, 10-16, 74-77, 102, 112, 118, 131,
    152, 270-80, 288
Monasticism, 71-73, 106-7, 118, 159-68,
    205, 251, 271
Montanism, 69
Moses, 171, 197

Napoleon, 243, 245
New Testament writings, 24-26, 28-29,
    40, 44-45
Nietzsche, Friedrich, 248

Old Testament, 5, 15, 28, 143, 149, 228,
    229, 279
Origen, 45-46, 57-59, 73, 80, 88, 223,
    264
Orpheus, 96

Otto of Freising, 153

Papacy, 67, 115, 118, 120, 132-33, 152-59,
    181, 183, 186, 201, 205, 251-55, 272,
    283, 284
Paul, 9, 10, 12, 14-16, 20, 21, 22-25, 28,
    39, 44, 46, 59, 67, 75, 87, 101, 152, 158,
    178, 190, 192, 196, 263, 289
Pelagius, 57
Pentecost, 40
Pentecostalism, 284
Perpetua, 79
Persecution, 78-81, 181, 186, 213, 243, 273
Peter, 16, 45, 67, 75, 101, 118, 137, 143,
    152-53, 190
Peter (czar), 211
Philo, 88
Pietism, 224, 227-29, 274
Pilate, Pontius, 4, 9
Plato, 171
Priscus Attalus, 85
Prophecy, 20, 69
Protestant churches, 194, 198-204, 208-
    17, 249-50, 255, 259, 274-76, 282-84.
    See also Church; Confession build-
    ing; Confessions; Luther; Calvin
Puritanism, 225, 228-29

Quakers, 230

Rationalism, 266
Richelieu, Armand de, 200
Ritschl, Albrecht, 266-67
Roman Catholic church, 204-6, 210,
    250-53, 271-73, 274, 283-84. *See also*
    Church; Confession building; Con-
    fessions; Papacy
Rulership, Christian, 83, 100, 145-52,
    154, 209, 211-13

Sacraments, 16, 20-21, 28, 29, 38-39, 41,
    52, 55, 63-65, 73, 102, 104-5, 138-42,
    148-49, 154, 186, 191, 200, 249
Sage, the Christian, 73, 92, 93
Saints, cult of, 70, 71, 77, 132, 216
Salvation Army, 257
Sartre, Jean-Paul, 248